"[Whitacre] reveals the challenges and struggles of an ordinary single woman doing extraordinary work during a tumultuous period change in American history."

—Mary Lynn Bayliss, *Virginia Magazii*

"A work with many amusing or insightful
Life in an Uncivil Time is an excellent reac ...yone interested in America at midcentury or the Civil War."

—A. A. Nofi, *Strategy Page*

"Julia Wilbur's life and struggle took place more than 150 years ago but remain relevant. This book presents tensions that continue to challenge individuals who seek their life purpose while negotiating societal expectations in a landscape rife with racism and social injustices."

—Gwen Gosney Erickson, *Friends Journal*

"By illuminating Julia Wilbur's struggles to end slavery, join the emancipated in the fight against bigotry, and live a life of purpose, Paula Whitacre offers a rich biography and beautifully written history."

—Chandra Manning, author of *Troubled Refuge:
Struggling for Freedom in the Civil War*

"Paula Whitacre shines a light on a remarkable character, abolitionist Julia Wilbur, who . . . heroically confronted misogyny, racism, and fear in an effort to aid enslaved African Americans making the transition to freedom. Here this important and timely story is empathetically brought to life. I urge everyone to pick up a copy and delve deeper into a chapter of Civil War history that has been overlooked for far too long."

—Lisa Wolfinger, co-creator and executive producer of the
PBS series *Mercy Street*

"Paula Whitacre's biography captures the extraordinary life and times of this seemingly ordinary American woman."

—Carol Faulkner, author of *Lucretia Mott's Heresy: Abolition and Women's Rights
in Nineteenth-Century America*

"Paula Whitacre's scholarship expands our knowledge of the African American experience before, during, and after the Civil War. A fascinating look at Wilbur and Civil War Alexandria, Virginia."

—Audrey P. Davis, director of the Alexandria Black History Museum
and historical adviser to the PBS series *Mercy Street*

"Paula Whitacre has created a compelling portrait of a nineteenth-century abolitionist working on the front line of change. Julia Wilbur joins the ranks of tough-minded women who stood firm at the point where idealism meets reality."

—Pamela D. Toler, author of *Heroines of Mercy Street:*
The Real Nurses of the Civil War

"In resurrecting Julia Wilbur's life, Paula Whitacre vividly conveys the struggles, both mundane and momentous, that reshaped families and nations in the Civil War era."

—Nancy Hewitt, author of *Radical Friend:*
Amy Kirby Post and Her Activist Worlds

"In Paula Whitacre's talented hands, Julia Wilbur's life bursts from the page. She appears as an adoring aunt, an ardent activist, Harriet Jacobs's ally, a committed teacher, and, most of all, an eyewitness to the ending of slavery and the beginning of freedom."

—Jim Downs, author of *Sick from Freedom: African-American*
Illness and Suffering during the Civil War and Reconstruction

"Julia Wilbur is not a well-known abolitionist. That lack of familiarity is one thing that makes Paula Tarnapol Whitacre's *A Civil Life in an Uncivil Time* so interesting. . . . Readers who will appreciate this book include those interested in the Civil War, abolitionism, and early feminism. Residents of both Rochester, New York, and the DC area will appreciate the detailed descriptions and historical photographs of their communities. Finally, we can all be inspired by the significant contributions made by a woman who was brave, relentless, and—comfortingly—ordinary."

—Robin Talbert, *Washington Independent Review of Books*

A Civil Life in an Uncivil Time

A Civil Life *in an* Uncivil Time

Julia Wilbur's Struggle for Purpose

PAULA TARNAPOL WHITACRE

Potomac Books

An imprint of the University of Nebraska Press

For Bill, who believed from the start

CONTENTS

ILLUSTRATIONS

PREFACE

People often ask me about how I "found" Julia Ann Wilbur and her diaries, which she kept in various forms from 1844 to 1895. We connected through Alexandria Archaeology, part of Alexandria's extensive local history program, in 2010, when I volunteered to research the more than thirty Union hospitals that sprang up during the Civil War. Among other sources, I consulted Julia Wilbur's diaries on microfilm in the Alexandria Library's Local History and Special Collections Room.

One thing led to another—first I offered to transcribe the Civil War years of the diaries. Then I decided to learn what Julia Wilbur did right before the war to set the stage, then right after, then *long* before, etc. Finally, after peering at microfilm for a year or so, I visited the originals in the Quaker & Special Collections at Haverford College. Douglas Steere—respected Quaker thinker and activist and Julia's great-great-nephew (direct descendant of her youngest sister Mary)—donated the diaries to the college, where he taught from 1928 to 1964.

At the time of my first visit to Haverford, Julia Wilbur's papers lived in four gray boxes, about the size of shirt boxes (since transferred into six more neatly partitioned containers). I opened the first to find her pocket diaries, each a small, leather-bound volume. Nice. It was amazing to touch what I had only peered at through a microfilm machine. But I really jolted when I opened the next box. There sat several dozen packets of cream-colored stationary, about 5x7 inches in size, tied up with red ribbon, a parallel set of diaries that began in 1844 (more than ten years before the pocket diaries). In them she waxed on for many pages on one day, then wrote maybe just a line or two on the next. The collection ends abruptly in 1873, but in reading them and her other diaries, I assume later years got lost. Known to scholars and others who used the collection, these diaries surprised my colleagues in Alexandria and me.

But I had just spent two years transcribing the pocket diaries. If

I tackled this second set, I would probably still be typing today. A solution emerged. Friends of Alexandria Archaeology, a nonprofit group, and Haverford split the cost of scanning and uploading the pages onto a dedicated website. About twenty-five volunteers in Alexandria each took seventy-five pages, often many more, to transcribe. As a result, we transcribed, proofread (albeit still with typos), and compiled more than 1,800 pages in just over a year.

I fulfilled my original goal: transcriptions of Julia Wilbur's diaries are online and searchable through Alexandria Archaeology.

My goal grew, as this book attests. Beyond making individual diary entries available, I wanted to draw on them to tell Julia Wilbur's story and the story of an amazing time in our nation's history.

What would Julia Wilbur think about this endeavor? After working with the diaries for many years, I believe she knew she was preserving something special for posterity—although probably did not envision posterity to encompass so many of us. We have Professor Steere to thank for transferring the diaries beyond the family confines.

As I dug into the pages, I wondered, however, if I violated her privacy, particularly her painful experiences in 1860 and 1861 related to losing custody and virtually all contact with her beloved niece Freda (see chapter 3). I think not. She reviewed her diaries many times over the years. Later in life she started extracting entries into another record, which she titled "Journal Briefs." She easily could have taken out pages or crossed parts out in her look-backs. Moreover, she referred to thoughts deemed too personal or damning with cryptic comments along the lines of "People have wronged me today." And she only alluded to events most scandalous for the time, such as her sister Frances's marital difficulties. A few times, too, she wrote about rereading and destroying personal letters.

A note about the direct and indirect quotes in this book: all conversations, thoughts, and dreams attributed to Julia and others come from diaries, letters, or other source materials. I wrote out a few abbreviated words (such as "cd." and "wd." for "could" and "would") to ease the reading and have added explanations in brackets. A few terms discomfort us today (such as "colored"), but I have maintained the original in all cases.

A Civil Life in an Uncivil Time

Prologue

"The Saddest Sound I Ever Heard"

The church bells of Alexandria, Virginia, tolled the morning of Saturday, April 15, 1865, a strange time to ring even on Easter weekend. Julia Wilbur heard the news as soon as she woke up. President Lincoln was dead, shot in the head while at the theater. Of course, she didn't believe it.

When she went outside in the morning rain (the day before, the sun had shone brightly, the victory celebrations in full swing), she saw signs that confirmed the awful truth. The usual steamboat service linking Alexandria and Washington across the Potomac River had ceased. Union soldiers, who had lately relaxed their vigilance in the city they had occupied since the beginning of the war in May 1861, stood on tense guard at every corner. They lowered flags to half-mast and began to drape black cloth across military-held buildings.

Julia burst into the home of her friends, the Beldings, Northerners like her who had spent the war years in Alexandria. She could see by their smiling faces of welcome over the breakfast table that they didn't yet know the awful truth. She told them. Mr. Belding ventured out and soon returned with tales of "secesh" (secessionists, Confederate sympathizers) under arrest, of rumored rebel cavalry a few miles to the west, and of general confusion and uncertainty.

The *Alexandria Gazette* reported, "As the particulars became known, men gathered in groups—heard with wonder and amazement—and expressed their indignation."[1] Not everyone was indignant, however. Julia heard, second-hand, that the mayor said, "The President died serving the devil." He managed to explain himself to the military governor, as the rumor went, but others heard using "disloyal language" were arrested.[2] Soldiers went house to house to make sure every resident displayed something black on the door or windows.

Those not inclined to express their condolences had a choice: mark their house or expect it to be torn down. Before nightfall the *Gazette* reported, "Every house occupied within the limits of the city displayed an emblem of mourning."[3]

The soldiers had no need to prod the black population to express grief. As Julia wrote in her diary, "every cabin, shanty, and shed" displayed a symbol of mourning, even a small shred of black wool or cotton. She went among the dwellings where freedpeople—men, women, and children who had escaped from slavery during the war into Union-occupied Alexandria—lived. One young man told her, "I would rather have been shot myself"; another person lamented "Uncle Sam's being killed." She wept right alongside them. "There is no consolation to offer," she wrote. "We all suffer alike."[4]

And those bells, "giving forth the saddest sound I ever heard. Tolling, yes, tolling for what seems to us the greatest calamity that could have befallen us."[5]

With boat service resumed, late Sunday night, the day after Lincoln's death, Julia crossed the river into Washington, where "the air seemed full of treason." Side by side with mourning on the streets, lately filled with celebrations to mark the recapture of Fort Sumter in South Carolina, the fall of Richmond, and the surrender at Appomattox, some people expressed glee. "Numbers have been heard to say that they are glad, that Lincoln ought to have been shot years ago, & they have not been arrested either," she observed.[6]

Rumors flew across town. An initial reward of $10,000 for apprehension of the conspirators soon increased tenfold. Word of two men found in a cellar dressed in women's clothes—the culprits?—had everyone rushing to Georgetown, only to find out that the men were probably army deserters. A detailed description of John Wilkes Booth circulated, down to his "hair, jet black, inclined to curl," but he eluded discovery for almost two weeks, ultimately killed in a barn near Bowling Green, Virginia.[7]

Presidents had died in office in the nation's history before but never so violently, so suddenly, and certainly never as a climax to such tumultuous national events. Cabinet members and other officials, in shock themselves, pushed Lincoln's traumatized widow aside as they hastily planned public mourning for the slain leader. The following Tuesday, Julia arrived at the White House early to avoid the long wait or risk not getting in at all. In double file mourners passed through an anteroom, a hallway, the Green Room, and finally into the East Room, where the president's body lay and black cloth swathed the chandeliers, mirrors, and picture frames. She walked slowly, looked at the president ("dressed in a full suit of black. His face is very white but wears a natural expression"), and exited, not allowed to linger.[8] Outside the line grew ever longer. Blacks and whites stood side by side—rather than the more expected practice of the time to make blacks wait separately and at the end.

Later that evening Julia went out again to see what was happening and spotted Gen. Ulysses Grant, barely recognized as he walked along the street in a dingy uniform. Originally scheduled to attend Ford's Theater with the Lincolns on April 14, the Grants had declined with excuses, Mrs. Grant not interested in a social evening with Mrs. Lincoln. They instead traveled to New Jersey, where their family lived at the time. After the calamity Grant slipped back to Washington, apprehensive that he too was a murder target.

Any public gloating over the demise of the president receded as funerary events took over the capital. A few days later Julia realized, "I have not seen a drunken person today nor heard one unfriendly remark about the President." She stood at the top of Pennsylvania Avenue and watched the slow procession that accompanied Lincoln's casket from the White House to the Capitol, where he lay in state until his slow train journey back to Illinois. The procession took almost two hours, as military units, bands, fraternal orders, workers' associations, and other organized groups paid their public respects—an estimated forty thousand marchers watched by multiples of thousands more. "I feel crushed with a great misfortune & this seems to be the general feeling," she said.[9]

Julia sought tangible mementoes—relics as people called them—to make some sense of the tragedy. She bought pictures of Lincoln and of Secretary of State William Seward, stabbed by another conspirator in a botched assassination attempt. Along with her friend and fellow

New York abolitionist Lucy Colman, she called on Josephine Slade, an African American woman whose father served as the president's valet. Miss Slade gave her a piece of "white rosette" worn by one of the pallbearers on his lapel; she also acquired pieces of black cloth and trimming used to decorate the casket. A few days later Colman gave her a lock of Lincoln's hair, Julia said.[10]

Whether these items were authentic and how or whether Colman had a piece of the murdered president's hair (much less enough to parse out to her friends), we do not know.[11] They did not last in Julia's personal effects. However, an April 1865 letter to her sister Mary did survive. Two weeks after the assassination Julia wrote Mary, "We have hardly recovered from the dreadful shock sufficiently to go about our business as before."[12] Julia's description of the aftermath of Lincoln's death clearly left a deep impression on Mary, who preserved this sole letter from among the dozens she received from Julia over the years.

More than a decade earlier, when Julia Wilbur taught school in Rochester, New York, President Millard Fillmore came to town. Because she disagreed with his acquiescence to slavery, she chose not to go see him, "although this may have been my only opportunity for seeing a live President."[13] Little did she know she would see a president, Abraham Lincoln, both alive (at public receptions and his second inauguration) and dead, as well as Presidents Johnson, Grant, and others over the three decades she spent in Washington from 1865 until her death in 1895.

At the war's onset in 1861, Julia lived in upstate New York with her father and stepmother, single, forty-seven years old, aimlessly figuring out how to spend her days. Instead of accepting her fate as the maiden aunt of a large family, she launched something wholly new, never to return permanently to New York again.

An ardent abolitionist in spirit, Julia moved to Alexandria in 1862 on behalf of the Rochester Ladies' Anti-Slavery Society. There the Civil War transformed her, as it did many Americans, white and black, women and men, soldiers and civilians. She had to figure out how to turn good intentions to assist freedpeople into actions that made a difference. She arrived with no official position or instructions nor a place to live or friends to orient her. By fighting for what she saw was just, often against those in positions of authority, she transformed herself into, in her own words, "a sort of missionary-at-large, a woman-of-all-work."[14] After the war she worked with the Freedmen's Bureau (officially the Bureau of Refugees, Freedmen, and Abandoned Lands), pushing the government to extend support to the newly free. Then in 1869, to remain in Washington, where she knew she could live a more independent life than back home, she sought a job in the Patent Office, part of the first generation of women in the civil service. She worked until a few months before her death at age eighty.

Julia Wilbur witnessed a changing world and had to figure out her place in it—from the mid-1800s, when the end of slavery seemed improbable at best, to the intense years of the Civil War, to Reconstruction and the fight for women's suffrage. We have little other family correspondence beyond Julia's letter to Mary after Lincoln's death, but diaries Julia kept for more than five decades, along with letters she wrote to abolitionist friends, do survive. Through them we witness when she bravely entered new situations and experienced setbacks along the way.

As I read her words, I wonder what I would have done when faced with her choices. How would I have reacted? Maybe you too will wonder about the choices you would make.

I

Before the War

CHAPTER ONE

"A Peculiar Period in My Pilgrimage"

May 1, 1844, dawned gloriously bright, the air loaded with the scent of orchards and the promise of spring after a hard New York winter. At eight in the morning Julia Wilbur nervously entered the offices of the Rochester Board of Education in the Reynolds Arcade, one of the city's finest new buildings, and faced three of its members, all men. They quizzed her on reading, on numbers, on geography. They grilled her on the short "e" and the long, the whereabouts of St. Helena, and other topics of academic significance. Satisfied, they issued her a certificate attesting to her ability to teach the city's children. Julia accepted their good wishes while also wondering how comfortably she could live on a teacher's salary.

She was twenty-nine years old when she began her new job at School No. 12, built just two years earlier, and started a diary-writing habit that stretched until the end of her life at age eighty. From her family's farm in the village of Rush, fifteen miles south of Rochester, she moved to a city dubbed the "young lion of the West," founded in the wilderness alongside the Genesee River just a few decades earlier, now a boom town after the completion of the Erie Canal in 1825.[1] Seen through the eyes of a British visitor, "every thing in this bustling place appeared to be in motion."[2] The city multiplied in population, from about 1,500 people in 1820 to almost 37,000 by 1850 and 48,000 a decade later.

Free public education had only come to Rochester a few years earlier. From the beginnings as Rochesterville, named after cofounder and Revolutionary War veteran Nathaniel Rochester, until the early 1840s, children attended a motley collection of schools paid for mostly by their families, the "poor fund," or the occasional philanthropic benefactor. Public sentiment favored a new system, reflecting the Common

School Movement led by Horace Mann in Massachusetts. Everyone praised its progressive ideas: uniform curricula, supervision of teachers, and more consistent municipal financing. Ten civic-minded men formed the first board of education in 1841, two from each of the city's wards, and hired a superintendent named Isaac Mack, a miller by trade. Shortly after their appointment, the board and Mr. Mack already had to respond to charges about their "extravagance in the erection of large and expensive school-houses" and about their efforts in recruiting suitable teachers.[3]

The leaders grappled with these and other issues that bedevil school systems today, including inequitable funding in wealthier versus poorer neighborhoods, racial integration versus segregation, and discipline. Superintendents came and went. School leaders soon figured out two advantages of female teachers over their male counterparts: a greater supply and lower wages.

Julia, a single woman who had attended a patchwork of schools without a complete high school education, reflected a standard teacher profile of the 1840s. She had her first experience teaching during the summer when she was fourteen years old (and wondered later what she possibly could have imparted to her students). Like most teachers of the time, she had scant preparation for classes that could have included fifty or more pupils, and she initially found School No. 12 a daunting experience. She could rely on a burgeoning industry that supplied new books and methods—how to impart the rules of grammar, how to decipher the mysteries of arithmetic—each hailed as the next best thing. But with attendance spotty, class size enormous, and the school calendar ranging from a few months to most of the year depending on funding, poorly paid teachers worked under tremendous pressure to prepare students for their exams—administered orally and in public. She persevered, but many colleagues, male and female, fled the profession.

Julia managed to get through the first few weeks only to realize on Sunday evenings, with some dismay, that Monday morning and another week came all too quickly. Over time, however, from among a sea of wild pupils and less-than-inspired academic performances, she saw a few promising signs, especially among some of her girls.

On her first anniversary as a Rochester public teacher, she realized she enjoyed the camaraderie, although her contentment with the profession waxed and waned over time—and eventually mostly waned as the wage inequity with men ate at her.

Throughout her thirties and into her forties she taught in five public schools, sometimes taking on oversight of the library and the physical premises. She became active in the Teachers Institute, which offered the equivalent of professional development to teachers, and served as "editress" of its publication for a time. She also tried to establish two small privately funded schools, known as select schools, one on Court Street in Rochester and one in the town of Lockport, but could not sustain them.

Julia Ann Wilbur was born August 18, 1815, in the village of Milan, further downstate between Albany and New York City. Ancestors from both sides of her family (father Stephen Wilbur and mother Mary Lapham) came to New York from Rhode Island, banished from Massachusetts in the seventeenth century as Quakers. Stephen's father, Jeptha, operated a gristmill and served as one of three "overseers of poor," in recognition of his stature in the community. In the days before New York State outlawed slavery in 1827, his responsibilities included attesting to whether freed slaves could support themselves.[4] The Laphams, on Julia's maternal side, lived in neighboring Stanford, and she claimed a connection through them to the Great Nine Partners, the earliest settlers in the area. As fellow Quakers sharing a New England background, the two families probably had contact so that Stephen and Mary could meet and marry.

Stephen and Mary had two daughters, Angeline and Elizabeth, older than Julia, when the family moved to the Columbia County village of Chatham, where Julia later described her father as involved in "mercantile and milling."[5] Keeping with the custom of another child at regular intervals, the family grew to include Theodore (1817), Frances (1819), Henry (1821), Sarah (1824), and William Penn (1826). In 1829, at age fourteen, Julia attended Nine Partners Boarding School, a well-established Quaker school previously attended by noted Philadelphia reformer Lucretia Mott.

But as Julia later described her parents' circumstances, "In the prime of their lives, misfortune came upon them" when her father was stricken with an eye disease, probably trachoma.[6] For four years he lived in total blindness, traveling to Hartford, New York, and Philadelphia in search of treatment. Modern-day medicine cures this bacterial disease of the cornea with antibiotics; the attempted surgeries and various solutions of the day never totally restored his sight. For the rest of his life Stephen Wilbur distinguished shapes and rode a horse but could not read or discern faces. He would assume his position at the head of the family dining table but had to ask if everyone else had sat down.

Stephen decided he could no longer operate in business. In July 1828 he purchased 124 acres of land in Rush that adjoined a farm owned by his brother. At some point soon after, the family moved to the town of about two thousand, into an existing house about three-quarters of a mile from the main road. The Wilburs and other farmers in the surrounding countryside supplied wheat to Rochester's flour mills, sent out along the Erie Canal.

In the early 1830s Angeline and Elizabeth married a pair of brothers—Alfred and Morgan Van Wagoner—and moved to farms on the way to Buffalo. Two other sisters were born, Ella (1832) and Mary (1834), bringing the family to ten children over a span of twenty-four years. But in 1834, six weeks after giving birth, Mary Lapham Wilbur died at age forty-three, leaving a forty-seven-year-old widower and ten children "motherless," as Julia lamented for the rest of her life, even through Stephen's two subsequent marriages.

When her mother died, Julia was nineteen and of prime marriageable age. How did her mother's death affect Julia's own life course? Her older sisters lived with their husbands, and her father was nearly sightless. Children ranging in age from six weeks to seventeen years needed care, especially the infant Mary and the toddler, two-year-old Ella. In 1836 Stephen married Sally Rundell Tanner, a widow in her late forties, but she did not seem to connect emotionally with the children, at least not that Julia expressed. Julia spent her twenties helping to run the household. By the time she moved to Rochester in 1844, her father must have concluded he did not need her at home, for it is hard to imagine her leaving otherwise. Her sister Sarah in particular moved into the role of principal caregiver for the younger siblings.

The only known photos of Julia Wilbur show her middle-aged. We see a plain but certainly presentable person, slim and well-groomed, dark-haired with gentle eyes, about five feet tall. Still she labeled herself "unattractive in appearance and repulsive in manner," even as a young woman.[7] She didn't describe most of her family members for us to know if, for example, particularly attractive siblings exacerbated this low self-image. She claimed she lacked confidence but said other people criticized her for acting like a know-it-all—perhaps a reaction to her tendency to voice her opinions, whether welcome or not. Surely the prevailing views of "the cult of true womanhood," which glorified subservient women, led to some raised eyebrows in her direction. And as her siblings and even her father found new life partners—her father outlived all three of his wives—maybe the mark of "spinster" affected how she saw herself.

Yet Julia bemoaned the fate of women who thought marriage would open new worlds. To her, if anything, marriage closed things off. When she visited a former schoolmate excited about setting up "housekeeping" as a new bride, Julia listened but privately mused, "She seemed perfectly happy. Long may she continue so."[8] She clearly thought her friend would face a different reality soon enough. A married friend wrote from the West, trying to reestablish contact out of loneliness and misfortune—another example to Julia that marriage, far from a solution, could create its own problems. She especially expressed sadness for women who entered marriage, usually to older widowers with children, out of economic necessity "for the sake of a home" (a situation that may have applied to her two stepmothers, both childless widows when they married Stephen Wilbur).[9] But she judged from a privileged position—not wealthy but with means to support herself and with her farm and family as a backup.

Julia never mentioned a suitor but did seek connection with others. "I certainly am made with a nature to love others. I love my friends most intensely. I sometimes think if they would return but half of it, I might be happy," she wrote in early 1848.[10] She stayed close to her siblings, nieces, and nephews, especially her youngest sister Mary, whom she helped raise, and Frances, with whom she lived later in life. She loved spending time with her brother Theodore, an artist and store clerk living in Rochester, and his wife Charlotte, who owned a "hair jewelry" shop, selling ornaments and wigs to Rochester's most fashionable women, her work "not excelled by any in the United States, none better made in the City of New York."[11] Although Charlotte led a far more flamboyant life than Julia could aspire to or even wanted, the two remained close, even after Theodore died of typhoid in 1858 and Charlotte remarried. Julia took a particular interest in their son Neddy and daughter Mary Julia, known as Sis, whom Julia described as so beautiful that she could get into trouble—as she did, marrying three times and alternating between wealth and poverty in her adult life.

Julia also formed attachments with female friends, many of them fellow teachers. "Miss D" shows up with great affection, and at one point they planned to board in the same place. When her friend contracted consumption and left Rochester, Julia lamented, "All my plans of happiness are frustrated."[12] Was this love of a romantic or sexual nature or was Miss D instead a well-thought-of friend? She gave no indication. Miss D eventually recovered and married.

On her thirtieth birthday on August 18, 1845, Julia felt herself moving into a new phase of life, or as she said, "a peculiar period in my pilgrimage." She saw youth passing her by, as was, most likely, marriage and motherhood. While her family still made demands on her time and attention, she admitted her good fortune, especially when the typical woman lived in a household-circumscribed "sphere." She realized this relative freedom came with an obligation to those around her. Over the next few years that sense of obligation extended beyond her family as she became more involved in abolition and other social causes.

Living in Rochester in a series of boarding houses and occasionally with family members gave Julia far more independence than most women had at the time. She lived in at least fourteen places from 1844 to 1858. In addition to staying with Theodore, a cousin in

Rochester, and a sister in Somerset, she rented rooms and ate meals with people beyond her circle. For example, in 1851 Julia stayed with Abigail Bush, a women's rights leader whose husband had gone to California in search of gold; at another point, she stayed with a "Mr. and Mrs. R." For them the extra money from a lady like "Miss Wilbur" might make the difference in eking out an existence. The census records of Rochester, or any city of the time, reveal how many unrelated people lived together in the nineteenth century, whether in hotels, boarding houses, or extra rooms in private homes. Many abandoned or widowed middle-class women took in boarders as one of the few socially acceptable ways to bring in much needed income.

The city offered opportunities to learn about, and get involved in, the social movements of the day: temperance, abolition, and women's rights, as well as more spiritual pursuits that ranged from Protestant revivalism to communication with the "other world." The most famous supporters of these causes made Rochester a regular stop on their circuits. Scientists, musicians, and pontificators also shared their talents at Corinthian Hall, Minerva Hall, and other splendid public places built by the city's business leaders.

When Rochester was barely a decade old, missionaries from New England started to circulate through western New York, and local bible societies and churches formed. But nothing prepared the region for the magnetic preacher Charles Finney in the 1830s. Originally invited to Rochester by a city leader concerned about the godlessness he saw accompanying Rochester's growth, Finney considered the city "a very unpromising field of labor."[13] He dug in. He preached an exhausting schedule of revival meetings throughout the week, three times on Sunday, emphasizing that individual free will could combat sin. He won over large numbers of converts with his mesmerizing speaking style and presence before he moved on.

Many other religious movements and people flourished in the "burned-over district" of upstate New York.[14] In 1833 farmer and lay preacher William Miller proclaimed that his reading of the Bible indicated the Second Coming in 1844, giving himself a good decade of fame. A pamphlet from a Millerite meeting remained among Julia's effects when she died, but the only handwritten comment describes what her sister Sarah wore that day. She noted when the promised doomsday of October 22 came and went, the "world seems going on yet pretty much as usual . . . to the great disappointment of many deluded persons."[15] Methodists, Baptists, Presbyterians, and Unitarians all found fertile ground and established churches in the Rochester area. Quakers, both Hicksite and Orthodox, established meetinghouses. Joseph Smith, the Mormon leader, gleaned his first inspirations in the woods outside his home in Palmyra, about twenty-five miles from Rochester. Then there were the Fox sisters, Maggie and Kate, known for their rappings and séances with the spirits. Thousands of people believed in their extraordinary powers, including, by the late 1840s, some of Rochester's leading abolitionists and other reformers.

Julia sought solace from religion but never found a deep connection with Quakerism or any other single system of belief, not for want of trying. She said in 1847, "I used to wish that I could believe as others do & unite with a church & think it all right. But I see something of good in all of them & all of good in none."[16] In Rochester and throughout her life she attended church services, often several different sects on a given Sunday, including African American churches, where she might find herself the only white person in the congregation. She sought wise words to inspire her; boring, mean-spirited, or otherwise not up-to-snuff sermons disappointed her greatly. She occasionally attended Quaker meetings but was not one to gain much from silent contemplation. And she found the Fox sisters a humbug.

Closely tied with religion, the temperance movement drew crowds, newspaper headlines, and the formation of numerous societies and groups in Rochester and elsewhere. The pro-temperance Wilburs supported the cause more from concern for the consequences of alcohol abuse than to detoxify any family members. But other families experienced alcoholism first-hand. From pre-Revolutionary times many towns and villages revolved around a tavern, and liquor permeated home, work, and other aspects of daily life. It was cheap and plentiful, sold alongside coffee and sugar. Whiskey warmed the body on a cold day, and beer quenched thirst on a hot summer afternoon. By the early 1800s, however, drinking patterns reflected changes in society, with more drunkenness, especially by white men, rather than the more moderate albeit continual drinking of years past. Adults drank an average of seven gallons of pure alcohol each year in early nineteenth-century America, more than double the amount today.[17] Women and children often bore the results of men's excesses through abandonment, domestic violence, and poverty.

Ministers and physicians made moral and health-related arguments against alcohol abuse. Speakers, often former victims of "demon rum," led thousands to "take the pledge." In addition to the message of the speeches, temperance events provided a way to pass a few hours out in society. Julia saw many temperance celebrities who came to Rochester, including John Gough, a young, attractive superstar known as much for his eloquence as his notorious backsliding. In 1844 Julia heard the "celebrated Lucretia Mott" preach at a Quaker Hicksite meeting. Mott called the temperance cause "the glorious reform of the day" but couldn't resist pointing out to the audience, "Its unparalleled success should be the beacon to start to encourage us in the promotion of the other great reforms of the day." Reaction to Mott varied: "The effects of this preaching were very apparent, some being very much disturbed. Others were evidently highly delighted."[18] We can count Julia among the delighted.

As an unintended by-product, temperance cultivated a group of people who wanted to change society, especially women who might otherwise have stayed on the sidelines. Susan B. Anthony entered the world of activism via temperance. Working and starting to burn out as an overworked, underpaid teacher in Canajoharie, New York, she gave her first public speech in 1849 before the town's Daughters of Temperance. She urged the Daughters to move beyond trying to convince "our own kindred" to avoid the "corrupting influence of the fashionable sippings of wine and brandy"—in other words, to leave the proscribed domestic sphere and work to change society as a whole.[19] Soon after, Anthony resigned from teaching and came to Rochester, where her Quaker family had moved a few years earlier, and became a full-time lecturer and organizer. The refusal to allow women to speak at a Sons of Temperance meeting led her to organize a protest and form the Women's State Temperance Society. Its meeting in Rochester in 1852, which Wilbur attended with two of her sisters, had an overflow crowd, rousing speeches by Anthony and others, and, perhaps most shocking of all, the appearance of "the Bloomer dress" on stage. The press delighted in describing the few women, including Elizabeth Cady Stanton, who defied fashion convention and wore Bloomers, wide pants covered by a skirt that stopped above the ankles. Stanton and several other speakers used temperance as an entrée to discuss a woman's right to divorce, "that the drunkard will have no claims on wife and child," and other social issues.[20]

Even before Anthony moved to Rochester, the city was at the center of the women's rights movement. In 1848, two weeks after the Seneca Falls Convention, which produced the Declaration of Sentiments (signed by Mott, Stanton, Frederick Douglass, and ninety-seven other people, including Julia's aunt Maria Wilbur), the Rochester contingent organized a follow-up meeting back home. In another example of how these movements interconnected, many potential attendees already planned on attending the annual Emancipation Day celebrations on August 1 to mark the end of slavery in the West Indies. Their meeting went so far as—earth-shattering at the time—to name a woman to serve as president of the gathering (Abigail Bush, with whom Julia briefly lived as a boarder).[21]

Julia expressed support for the cause and attended some of the public meetings, but abolitionism, more than women's rights, captured her energies at this point. She attended Emancipation Day but not the meeting the next day, although she regretted missing it when she heard more about it. More than joining organized women's rights groups, she tried to advocate for those rights in her own life. Her outrage over the discrepancy between male and female teachers' wages led her to publicly take on the issue with the New York State Teachers Association. In 1857, a thirteen-year veteran teacher, Julia attended the association's annual meeting in Binghamton and offered two resolutions:

> *Resolved* that as the present compensation of female teachers is generally about one-half or one-third as much as men receive in the same employment and under the same circumstances, it is a fact mortifying to woman and calculated to degrade her

in the estimation of the community, and thus it is alike inconsistent and unjust.

Resolved that there is no reason, if a woman performs it
equally as well, why she should not be paid equally as much.[22]

"The spirit moved me & this was my first speaking in public.
A spicy time," she commented.[23] The men who led the association
acknowledged the salary discrepancy—it was hard not to—but almost
all of them chalked it up to the way society operated. Julia pointed
to one example of a widow who took over as principal from a man
who received $600 per year while she earned only $400, despite also
having to support a family. Anthony, also in attendance, backed her
up. (At an earlier meeting of the association, Julia publicly supported
Anthony when she called for racial integration in public schools.)
The first resolution passed; the second did not. The majority recognized the inconsistency but would not fix it.

An advantage of the teaching profession, then as now, oft-touted
especially by opponents to the raising of teachers' salaries, is the school
calendar's vacation time. True enough, with no legally required mini-
mum number of days to attend, Rochester's schools closed for Christmas and other holidays, for large public gatherings (a national Whig
convention, a visit by President Millard Fillmore), and sometimes
for lack of funds to operate. Shortly after the 1857 teachers' convention that considered women's pay, with school out of session, Julia
left with her sister Angeline and brother-in-law Albert on a trip to
Michigan, Chicago, and St. Louis. They visited family members who
had moved west, especially their beloved youngest sister Mary, who
lived in Michigan with her husband Joseph. Julia returned to School
No. 4 in Rochester for the 1857–58 school year, having seen more of
the world. She did not know it at the time, but it would be her last
stint as a schoolteacher.

CHAPTER TWO

"Slavery Is an Evil That Ought Not to Exist"

On July 23, 1845, the *Rochester Daily Advertiser* published three lines about an event taking place that day and the next: "Frederick Douglass / The eloquent fugitive from Southern slavery, will lecture at Talman Hall, in this city, on Wednesday and Thursday next, at 3 o'clock p.m." Douglass, on the cusp of fame, had published *Narrative of the Life of Frederick Douglass, an American Slave* two months earlier, although it wasn't yet the best seller it would become. Instead in 1845 he traveled alone on a lecture tour in New England and New York, from early July until shortly before a scheduled trip to England and Ireland the following month. The tour put him at risk since he had publicly identified his former owners and proclaimed his status as a fugitive in his book, although he traveled safely.[1]

In Rochester Douglass lectured in Talman Hall, built by the abolitionist couple John and Mary Talman on land she had inherited from her father, wealthy early settler William Fitzhugh. Two years later, when Douglass sailed back from Europe as a celebrity and a free man (his legal freedom funded by British supporters), he moved his family to Rochester. He even returned to Talman Hall, where he published the *North Star* and *Frederick Douglass' Monthly* newspapers.[2]

Julia Wilbur attended both his lectures, enthralled, though still identifying Douglass in her diary as "the eloquent fugitive slave" and not the acquaintance and hero he later became to her.[3] The morning after the second lecture, she and her students joined in a celebration of the sixteen public schools in nearby Washington Square. More than two thousand boys and girls sang (according to a news report, this "added not a little to the interest of the occasion").[4] They sat along a specially constructed three-hundred-foot-long table for a "Pic Nic," under a banner stating "Knowledge Is Power." As she became more involved in abolitionism, Julia embraced that motto.

In the mid-1800s, Rochester was a city of change. Its population boomed, with new residents bringing in fresh ideas and ambitions. After the mid-1820s Erie Canal barges easily transported goods to and from Rochester. By the 1840s trains connected to Boston, New York, and Philadelphia, as well as linked people in the outlying countryside to the city. Situated near Lake Ontario across from Canada, Rochester served as the last U.S. stop on the Underground Railroad for many blacks escaping slavery. Movements in support of temperance, abolition, and women's rights grew, overlapped, attracted many of the same supporters, and developed inevitable schisms based on personalities and points of view. Local reformers, many of whom chose to move to Rochester in adulthood, gained national renown, including Isaac and Amy Post and Lucy Colman, in addition to Douglass and Susan B. Anthony. Historian Nancy Hewitt describes Rochester at this time as a place where "social change, social activism, and women's activism converged in particularly vivid forms."[5]

An old but undated list of "Abolitionists of Rochester Monroe Co.," found in the papers of the Benjamin Fish family at the University of Rochester, lists about twenty-five women and men, individuals and families, a few blacks but mostly whites.[6] It makes no mention of Julia Wilbur. She was not one of the leaders who made the list. She sat in the audience rather than on stage; she attended meetings rather than organized them. But she faithfully showed up, often after a day of teaching, to the many anti-slavery lectures and conventions held in Corinthian Hall, Minerva Hall, the Unitarian Church, and other places around town. As the abolitionist community split on tactics, she tried to maintain relations with Rochester's two main groups in the 1850s, earning scorn by both.

Activity among the organized anti-slavery groups in which Julia participated peaked in the 1840s and 1850s, but the groundwork began earlier. African Americans moved to Rochester shortly after its settlement, most prominently a community leader named Austin Steward. White competitors vandalized a grocery store he opened. Indeed many in Rochester's majority did not welcome him or the rest of the black population, as tiny as it was (at its prewar peak in 1850, some 1.5 percent of the total population).[7] But the African Americans persevered in opening churches, businesses, and a Sabbath school. Some, like Steward, had escaped slavery, whether from the South or New York State itself, and helped others move to freedom.[8] In 1834 members of the AME Zion Church formed the city's first female anti-slavery society, similar to groups formed by African American women in Philadelphia, Salem, Massachusetts, and other cities. Whether these Rochester women's efforts soon ceased or were simply not covered in the mainstream press, they did not leave a record of their activities.[9]

More visible, perhaps because its membership consisted of well-connected white women, the Rochester Female Anti-Slavery Society formed in 1835, proclaiming in the *Daily Democrat* that "we can act most efficiently in the way of organized effort."[10] Most members were wives of the founders of the all-male Rochester Anti-Slavery Society. Their principal "organized effort" in the 1830s consisted of circulating and sending petitions to Congress on such topics as the elimination of slavery in the District of Columbia and in new territories in the West. Their documents joined thousands of others until Southern members of the House of Representatives imposed a "gag rule" that tabled all anti-slavery petitions without their being read into the record. Women's groups throughout the North continued to petition Congress after the gag rule, even increasing the numbers for a while. By the end of the 1830s, however, local clergymen and the press criticized the organization with various women-out-of-their-sphere tirades. Perhaps the combination of male criticism and frustration about the gag rule led to the group's dormancy.

Although they did not flourish for long, the black and white women's groups of the 1830s represented the first organized efforts by Rochester women to end slavery.

At that time Julia lived in Rush, new to upstate New York and helping tend the household. She would have had no formal contact with these groups, although she may have heard about them from an aunt and uncle, Maria and Eseck Wilbur. Later she would meet several of the women when they took up the cause again, forming the Rochester Ladies' Anti-Slavery Society, which Julia joined in 1852.

Nationally the most vocal anti-slavery message first came from the American Colonization Society, formed in 1816. The group advocated emancipation but also the removal of formerly enslaved (and, if some supporters had their way, free) blacks to Africa or the Caribbean. U.S.-born blacks understandably took issue with this solution and began to organize anti-slavery societies in Northern cities. In 1829 David Walker, a free black from North Carolina who had moved to Boston, published *Appeal*, a pamphlet that advocated a violent overthrow of the system of slavery.

William Lloyd Garrison also entered the abolitionist arena. Garrison, white, spare in appearance and strident in tone, was, as biographer Henry Mayer noted, "one of the first Americans, after Thomas Paine, to make agitation his professional vocation."[11] After being hounded out of Baltimore, Garrison published the *Liberator* newspaper in Boston. He received death threats, mobs vandalized his office, and preachers denounced him from their pulpits. But supporters respected his uncompromising stance. When Julia finally saw him and other leaders she had read about, she was starstruck: "I have at last had the pleasure of looking upon Garrison & [Wendell] Phillips & a host of other worthies that it has long been my desire to behold."[12]

Rejecting colonization, Garrison helped launch the American Anti-Slavery Society in 1833. The society split seven years later. Fierce debate about whether a woman from Massachusetts, Abby Kelley, should serve on a leadership committee precipitated the split. More fundamental differences divided the factions. With little progress— indeed regularly confronted with public indifference, insults, and violence—the abolitionists had to face the reality that slavery was as entrenched as ever. What should they do? To the Garrisonians (who supported Kelley and women's rights in general), the path rested on "moral suasion": that is, persuasion and an appeal to morality, rather than working within the corrupt political system, would end slavery. The opposing camp, led by New York businessmen Lewis and Arthur

Tappan, favored what it saw as a more practical and realistic approach: end slavery by working within the political system and—for heaven's sake!—don't mess things up by adding women's rights to the mix.

In the general population neither path won over many converts. Most white Northerners, even those who opposed the concept of slavery, were not abolitionists. They might disagree with the practice in theory, but they did not see it every day, and whether recognized consciously or not, they benefited from it economically. Further, most whites, no matter their views on abolition, were blithely open in their prejudice against blacks. Only occasional events pierced their complacency and gave a human face to a practice that had enslaved almost 4 million people (about one-eighth of the U.S. population) by 1860, such as the publication of *Uncle Tom's Cabin* or well-publicized cases to save individual blacks from a return to slavery.[13] Like most families, the Wilburs held varying views on the issue, ranging from abolitionist support by Julia, her father, and several siblings to indifference by most of the rest to sympathy for the South by at least one brother-in-law.

Two years before Julia moved to Rochester, the Western New York Anti-Slavery Society formed in 1842. Radical for its time, men and women, black and white, worked together to sustain the organization, known as the WNYASS. The Quaker members became so active with "worldly," or non-Quaker, groups that most either chose to leave the Friends or were asked to do so. They favored Garrison's moral suasion and radical stance, even supporting "dissolving our connection with slaveholders"—that is, a breakup of the United States—especially after the annexation of slave-holding Texas in the aftermath of the Mexican-American War.[14] Years before the Civil War extremists in both the South and North considered "disunion" as a solution to the polarization over slavery.

Among WNYASS members, Isaac and Amy Post, later supporters of Julia in Alexandria, stand out. From Long Island, in 1836 they moved to Rochester, where Isaac ran a pharmacy. They opened their home to family members and friends, both black and white; Amy told a historian in the 1880s that their record for the greatest number of fugitive slaves hidden on their property at any one time was twelve.[15] They welcomed Frederick Douglass as early as 1842; later he acknowledged to Amy, "You loved me and treated me as a brother before the world knew me as it now does."[16]

Once a protégé of Garrison, Douglass realized the need to strike out on his own. He discussed and began to raise money for his own newspaper while in England. When it became clear he could not publish his own paper near Garrison and the *Liberator* in Massachusetts, he sought another home. Friendship with the Posts and their circle, as well as Rochester's small but vibrant black community and its proximity to Canada, planted the idea of Rochester because he knew "of no other place in the Union where I could have located with less resistance or received a larger measure of sympathy and cooperation."[17] Isaac helped him find a place to move his family from Lynn, Massachusetts—his wife Anna and (at that time) a daughter and three sons. William Nell, a black abolitionist from Massachusetts, also moved to join Douglass in his new publishing enterprise and lived with the Posts.

The Posts were known for their open-mindedness, their support for African American and women's rights, and, incongruently or not, their strong belief in spiritualism and the rappings of the Fox sisters. In addition to Douglass and Nell, they welcomed John S. Jacobs and his sister Harriet in Rochester, with Harriet living with the Posts for more than a year. Amy later encouraged Harriet to write about her escape from slavery in *Incidents in the Life of a Slave Girl*, which led to her fame and eventually to her work in Alexandria in the 1860s alongside Julia Wilbur. But that remained for the future. In the 1840s John, who had also escaped slavery, was the more politically active of the two siblings.

Julia began her involvement in abolitionism by attending public lectures, like the Douglass lectures at Talman Hall in 1845. By early 1849 she had gone from lecture hall to front-room parlor when she attended a WNYASS meeting at the Posts' house, the first time she records meeting them. The next month she was home in Rush, helping pave the way for meetings in the nearby town of East Avon by Frederick Douglass and John S. Jacobs.

The abolitionist lecture circuit was a hard one. Visiting speakers sought volunteers to help them go "house to house, town to town." Sometimes locals like the Wilburs stepped up to make arrangements, spread the word, and host the speakers. If not, they arrived in a strange place and had to find everything themselves: lodging, food, a meeting space, and an audience. Things could get dicey for an abolitionist, especially an African American man who showed up alone in a small town. During one tour Jacobs reported his reception ranged from a lecture in Eagle Harbor, where "the audience was quite disorderly, being in part made up of some boatmen whose highest idea of manliness seemed to be disturbance"; to Johnsons Creek, where he had to light the fire in the meeting house himself; to—hallelujah, relief—Holley, where a supporter made the arrangements and the Presbyterian minister canceled his own meeting to bolster attendance for Jacobs.[18]

As for the Douglass-Jacobs event in East Avon, according to Julia, "Notice was pretty extensively circulated," but only eleven people showed up for the afternoon lecture, although "there was a greater turnout than we expected" that evening. (Douglass gave a more pessimistic view of the lecture tour in the *North Star*, without mentioning the Wilburs or East Avon specifically.) The Wilburs hosted the two men for dinner. "Indeed, we consider this visit quite a chapter in our lives," Julia wrote. It is safe to say this was the first, and perhaps only, time two black men ate in their home. She expressed perhaps too much surprise that "they appeared intelligent on almost any subject & are very agreeable in conversation"; in fact, through slavery and abolition work, both men were far more traveled and worldly than she.[19]

In April Julia returned to Rochester, bringing her sister Mary, then fifteen years old, and setting up a select, or private, school on Court Street with five students. She and Mary lived with their brother Theodore and sister-in-law Charlotte. This arrangement lasted only a few months but proved a good base from which to take advantage of what Rochester had to offer, such as the Anti-Slavery Reading Room in Talman Hall.

The WNYASS had set up the reading room the previous year: "Desks, table, show-case; and a carpet was purchased by the Ladies' Society.

A good supply of newspapers from the exchange list of the North Star . . . was placed in the room, conveniently arranged, and open for all to read free of expense."[20] Despite high hopes, the room drew few readers under the first managers, two WNYASS activists.

John Jacobs took over the reading room in hopes of generating more interest. When he lectured or was otherwise occupied, Harriet minded the room. Julia stepped in one day and "had a chat with Miss Jacobs. She is sister to J. S. Jacobs & quite an interesting person."[21] At the time, she recorded a not entirely accurate version of Harriet's life and her escape from slavery. Later Julia would learn much more about the woman she met in the reading room in 1849 when they re-met in Alexandria in 1863.

On another occasion Julia and Mary visited the Douglass home on Alexander Street. At this time, people called on each other without a specific invitation as long as they came at socially acceptable times. There they met another set of sisters—Julia and Eliza Griffiths, two "fearless spirits" from England with whom Wilbur said she was "hoping to become more acquainted."[22] Like most people in Rochester, Julia didn't quite know what to make of these two women, who had hosted Frederick Douglass in Great Britain and now swooped into the Douglass household and the *North Star* office with no apparent plans to leave.

During the visit they must have discussed the schooling of the Douglass's older daughter, Rosetta. The day after, Julia recorded in her diary, Rosetta came to her school on Court Street. "Expecting several others would leave, but they have not yet," Julia reported with bated breath. The status quo lasted a week when "two of my red-haired scholars have left, though quite reluctantly on their part." At first Julia thought she had had the last laugh: "The beauty of it is, they are placed in another school so near they associated with my scholars both white & colored during play hours. Alas for poor Mr. B [the students' father] I am afraid he will not be able to preserve his children from coming in contact with the growing humanity of the age."[23]

Back in 1846 an African American minister had sent his two daughters to their neighborhood school, which happened to be No. 12, where Julia taught. A white trustee insisted they leave. At the time

Julia lamented the action but apparently did not fight it. This time she tried to keep her own school going with Rosetta as a student. But she had to close it at the end of July 1849 as more students left. "I kept it going 3 months," she wrote. "In reality, it has continued to be a serious detriment as far as pecuniary affairs are concerned."[24] Not sure what to do next, she moved to the farm of her sister Elizabeth and brother-in-law Morgan Van Wagoner, where she spent most of the next school year teaching their children and helping around the house.

Shortly after Julia closed her school, Frederick Douglass sent Rosetta to a more established female seminary in Rochester. The school director accepted Rosetta, but parental outcry led her to move the girl into a classroom by herself. Douglass, outraged, pulled his daughter out, eventually hiring a tutor to teach her and his other children at home.

Since Rochester's public schools had opened in the early 1840s, African American parents complained about segregation and poor conditions. Douglass lent his voice and newspaper to the ongoing opposition. At the end of December 1848, as reported in the *North Star*, "a large number of respectable citizens" held a meeting at the court house to protest segregated schools. A member of the board of education, while complaining that a "public meeting was not the proper way to redress these grievances," said he had voted for segregated schools because he "was informed that a portion of your population desired it." The "portion" informed him this was not the case, and, moreover, the building assigned as a black school was an "unhealthy, dark and dirty hole, which has been used for a number of years as an ice house." These parents asserted their rights as taxpayers and the right of every child to attend district school, noting the law "makes no reference to the color or origin of the children entitled to this privilege."[25] In 1857 the board of education adopted a policy to integrate the public schools, among the first in the nation to do so. In practice, because of Rochester's small black population, this policy meant only a handful of black children might attend a particular district school, and some even noted the change saved money without the expense, however substandard, of separate facilities.

While Douglass continued to maintain friendships with individual members of the WNYASS, change was in the air. He had already distanced himself from Garrison and other Massachusetts leaders when he moved to Rochester; now he questioned the viability of moral suasion, announcing a "Change of Opinion" in the *North Star* toward political abolition—that is, working within the existing power structure rather than expecting people's moral principles to come around to oppose slavery.[26] The Griffiths sisters had remained in the Douglass household, but Eliza married and moved to Canada, leaving the more flamboyant Julia in Rochester. The already controversial trio of Douglass and the Griffiths sisters became a twosome, with a great deal of tongue-clucking that a married black man and single white woman were publicly seen out and about. Julia had a desk at the *North Star* and immersed herself in its editorial and business operations.

Between 1843 and 1850 the WNYASS held anti-slavery fairs, but its fundraising steam began to sputter. After a fair held during a snowstorm in January 1850, Amy Post praised the post-fair celebratory meal, where "at least two hundred persons of both sexes, and all colors and classes sat down together."[27] Where Post saw camaraderie as a sign of success, Douglass saw failure from a financial standpoint, as the event had disappointing sales. The group moved away from holding its own anti-slavery fairs and decided to contribute items to a huge fair held annually in Boston. But a Boston fundraiser would certainly not apportion any of the proceeds to Douglass in Rochester.

The *North Star* needed money. Always financially precarious, it lost Garrison-oriented subscribers and funders. Griffiths began to look around for new ways to build support and bring in much needed revenue. She turned to the Porter family. Susan Porter had been involved in the first society of white anti-slavery women back in the 1830s. Over the years she and her husband had built a comfortable life in Rochester and remained active in abolition circles, including offering Underground Railroad shelter to fugitive slaves.

On August 20, 1851, a small group of women met at the Porters' home to form the Rochester Ladies' Anti-Slavery Sewing Society (RLASS). Proclaiming in its constitution that "slavery is an evil that ought not to exist, and is a violation of the inalienable rights of man," the group stated "its object shall be, to raise funds for Anti-Slavery purposes." Since sewing was ancillary, the members soon dropped the activity from the name of their organization. Susan Porter became the first president; her sister-in-law Maria served as treasurer throughout the organization's almost two decades; the secretary was Julia Griffiths. The six directresses, as they were called, included Julia Wilbur's sister-in-law Charlotte, who periodically hosted the group's biweekly meetings.

Compared with the WYNASS, the RLASS was the Establishment, keeping in mind that abolitionists of *any* stripe constituted a small minority in Rochester.[28] Its members were white, economically comfortable, and less vocal on women's rights than their WYNASS counterparts. Griffiths herself, while living the life of a strong, independent-minded woman, stressed, "I am not a 'woman's rights' or a public speaker."[29]

Douglass admired and remained connected with the Posts and other WNYASS members, but he turned to the RLASS for support. When he thanked the group for a donation after its first anti-slavery fair in March 1852, he challenged, "It is to the Rochester 'Ladies Anti-Slavery Society' that I look for important services to the anti-slavery cause in Rochester. . . . It is for you to call conventions, secure eloquent speakers, and make all needful arrangements for spread of the anti-slavery truth here. Should you fail to do this, the work will fail, or others will take it up."[30]

That was a tall order for a group that at the time consisted of nineteen members and whose constitution, in addition to its anti-slavery language, included the requirement that the biweekly meeting hostess provide a supper that consisted of "tea, bread and butter, one kind of plain cake, and a simple relish." But the ladies rose to the occasion.

Wilbur spent the long winter of 1852 teaching at a school in Lockport, where she wrote she found no one sympathetic to abolitionism. (In fact quite a few abolitionists lived there, so it is curious she did not connect with them.) She gladly returned to Rochester and a job at a public school on Reynolds Street. Probably through Charlotte, she joined the RLASS, "formed last winter and favorable to the views entertained by Douglass." She quickly discerned the difference between it and the WNYASS. The former, as Julia observed, "has more influence & Respectability . . . but I doubt there is that self sacrificing like martyr spirit among its members."[31] Despite attending meetings of both groups and vacillating between which orientation she preferred, she became one of six directresses, with the assigned task, as enshrined in the RLASS constitution, to "make all purchases, and to cut and prepare all the work for the Society."[32]

At the second RLASS fair, held at Christmastime 1852, Julia jumped in and made her first sale: a night cap to a young man. The fairs, often timed for holiday gift giving, could earn hundreds of dollars, a tidy sum for the time. Donated items came from Rochester and other U.S. communities, with a special allure around items from abroad; the "British tables presented an elegant and attractive appearance."[33] Customers could help the abolitionist cause while they purchased baby frocks from Dublin, *papier mâché* from Manchester, and even, one year, a surprise donation of toys and coral from Mexico (although "owing to some remissness in packing, the Toys were all, more or less, broken, and the Coral was somewhat shattered").[34] The group profusely thanked contributors in its annual reports, no doubt with the next year's event in mind.

The group (or mainly Griffiths; in its early years "group" and "Griffiths" were sort of the same thing) hit upon a new fundraising idea: a book called *Autographs for Freedom*. At the time many adults collected the autographs of friends and celebrities. Capitalizing on this trend, the RLASS women envisioned a book in "an elegant and substantial style. . . . The beauty of its exterior will commend it as a suitable Christmas or New Year's gift."[35] The women, including Wilbur, wrote to famous anti-slavery people to ask them for a poem, essay, or other contribution and, most especially, their signatures to reproduce in the book. In the wake of *Uncle Tom's Cabin*, the cover page of the first British edition bylines "Mrs. Harriet Beecher Stowe and Thirty-Five Other Eminent Authors." Other contributors included abolitionist senator Charles Sumner, editor Horace Greeley, and poet James Greenleaf Whittier.

With her characteristic *chutzpa* Griffiths ignored the animosity between Douglass and William Lloyd Garrison and wrote directly to Garrison to solicit his participation. "We need not assure you that your name is of great value to any good cause to which it is given," she purred, ending the flattery with her characteristic bluntness: "Communications for the Autographs must be in the hands of the Secretary by the last of August. Hoping for a speedy response, I beg to remain, Most respectfully yours, Julia Griffiths, Secy."[36] Garrison's autograph appears in neither the first nor the second edition, published the following year.

As the 1850s continued, RLASS membership never grew much, but the group sustained a high profile. Speakers in their lecture series included Rev. Henry Ward Beecher, Harriet Beecher Stowe's brother and a celebrity preacher in his own right; James McCune Smith, the country's first African American physician; Horace Greeley, the editor of the *Tribune* in New York City; and prominent anti-slavery members of Congress. Douglass gave one of his most enduring speeches at an RLASS-sponsored event at Corinthian Hall in 1852—"What to the Slave Is the Fourth of July?," which he deliberately delivered on the *fifth* of that month.

Despite a flat membership roster, the society's treasury did grow. After initial earnings of about $400 per year, treasurer Maria Porter reported annual revenues of more than $1,300 by the mid-1850s. An annual contribution to Douglass always represented the largest share on the expense side, and smaller amounts were directed to individual fugitive slaves, to Underground Railroad leader Jermain Loguen in Syracuse, to an anti-slavery newspaper in Kentucky, and to other causes. The RLASS also funded onward journeys of fugitive slaves, recording either a collective sum ($530 in 1858) or individual contributions (in 1859, for example, January 7, three fugitives, $8, or January 14, four fugitives, $7).[37] A few individual members sheltered escapees on their property, although the Wilburs did not.

Supporting escapes and broader principles of justice, RLASS members acted on brave-for-the-time sentiments. But they, like many white abolitionists, had a hard time recognizing blacks as individual people with the same strengths and weaknesses as whites. Articles and letters abound sympathetic to the cause but with references along the lines of "these poor unfortunates." Julia put Douglass and other black leaders on a pedestal while she could also be patronizing, especially when encountering poor blacks with no or little education. Surely she knew what was best for them, she wanted to believe. She shared the prevalent disrespect of Frederick Douglass's wife, Anna, by many white visitors, interpreting Anna's diffidence as coarseness. Yet Anna, a free black in Baltimore without a formal education, masterminded and financed Frederick's escape from slavery in Maryland to New York and New England.

Julia Griffiths, meanwhile, peppered the Garrison-leaning women of the WNYASS to join the RLASS. In October 1852 she wrote a conciliatory letter to Amy Post, inquiring about her and her family's health and asking her "dear friend" to read the RLASS constitution: "I do want you to be with us—and of us. . . . *Can you say no?*"[38] Apparently Post could, and did, say no, although she later provided clothing and moral support to Wilbur as the RLASS-sponsored agent in Alexandria.

The Garrisonians did not like Griffiths, no doubt because they mistrusted her belief in political abolition and her influence with Frederick Douglass. In turn their antipathy may have hardened Griffiths against anyone who sympathized with them, including Wilbur. After earlier falling under Griffiths's spell, Wilbur began to find herself in disagreement with her. When the two women traveled together to an anti-slavery meeting in Syracuse (one of the few times Wilbur traveled for this purpose), she commented, "Miss G despises the Garrisonians & I have a very profound respect for them, being one of 'em. . . . But Miss G has her opinions & I have mine."[39]

They locked horns at RLASS meetings, with Wilbur discovering that no one else would speak up against Griffiths. "If all the rest are afraid to do it, I am not afraid. I presume I have forfeited her friendship but I cannot help it," she wrote, without describing the specific disagreements. On the occasions that Griffiths did not attend a meeting, Julia observed, "Ladies all expressed their opinions freely about the matter of things & people & why? Because they had not the fear of Miss Griffiths before their eyes."[40]

In 1855, the outcry about her relationship with Douglass too strong, Julia Griffiths returned to England. She continued to wield her pen and express her views from afar. Wilbur was asked to serve as RLASS secretary in her stead, although several of the members protested "on account of my being a Garrisonian."[41] She took the criticism personally and agonized about whether to accept the position. Ultimately the RLASS amended its constitution to allow for two secretaries: Wilbur initially occupied the position of recording secretary, and Griffiths became corresponding secretary.[42]

All along Julia tried to straddle both the RLASS and the WNYASS. When she first joined the former, she noted, "They have little sympathy with the old society but I can sympathize with *both*."[43] She went to both groups' meetings, sometimes on two sequential days. One result: suspicion by both.

Just as the RLASS women questioned Julia's Garrisonian leanings, some WNYASS members distrusted her. In 1856, when she boarded for a time with William and Mary Hallowell, the son-in-law and daughter of the Posts, she unsuccessfully approached Amy Post to support the RLASS, but according to one account, "Post and her friends were immediately suspicious of Wilbur's motives and did not believe the RLASS had changed."[44] Julia did not record this overture in the diary, but she did describe a "remarkable letter" from William in March 1856 "accusing me of . . . being false to their society & all this when I have long considered myself one of them."[45]

Meanwhile, William Nell, the Massachusetts abolitionist who lived for a time in Rochester, wrote Amy Post with a more forceful warning against Julia. "My own sentiment towards Miss Wilbur has been one of distrust—the position she occupies of close fellowship with Your enemies materially unfits her for confidence of Your Circle. . . . She may not give any occasion for her friends to find fault but she certainly has a wide field for annoying both parties."[46] Let's hope Julia never knew about this personal invective against her. We do not have any indication of Amy Post's paying any particular heed to the warnings.

Teaching, activism, attending lectures, and family made for a full life. Julia's sisters Sarah, Ella, and Mary married in the mid-1850s, leaving Julia the only single sister. When her stepmother died suddenly of "dropsy of the chest" in late 1857, Julia went back to Rush to "prepare her [Sally's] clothes" for burial, even if she did not much grieve for the woman to whom she was never close. Out of social propriety and concern for her father, she hoped "everything will be done perfectly right."[47]

But all changed in April 1858, when she received word about the serious illness of Sarah, who had given birth to her second daughter four days earlier. Julia returned home, where Sarah's husband, Revilo Bigelow, farmed with Stephen. Sarah died, leaving the infant, still unnamed, and a two-year-old daughter named Alfreda, nicknamed Freda. "My duty seemed to be in two places," Julia agonized, but caring for her father and Freda clearly won out over her teaching life in Rochester.[48] She moved home to Rush.

The eighth annual report of the RLASS began with the following news: "We have to regret the removal from the city of our Corresponding Secretary, JULIA A. WILBUR, thus depriving the Society of a most efficient and ever faithful worker." By then Julia had moved to Rush, taking on a new role as Freda's surrogate mother.

CHAPTER THREE

"My Plans Overthrown. Life All Changed."

When Julia's sister Sarah died, leaving two-year-old Freda and an unnamed infant daughter, it fell to Julia—or she chose to have it befall her—to pick up the pieces. It almost destroyed her.

Sarah, eight years younger than Julia, had taken over as sister-in-charge at the family's farm in Rush when Julia moved to Rochester to teach in 1844. Together in 1851 they traveled for six weeks, visiting spots in Dutchess County where their parents and grandparents had lived. Sarah was gentle, easy to get along with. When Sarah married Revilo Bigelow, the brother of their neighbor down the road, in 1855, all seemed copacetic. "Everything passed off pleasantly," Julia commented, and the newlyweds took a trip to Lockport before settling into married routine.[1] The next year Sarah gave birth to Freda, and the threesome moved into the Rush farmhouse to help out. Already an aunt to twelve other children (her sister Elizabeth accounted for nine of them), Julia had a new niece to dote on, and she did.

Sarah's second pregnancy went deeply wrong. Julia returned to Rush as soon as she heard Sarah was failing. It came out that Sarah had hidden that she had not felt well during her last two months of pregnancy; "her legs pained her and she was quite lame"—a possible symptom of a blood clot. All sorts of diagnoses floated around. The Avon doctor said she had "neuralgia"; Julia thought she had "milk leg" or, to be more clinical, venous thrombosis. A doctor from Rochester finally proclaimed, "Her disease was puerperal fever and it was badly managed."[2] At the time, this post-childbirth bacterial infection was fatal.

Whatever the cause, the family had to rally. It was agreed that Freda would remain at the Wilbur farm, cared for by Julia, who could also help her father, a recent widower himself. "My plans overthrown. Life all changed. My duty was plainly at home to care for Father & Freda," she wrote.[3] Julia's sister Frances and her husband, Abner Hartwell, married for more than a decade but without children, would care for the infant.

Julia, now forty-three, dug into motherhood with gusto. Freda became the daughter that she never had and never would. Moreover, the young girl provided an emotional and physical connection that Julia did not have with anyone else. Freda slept in Julia's room and came along on social calls and overnight visits to family members. "I have considered her my own. I have been with her constantly," Julia wrote. She already envisioned guiding her to maturity. "I do so wish to bring her up to be a good & useful woman, to protect her from unkindness & harshness."[4] It was not meant to be.

Freda's presence helped buffer the impact of two other tragedies. In August 1858 Julia's brother Theodore, the artist of the family, died of typhoid fever. His Rochester home was a place of comfort and fun where Julia had lived for a while and otherwise spent much time with him, his wife Charlotte, and their two children. As customary, family members flocked to their home, taking turns by his bedside.

One night, off sickroom duty, Julia and her sister Elizabeth walked over to a ceremony to mark the laying of the Atlantic cable and to hear read aloud the first telegraphic message between President James Buchanan and Queen Victoria extolling perpetual peace and friendship. (The line failed three weeks later, with eight more years needed to engineer a permanent solution.) It provided a good excuse for a summer celebration, with fireworks, a torchlight parade, and late-night rallies. At midnight, due to the flames, cinders, and general inebriation about town, fire struck. Five blocks of stores and one of the city's largest churches burned. "The fire was one of the grandest spectacles we have ever beheld—it carried terror as well as awe to the mind of every beholder," reported the *Rochester Union and Advertiser.*[5] But as proof of the severity of his condition, Julia realized, "Theodore noticed none of the noise."[6] He died the next day.

While the family still reeled, Sarah and Revilo's infant, finally named Sarah Alice, died in September at the age of six months. The news came out of the blue—"[brother-in-law] Alfred came to tell us the baby had unexpectedly died," the cause unknown.[7] Unlike in the case of her siblings Sarah and Theodore, Julia did not express heartrending sorrow at the loss of the infant. She had not often seen or gotten as attached to little Sarah Alice as she had to Freda. Maybe she connected the baby to the death of the mother. In addition, death of the very young, while still mourned, was sadly common compared to today.[8]

In this eventful time for the Wilbur family, two marriages took place. Julia's brother William Penn married Henrietta Fletcher, who "knows his peculiarities."[9] William Penn, then age thirty-two, had never married and wandered about looking for a livelihood; the couple moved to Michigan and a hard farming life. And Stephen Wilbur married for the third time; the bride was Laura Winegar, a widow fifteen years younger than he. It is a little unclear what the courtship ritual entailed because, suddenly, Julia wrote, "Father came from Mt. Morris [a nearby town] with a new wife."[10] Laura returned with Stephen to Rush, a virtual stranger but now the official mistress of the house.

As much as Julia missed Theodore, as much as she rued her father's marriage, her biggest source of anxiety centered on Freda and Revilo. For just as she was becoming attached to Freda, just as they had settled into a rhythm of mother and child (although Freda called her Aunty), Revilo started to make noises that he would reclaim his daughter. True, he had agreed to the arrangement and moved back with his own family in Groveland, in Livingston County, about thirty miles to the south. But Revilo—a dastardly sounding name given the circumstances—changed his mind. Today we would assume a widowed father would raise his own daughter, no matter that our sympathies might lie with Julia. But she saw Revilo's decision as wrenching Freda from the home where the girl had grown up and from the family of her mother. No doubt Julia's own feelings as a motherless child entered into her thinking.

In July 1859 Revilo told Julia what he had already shared with others—he would soon move Freda to Groveland. She began an unsuccessful campaign to keep Freda in Rush, but "he seems hard as a stone & as cold as ice."[11] No matter what the day brought, "A shadow rests on all pleasant things here." She even wrote, "I think I can realize what a *slave mother* must feel when she considers that her children are at the disposal of another" and expressed sympathy for Margaret Garner.[12] Three years earlier Garner had made headlines when, in attempting to escape slavery in Kentucky, she killed her daughter rather than subject her to return to bondage. Of course Freda was not being sold into slavery, and Julia was not her mother. But she empathized with Garner's powerlessness.

In early December Revilo told one of Julia's sisters he would come for Freda within the next few weeks. The impending separation absorbed Julia. When John Brown was hanged on December 2 for leading the raid on the Harpers Ferry arsenal earlier that year, Julia felt he was a "noble old man, he will not die in vain!" but admitted her "own trouble prevents my thinking much of others," as this was the day she learned Freda would soon leave. Her father, while sympathetic, offered no concrete help to keep his granddaughter in his household.[13]

Revilo married Nancy Sinclair Haynes, a widow with three children of her own. Julia went to see her, and they took an immediate dislike to each other. "She was flippant and unfeeling in words," Julia wrote, and her house looked untidy. Worse yet, Nancy said, "I told him [Revilo] if I took him, I should take all he had," and "all" included Freda.[14] By the end of 1859 Julia pled for an extra few days with Freda, and she and Revilo squabbled over whether and how much Revilo should reimburse the Wilburs for some of Freda's and Sarah's household items that he would take to Groveland. But Revilo held the cards—he would have custody of Freda.

On December 31, 1859, Revilo came to the door for his daughter. "They have taken her away. When they carried out Sarah's trunk that contained her things, it seemed like they were carrying out a coffin."[15] Revilo and Freda left, returned a few minutes later for a satchel left behind, then drove off again.

The quiet was immense. Think of a house far off the main road on a winter's afternoon. No noise of traffic, electronics, music—a house that had contained the noise of a small child who was now gone. "Few words have been said in this house today & those in suppressed tones," Julia wrote. She moped; she grieved: "My energies are all gone, my faculties are impaired & I do not feel able to undertake any business & least of all school teaching."[16] She had a vicious run-in with Revilo and Nancy in Groveland that devolved to a fight about money, with Freda the real bone of contention. It ended when Nancy demanded that Julia leave.

At home Julia stayed away from politics and reform. In March 1860 she visited Rochester for the first time since Freda had left. Returning to the place she had easily lived on her own for more than a decade, "the noise & bustle of the city worries me." She went to a doctor for her "weak body & still weaker nerves." When she explained her symptoms, he said there was "no organic disease of the heart, but all these bad feelings will leave me if I can stop thinking of my trouble & become reconciled to what I cannot help."[17] Easier said than done. Julia ratcheted down her expectations. Maybe if she could just see Freda every so often, she could get by. But Revilo expressed no interest in that relationship either.

Julia stayed with her sister-in-law Charlotte and visited Charlotte's hair business the next day. This was not her cup of tea—"Spent 2 or 3 hours listening to the frivolous talk of ladies preparing for a party. If I had to hear all that C. does, I should be disgusted with womankind."[18] She saw little things she could have purchased for Freda. She went out to lectures, including one by then famous author Grace Greenwood, and visited friends and family. But she did not seek out RLASS members, Frederick Douglass, or other abolitionists upon whom she used to call regularly.

Julia realized she needed more time away from Rush. From Rochester she visited her family in Lockport and Somerset, dwelling on the fact that Freda had accompanied her the last time. Indeed she saw reminders of Freda no matter where she went and what she did. It became deeply personal. "This deep love, this intense yearning for her happiness & comfort, does it mean nothing? Will it avail nothing? Has God given me such affections to be wasted?"[19] She frequently dreamt about Freda and started to mark in her diary how many weeks had elapsed since she had last seen her, a practice she continued for years. She talked to Revilo's minister about intervening,

thinking he might have some sway. She tried to glean any information she could about Freda's well-being from common acquaintances.

By the end of May the encounters around Freda turned soap opera-
ish. One afternoon, when the Wilburs realized Revilo and family were
visiting his brother Harvey, they quickly went down the road. Revilo
and Nancy tried to physically block them from seeing Freda. Another
time, Julia rode to the school Freda briefly attended—unfortunately
the teacher was Nancy's sister, who told Julia, "I have to tell you to
leave. I have orders not to let you see Freda." It was becoming a bit
of a community scandal. When Julia stopped in Lakeville on the way
home from the school, she saw a cousin of Nancy's, and Julia noted,
"She thinks they [Revilo and Nancy] do wrong & wicked. . . . She
says there are but few persons there who take their part."[20]

But life went on. With Theodore dead about a year, Charlotte told
Julia she planned to marry a daguerreotypist named Lewis Griffin.
Julia knew him and had gone to his studio for her portrait, but she
worried about a stepfather's effect on her niece and nephew. Again
Julia observed marriage often came down to practicalities, even for a
successful businesswoman like Charlotte. "Had a talk with C. today.
She feels confident that [Griffin] is going to better her situation &
also her children's, & I do so hope she will not be disappointed."[21]
Julia soon became fond of Griffin and appreciated that Charlotte
remained close to the Wilburs, even stopping to visit after the wedding on the way from Rochester to Lewis's hometown of Genesee.

Meanwhile, Julia's brother Henry and wife Ann moved into the
Rush farmhouse. Julia and Henry did not have a close relationship. When Henry married Ann Austin in 1846, Julia did not know
about it until two days after the wedding. At one point she bewailed
a member of the family who forgot "his family, himself & his god,"
likely referring to Henry given the context, while she considered Ann
"very gay & frivolous."[22] Within ten years Henry and Ann had lived
in at least four places—with Theodore and Charlotte in Rochester
in 1850; in Kendall, New York, where her parents lived; in Adrian,
Michigan; back to New York—perhaps with their expectations unmet
each time. Their journey was common for the time. We often assume
people move more often today compared with the past, but Henry

and Ann's experience, and indeed Julia's frequent changes of boarding houses in Rochester, typified the lives of many Americans who were not part of the elite.[23]

Stephen Wilbur took Henry and Ann in and probably appreciated Henry's help on the farm with Revilo gone. The house filled with him, Laura, Julia, occasional servants, and now Henry and Ann and all their "goods and chattel." Julia complained, "If H. & Ann had staid in Michigan instead of coming here, we might have had some small chance of comfort left even yet, but they have involved us in still deeper trouble. . . . I think Ann had done that which a long life of good deeds can never atone for."[24] Something awful seems to have taken place, whether financial or related to social proprieties, but we unfortunately do not know what exactly occurred. We do know Ann usurped the choicest spaces in the house, refused to do her share of the chores, and traveled back to Kendall or elsewhere whenever she wanted with no notice. With sister-in-law Ann and stepmother Laura ensconced in Rush, Julia's sisters found reasons not to visit often.

A nineteenth-century farm demanded a lot of work, and Julia felt the housework fell unduly to her. At various times female servants lived in the house, but they came and went. In at least one case, her father declared the Wilburs must be their own Bridgets ("Bridget" referred to an Irish servant).[25] Julia spent a good part of her day cooking, washing clothes, cleaning the kitchen, and gardening. Although she complained, she relished the relief in occupying herself. She read, visited friends, and sewed, and she found solace in tending the cemetery. She complained about lack of money. Except for selling grapes she grew on the property and perhaps earning a bit by sewing for friends, she did not receive the income she earned as a teacher, even if she had complained about its inadequacy at the time. She probably could have returned to the Rochester school system but did not seek out a position.

Instead she mourned—"I found some dear little worn out Shoes. . . . I can kiss these & cry over them, but will I ever kiss again those dear little feet they once contained?"[26] Julia's post-Freda life is anguished and raw. Her diary served as the place where she could pour out her feelings because she could not do so with anyone else in the house.

Her father talked to Revilo ineffectually on her behalf but basically told her to get over it. We can assume Laura did not comfort her or miss Freda, nor did Henry and Ann. Her sister Frances was the most sympathetic but lived with her husband's family, so the two women did not have daily contact.

The 1860 federal census listed the household as containing Stephen, Laura, Henry, Ann, and Julia, along with two servants. Julia identified herself as a "Teacher of Com. [common] Schools." She did not teach, but she asserted an identity when she had a profession and a purpose. This proved a step in the right direction, however dark things looked at the time.[27]

"At Alexandria . . . the Potomac Rolls Its Majestic Stream"

Julia Wilbur called John Brown a "noble man." Prevailing opinion in Alexandria, Virginia, the place she would call home in 1862, had a decidedly different view about the man who raided the arsenal in Harpers Ferry in October 1859 in an attempt to overthrow slavery. "It was a wild and wicked plot, conducted by desperadoes and fanatics," reported the *Alexandria Gazette*, which devoted column upon column of print to the raid, the trial, and the public execution of Brown over the next eight weeks.[1] The paper took special pride in the performance of the Alexandria Rifles, the twenty-nine-member volunteer militia that hurried to Harpers Ferry and basked in public praise from the governor for its bravery. Although panicked about the possibility of armed revolt, the *Gazette* echoed the opinion of others throughout the South that the fact Virginia's blacks did not take up arms alongside Brown proved their satisfaction with the slave system.

African Americans made up about one-quarter of Alexandria's population of 12,652 in 1860, almost evenly divided between enslaved (1,386) and free (1,415), one of the largest free black populations in the state.[2] They kept opinions about Brown to themselves. Whites' claims to the contrary, most probably supported or at least sympathized with Brown's cause, if not his tactics. The repercussions of publicly expressing these opinions would have been frightening. But if they could have, they may have expressed solidarity similar to that of African American women in New York, who wrote to Brown's soon-to-be widow Mary, telling her, "In offering this word of sympathy to you now we desire to express our deep, undying gratitude to him who has given his life so freely to obtain for us our defrauded rights."[3]

Early settlers clustered in Alexandria because of its water access—in this case the Potomac River, rather than the Genesee River four hundred miles to the north in Rochester. Unlike Rochester, Alexandria barely grew for many decades of the nineteenth century. The population between 1820 and 1840 increased by fewer than three hundred people.

By the 1850s Alexandria enjoyed good times, a boom in the boom-and-bust cycles that characterized its economy. The white and black populations both increased. Canal and railroad traffic bustled. In 1852 alone, builders constructed new warehouses, a block of brick stores "with cast iron heads over the windows and doors and all the modern improvement," a sprinkling of new homes, both of brick and timber, a bank, and much more.[4] A locomotive and car works supplied rolling stock to the Manassas Gap, Baltimore and Ohio, Orange and Alexandria, and Hudson River Railroads. "It is our candid and deliberate judgment and opinion, that a better and a brighter day for the city is now dawning," wrote a visitor in November 1859 in an account the *Gazette* deemed worthy of publication.[5] Eighteen months later a different dawn brought a different fate for Alexandria.

People had witnessed dawns on this land for thousands of years. Native Americans traveled through the area, fishing along the river and the creeks that ran into it. The oldest archaeological find to date is a spearhead called a Clovis point, more than ten thousand years old, proof of activity millennia ago. British settlement began in the mid-1600s, when Margaret Brent received a seven-hundred-acre land patent, unusual for a woman at the time, and Robert Howson received six thousand acres for bringing 120 settlers from England to America. Howson sold his holdings to John Alexander for three tons of tobacco. Thus the Alexanders became the largest early landowners, and the town, when it formed in 1749, took on the family's name, as well as an identity evocative of the ancient city on the Nile.

Warehouses and wharves handled tobacco and, once that crop exhausted the land, wheat and products like flour, crackers, and whiskey. Young surveyor George Washington signaled future development on a plat he drew in 1748 in preparation for the auctioning of town lots: "Note that in the Bank fine Cellars may be cut. From thence wharves may be extended on the flats without any difficulty and ware houses built thereon as in Philadelphia."[6] In keeping with Washington's vision, prominent families built stately brick homes along King, Queen, Pitt, and Alexandria's other main streets named in a general nod to nobility and specific VIPs. The upper stratum of society supported private schools, churches, and a lecture hall and library. Many of these buildings became Union hospitals, offices, and residences from 1861 to 1865.

Washington, living on his plantation at Mount Vernon starting in 1754, became the town's most famous citizen. (A close second: Robert E. Lee, who moved to Alexandria with his prominent but penurious family in 1810 at age three; married Mary Custis, a step-descendant of Washington, at age twenty-four; and moved to her Arlington House estate.) Mount Vernon lay about ten miles south, a several-hour ride by horse, but Washington kept a house on Cameron Street to use when in town and to accommodate friends and family.[7] He bought a pew at Christ Church; voted in Alexandria; and frequented its taverns, apothecary, and other businesses. The lingering spirit of Washington remained strong during the Civil War, when Northerners, including Julia Wilbur, visited Mount Vernon and Christ Church.

In the days before the creation of the national capital, Alexandria aimed to become the legal, commercial, and social center of the region. A French traveler reported in 1780, "At Alexandria . . . the Potomac rolls its majestic stream with sublimity and grandeur. . . . This town is rapidly on the increase, and . . . cannot fail of becoming one of the first cities of the new world."[8] However, another warned, "There is a great display of luxury but it is a tawdry sort of ostentation: servants in silk stockings, men wearing silk stockings inside their boots and women most elegantly arrayed and with feathers in their hats."[9]

When President Washington chose the location for the nation's capital midway between North and South and straddling both sides of the Potomac, Alexandria leaders welcomed inclusion in the new District of Columbia. On April 15, 1791, a procession marched to Jones Point, south of town, to place the first boundary stone of the new federal district, originally envisioned as a diamond resting on one of its corners. Over glasses of wine, the participants toasted, "May the stone we are about to place in the ground remain an immovable monument of the wisdom and the unanimity of North America."[10] The cornerstone remains in place, but the rest of their toast proved illusory. The promised benefits never accrued, and Alexandria "retroceded" back to Virginia in 1847. By then Baltimore had overcome Alexandria as the region's main port.

One line of business flourished while the rest of the local economy languished—the buying and selling of slaves.

In 1827 New Orleans–based Isaac Franklin and Alexandria-based John Armfield, Franklin's nephew by marriage, joined forces to make slave trading an efficient and lucrative business. Before they launched their endeavor, slaveholders had gathered at the beginning of each year in Alexandria's taverns and made deals among themselves or sold slaves to itinerant traders. Franklin and Armfield changed the business model. Financially stretched property owners in Maryland and Virginia received visits from their agents or read their frequent newspaper advertisements offering "highest prices" for slaves. Many slaveholders—and slaves—found their way to the traders' establishment on Duke Street, one of Alexandria's main east-west arteries and less than a mile from the river. Armfield entertained the owners in fine parlors in the main house, while the enslaved waited out their fate in holding yards in the back. He bought slaves "wholesale" in Alexandria, shipped them via company-owned boats or marched them by foot to New Orleans and Natchez, where Franklin handled the "retail" side, auctioning off individuals in Louisiana and Mississippi.

Some observers commented on what they saw when blacks left the slave trader for parts unknown. "After having been confined, and sometimes manacled in a loathsome prison, they are turned out in public view to take their departure for the South," wrote one shortly after the business opened.[11] But Armfield, mindful of the importance of public relations, organized well-orchestrated tours of the enterprise for visitors from the North and foreign countries. Many, even those who professed themselves against slavery, seemed to believe all was on the up and up, relatively speaking. "In answer to my inquiries respecting the separation of families," wrote one observer incorrectly in 1835, "he [Armfield] assured me that they were at great pains to prevent such separation."[12] Some praised the quality of the clothing and food provided for the soon-to-be-sold. Others rightly criticized the very idea of auctioning off people (an illustration of an auction was part of the masthead of the abolitionist *Liberator*), but no organized attempt to close down the business, either locally or from elsewhere, occurred. In fact, their chosen line of work was legal. And while the slave traders never made it onto Alexandria's social A-list or the rosters of boosters of the library, schools, or other local civic endeavors, they retired as very wealthy men.

Alliances formed and reformed among the traders. In the 1830s, at the top of their game, Franklin and Armfield sold the business to one of their agents, who brought in his own business partners. Joseph Bruin, another former Franklin and Armfield agent, opened his own trading house a few blocks up Duke Street. Both firms advertised regularly and claimed to offer the best prices.[13] Slave-trading businesses that transferred people from the Upper to the Lower South also flourished in Baltimore, Richmond, and other cities. The sellers received much needed cash; the buyers, much needed labor. Historian Steven Deyle characterizes the domestic slave trade as "very much the lifeblood of the southern slave system and without it, the institution would have ceased to exist.[14]

The case of Mary and Emily Edmonson became Bruin's most famous transaction. In April 1848 the two girls, four of their brothers, and seventy others enslaved in Washington unsuccessfully attempted to escape on a ship called the *Pearl*. Like many of those on board, the Edmonsons had free-black relations, including their father. Most of the owners, aggrieved their "servants" wanted to leave them, sold the caught escapees. Bruin purchased the Edmonsons. He transported the girls to New Orleans, where they would have probably been forced into prostitution. Meanwhile, their father successfully made their case known in abolitionist circles, traveling to New York and connecting with the prominent Beecher family, among others. Fortunately for the girls, yellow fever hit New Orleans. Rather than risk his investment succumbing to disease, Bruin brought Mary and

Emily back, first to Baltimore and then to Alexandria. Their father and other supporters had extra time to raise money and negotiate with Bruin until the two sides made a deal in November 1848. The girls moved north to acclaim in abolitionist circles, although Mary died of tuberculosis soon afterward. Harriet Beecher Stowe acknowledged she drew on aspects of the Edmonsons' lives and of the Bruin slave pen in her novel *Uncle Tom's Cabin*. Julia Wilbur met Emily at least once, at an anti-slavery fair in Rochester.

The total number of people who left Alexandria under such circumstances is unknown, although Franklin and Armfield were said to transport more than one thousand people per year in their heyday. Slave manifests and other surviving documents record the names of a small percentage, but most remain anonymous, their voices and feelings lost. One exception is a letter from a young woman named Emily Russell, and it no doubt reflects the grief of thousands of others. "Mother! My dear mother! Do not forsake me; for I feel desolate," Emily wrote from Bruin's jail in 1848—rare that she could write, that she was able to pass a letter to her mother, and that her words survive.[15] The mother could not rescue her daughter, who died en route to Georgia.

Some locally enslaved blacks sadly passed through the traders' doors for sale down south. For most the businesses on Duke Street and periodic coffles of people leaving the city in chains represented a grim reminder of what *could* happen to them. Life for almost everyone in nineteenth-century America was economically and socially precarious, with virtually no safety net in the advent of a crisis. Added to this pervasive insecurity, blacks, including those legally free, walked a fine line in Alexandria as elsewhere. In 1831, after Nat Turner's rebellion in southern Virginia had resulted in the killing of 55 whites (and the reprisal killing of 120 blacks), the Alexandria black community felt obliged to issue a statement of "abhorrence of the recent outrage" and promised to "give public information of any plot, design or conspiracy."[16]

While Alexandria's majority white population welcomed the city's return to Virginia in 1847, African Americans probably did not join in the celebrations or the song written for the occasion with the chorus,

"Hurrah! We'll retrocede!" Life for a black person in the District was burdensome enough. Retrocession meant Alexandria's black population fell under the post–Nat Turner laws of Virginia. A school for black children closed. Black church activity was circumscribed. Those fortunate to gain freedom, whether through purchase or manumission, had to leave Virginia within one year, petition the legislature to remain (a lengthy and cumbersome process, with success not guaranteed), or risk return into bondage.[17] A liberated black with still-enslaved family members faced a tough choice.

For most of Alexandria's antebellum years, no organized white effort supported abolition or the rights of blacks. In 1827 the small but influential Quaker population launched an organization called the Benevolent Society of Alexandria for Ameliorating and Improving the Condition of the People of Color. It chose a conciliatory approach in action and language, appealing to the self-interest of slaveholders in ending slavery. But even that was too much after the Nat Turner rebellion. As locally prominent Quaker educator Benjamin Hallowell stated, "It was most prudent to suspend the meetings and they were never resumed."[18] In the late 1840s New Jersey Quakers purchased land next to Washington's Mount Vernon and created an agricultural community using free labor to dispel the notion the region could flourish only with slave labor. While indeed economically viable, their ideas did not catch on in the wider community.

Nonetheless, with a relatively large free population and many enslaved people having limited autonomy when hired out to other residences and businesses, African Americans in Alexandria created communities and bonds. In neighborhoods called The Bottoms and Hayti, free-black families earned their living from the trades and from physical labor. In another neighborhood appropriately called Fishtown, blacks worked seasonally to process shad and other herring from the then bountiful Potomac for export. A very small number owned their own businesses, including a male-owned barbershop and a female-owned grocery store.

Alexandrians at the beginning of the 1860s had no inkling of what the next ten years had in store for them. Things looked bright. While the initial furor about John Brown incited some to conclude that dissolution of the nation was the only way to protect slavery and their way of life, that opinion subsided after a few months. A torchlight procession in September 1860 proved, according to the *Alexandria Gazette*, the "intense enthusiasm" for the Union cause. Intense enthusiasm, that is, until Fort Sumter and Lincoln's call to arms.[19]

2

During the War

CHAPTER FIVE

"Civil War Is Upon Us"

The Confederate attack on Fort Sumter did what Abraham Lincoln and Jefferson Davis couldn't pull off on their own: it charged Rochester up to take on the Union cause and Alexandria to rally around secession.

In the November 1860 election, Lincoln carried Rochester but not with great gusto.[1] The following February, when his train passed through en route to the inauguration in Washington, fifteen thousand city residents braved the cold to see him, but more out of respect for the soon-to-be chief of state than partisan fervor. A large "Welcome to the President" sign waved, a band played "Hail to the Chief," and the depot was festooned with American flags. Lincoln stayed in Rochester for six minutes.

Julia Wilbur was a strong Republican, but she recorded a muted reaction to Lincoln's victory. Two days after Election Day, she wrote, "It is thought Lincoln is elected." Other family members were less enthralled, especially her brother-in-law Alfred Van Wagoner, a Democrat with Southern sympathies. The two often debated the issues of the day, Julia assuming she got the last word and no doubt Alfred thinking the same. She was in the midst of a visit to the Van Wagoners' farm in Somerset on Election Day, a trip she claimed to take as a "matter of duty" but in fact one that helped break her loneliness at home. When Alfred returned from voting, she asked, "What is the aspect of things?" He replied, "All black."[2]

Many people in Rochester—indeed throughout the North—shared Alfred's views upon the election of Abraham Lincoln to mollify the South and avoid disunion. In early December 1860 a mob threatened abolitionists in Boston, including Frederick Douglass and Wendell Phillips, when they held a meeting to commemorate the anniversary of John Brown's hanging. Thurlow Weed, an Albany newspaperman and Republican with a national reputation, vocally advocated conciliation. Northern congressmen suggested a series of well-publicized but unsuccessful compromises with their Southern counterparts.

Conciliation notwithstanding, on December 20, 1860, South Carolina seceded from the United States. The *Charleston Mercury* crowed, "The State of South Carolina has recorded herself before the universe." The mainstream press in Rochester noted the event more circumspectly, although Frederick Douglass saw war on the horizon with South Carolina's action. In Alexandria the *Gazette* reported as a "painful duty" the news of South Carolina's secession from the Union, which had been "created by the Fathers whose memory we reverence and whose principles we cherish."[3]

Julia Wilbur read the news but remained preoccupied with her own civil strife. "Disunion troubles do not disturb me. Home affairs are all that I care about now," she wrote on December 22, the day South Carolina's representatives were in Washington to demand the turnover of federal property to the state.[4] Lincoln, still in Illinois as president-elect, pronounced he would not interfere with slavery when he became president.

Julia had new worries added to her grief over Freda and her disagreements with her brother Henry, sister-in-law Ann, and stepmother Laura. In Michigan her sister Ella was seriously ill. Frances, the one sister who lived within walking distance, announced, without much enthusiasm, that her husband had bought a farm about seventy miles away from Rush in the town of Hartland, and they would move in the spring. Christmas 1860 passed quietly—no festive family feast, only the specter of the one-year anniversary of Freda's leaving and continued hostility in the Wilbur household.

Then another slap. On December 30, almost to the day of the anniversary that Revilo had come for Freda, Julia's father had Sam, the dog that Freda had adopted, killed. Whether he consciously knew the anniversary or was oblivious, Julia couldn't fathom. "They tell me it was feared that he would kill sheep, but I think this was a mere pretext." So Julia didn't even have Sam, "the good old dog that Freda loved & I loved for Freda's sake," to comfort her. Most farms have a motley crew of animals, and not everyone attaches to them emotionally, particularly in an era when few people kept animals as pets. Apparently the men in the Wilbur household did not number among the pet lovers. Henry had already chased away a cat Freda had liked to play with. When Julia confronted her father, Stephen professed not to understand the reason for the fuss. Even more disturbing than his attitude about the dog was his attitude about the child: "I believe he scarcely thinks of her & probably supposes that *I* have given her up." She definitely had not given Freda up. Her father grew impatient with her inability to accept the reality—Freda was gone, and Revilo didn't want any contact with them. To him it was unfortunate but time to move on. He wanted to "avoid disunion" at home.[5]

In early 1861 abolitionist and women's rights advocate Susan B. Anthony organized a speaking tour around the theme "No Compromise with Slaveholders." Wherever the "No Compromise" tour stopped, people attacked it. Opponents, including community leaders and policemen, "hissed, hooted, yelled, and stamped" in Buffalo, while in the small town of Port Byron, someone threw cayenne pepper on the heating stove, forcing everyone to leave or choke.[6] The *Rochester Union and Advertiser* could barely restrain its contempt, referring to "Susan" and not "Miss Anthony" in an article reporting about the event at the city's grand Corinthian Hall. While the paper did not glorify those who disrupted the gatherings, it expressed outrage that "an attempt was made by these agitators to hold a meeting here at this time."[7]

In March, undeterred, the abolitionist "agitators" planned another meeting. Corinthian Hall wasn't an option this time around; they held it at the black AME Zion Church, a stop on the Underground Railroad and the place that had harbored the city's first anti-slavery women's group almost three decades earlier. This meeting featured talks by Anthony, Frederick Douglass, Lucy Colman, and others. Julia, visiting Rochester, attended and even stayed with Colman for a few nights. It was good for her to get away from the farm. It hadn't helped her mood when she had stopped at the family burying ground on her way to Rochester, where "a terrible sense of loneliness came over me; it seemed not a hard thing then to lie down with those pale sleepers & leave the world to others who choose to struggle & live on."[8] We have no indication she seriously considered steps to "leave the world," but these are certainly the words of a sad person.

Julia's visit reflected the dissonance of her own life and of the times. The following day she visited a widowed acquaintance named Mrs. Hall and saw the irony in her hostess's views: "She is not Anti-S [anti-slavery] & thinks women are inferior to men in every way & this—while she teaches school—keeps house—has 3 children to care for & keeps boarders!"[9]

Next on the agenda Julia and Colman visited the home of Frederick and Anna Douglass, who then lived on the outskirts of the city. Douglass enthralled his guests with his account of John Brown. Like many abolitionists, Julia had read the conflicting opinions about Brown. She noted, "Today's visit enlightened me. I have heard about it from one who knew."[10] Although Douglass considered the 1859 raid "unwise, imprudent and dangerous," he said Brown still impressed him as a great man. Julia and the other visitors must have sat on the edges of the family's front parlor seats as Douglass related his secret meeting with Brown in a quarry near Harpers Ferry when he tried to convince Brown to abort the raid. Despite discouraging Brown, Douglass told his guests he was vulnerable to arrest because he knew about the plan beforehand. He had anxiously telegraphed back to Rochester to get "certain papers in his house secured," then fled the country in disguise to escape arrest as a conspirator.

Over the course of three days, Julia reconnected with her political leanings at the anti-slavery meeting, contrasted her views with those of the reactionary Mrs. Hall, and visited with an abolitionist icon. She also spent time with people, probably the majority then as now, who just wanted to relax and enjoy themselves. She accompanied her former sister-in-law Charlotte to a social evening at the home of some of Charlotte's friends. Julia sat on the sidelines while the rest of the guests played cards and drank champagne. "To see rational, accountable beings spend hours in this way, instead of trying to improve each other by intelligent conversation & social intercourse is, to me, a sad sight," she sniffed.[11] She preferred an evening hearing about John Brown, but clearly not everyone did.

Most Alexandrians eschewed the secessionist enthusiasm of the states further south. In the 1860 election John Bell, a pro-Union candidate who tried to avoid a position on slavery in the campaign, garnered the majority of local votes. "Most certainly the mother of States has spoken in unmistakable language in favor of the preservation of the Federal Union," suggested the *Alexandria Gazette* in reporting the election results. Lincoln received 2 votes out of 1,670 cast.[12]

More excitable elements stepped up the effort to strengthen the local militias. The Mount Vernon Guards, Alexandria Rifles (the group that had gone to Harpers Ferry post–John Brown), and Alexandria Artillery drilled and marched around town. Two teenagers announced a meeting to form a new rifle company on December 1, 1860. Four people showed up, including the two of them. Undeterred, they continued to recruit, and eventually more than one hundred strong, named themselves the Old Dominion Rifles.[13]

As the tide of secession grew, Virginia was the prize both the Union and Confederacy wanted. It had the largest industrial capacity in the South, as well as the largest white population and number of military-age white men.[14] According to the 1860 census, four of the ten largest Southern cities were in Virginia. Alexandria, with a population of 12,652, came in number eleven.[15]

With South Carolina and six other states already out of the Union, the Virginia General Assembly voted to hold a special session in Richmond in mid-February 1861 to consider secession. As its representative, Alexandria decisively elected a lawyer named George Brent, who campaigned in favor of remaining with the Union against a secessionist-leaning opponent. The convention started out with a majority of delegates opposing secession. Over the next few weeks secessionists, although the minority, recognized the advantage of shaking things up in the court of public opinion. They packed the audience galleries with supporters who cheered and jeered as needed. At night, according to one of the pro-Unionist delegates, they organized "a motley crew of free negroes, boys, and mad cops" who would gather under the hotel room windows of the Unionist men cat-calling the ultimate insult—"Abolitionist!"[16]

Meanwhile, in Alexandria the volunteer militias continued to drill, march, design their uniforms, and compete with each other to reap the most praise from their fellow citizens. The men took turns on patrol, with certain spots around town particularly desirable for their proximity to "the company of bright and pretty girls," as well as places to get a bite to eat or a glass of ale.[17] War and bloodshed barely entered into the picture.

Who had heard of Fort Sumter before December 1860? Certainly not the average Rochesterian or Alexandrian. Only a few civilian laborers occupied the fort on an island off of Charleston when South Carolina seceded in December 1860. The small federal military contingent quartered instead at nearby Fort Moultrie on the mainland. Commanding officer Maj. Robert Anderson knew any attack from the militias in nearby Charleston could ignite war and that his every step, whether forward or back, was critical.[18] He moved his group of fewer than one hundred from Moultrie to the better-protected Sumter. South Carolina demanded the men evacuate. A tense stand-off held until early March 1861, when Sumter began to run out of food. Should the government attempt to resupply the men, risking Southern ire, or leave, thus recognizing the Southern claim? Most of Lincoln's advisers and military leaders initially favored voluntary evacuation; the newly inaugurated president did not, and eventually his Cabinet came around. Expecting relief to arrive to Anderson and his men any day, the Confederates attacked Fort Sumter on April 12, 1861. On April 14 the federal troops surrendered.

That was huge. No matter the buildup, no matter the months of waffling and searching for compromise, the North saw the Confederacy had attacked. Lincoln issued a call for seventy-five thousand troops from the states, including three thousand from Virginia. With no draft until further into the war, he could not require a single man to serve beyond the mere sixteen thousand or so who formed the standing U.S. Army. Virginians saw Lincoln's request as bearing arms against fellow Southerners. On April 17 the Virginia convention delegates quickly passed an Ordinance of Secession stating that the "Constitution of the United States of America is no longer binding on any of the citizens of this State." Alexandria's George

Brent voted in the minority to remain in the Union but volunteered to fight for the Confederacy the day after the convention formally adjourned. Robert E. Lee resigned his U.S. Army commission and headed south, along with about one-third of the federal officer corps.

Brent's switch to the Confederacy reflected the views of his formerly Unionist-minded fellow Alexandrians. The militias reported large increases in their numbers. The *Gazette*, which had advocated for the Union for months, proudly declared that "we are gratified to be able to state, since the appearance of Lincoln's Proclamation, calling for seventy-five thousand troops to invade the South, the expression of sentiment is well nigh unanimous in favor of the maintenance of Southern rights."[19]

A formal vote to ratify the convention's ordinance was scheduled for May 23, a month hence, with the results a foregone conclusion. As another foregone conclusion, everyone knew the Union would try to move into Alexandria, directly across from Washington, as soon as Virginia formally seceded.

A reporter from Washington ventured across the river in mid-May to find that "birds were singing in the trees, and the echoes of their notes sounded as they do in the still air of a forest. . . . Nearly all the houses seemed deserted, and in one or two places I noticed that spiders have woven their webs across the door-ways."[20] Alexandria was not quite as depopulated as he reported to his readers, although many evacuated for what they expected would be a short period of time. They assumed they would return in a week or two, a Union-leaning shopkeeper named John Ogden later wrote to his daughter, once "Lincoln's hirelings, as they called the U.S. soldiers, would be driven out and Alexandria retaken by southerners."[21]

"Our friends and neighbors have left us," wrote Judith McGuire in her diary on May 4. "Can it be that our country is to be carried on and on to the horrors of civil war? I pray, oh how fervently I do pray, that our Heavenly Father may yet avert it."[22] She and her husband, headmaster at Episcopal High School about two miles outside of town (still in operation today), had already sent their children away and would themselves leave within weeks.

Across the Potomac troops from New York, Rhode Island, and

other Northern states poured into Washington daily. As a more visible reminder of the potential consequences of secession, the USS *Pawnee* loomed within sight of the Alexandria waterfront.

Not everyone fled or fretted. Some exalted in the expected showdown. Back in March a man named James Jackson had ordered a Confederate flag from a seamstress whose late husband had been a flag and sailmaker; it was this flag that led to the fateful encounter between Jackson and Col. Elmer Ellsworth of New York at the end of May and the first casualties of the Civil War. Jackson had recently arrived in Alexandria. The youngest of seven children, he had a little trouble settling down; according to a fawning biography published in Richmond a year after his death, the tall, dark-haired man "became involved in numerous hardy adventures" throughout Northern Virginia.[23] During the 1860 presidential campaign, he cut down the flagpole of a pro-Lincoln supporter in the town of Occoquan, so he knew well the symbolism of a flag. In late 1860 to early 1861 he invested $4,000 to refurbish and lease the Marshall House Hotel for five years, hoping to compete with the finer establishments in town. He didn't recoup his money, but the investment certainly earned him a different type of return.

The finished flag was huge, fourteen by twenty-four feet, the equivalent of three modern-day queen-sized sheets sewn together.[24] Jackson had it raised above the Marshall House on a forty-foot pole on the afternoon of April 17, the day the Virginia convention voted; the story goes the Lincolns could see it through a spyglass from the White House. Back in Alexandria people stood at the intersection of King and Pitt Streets near the hotel and cheered as the flag ascended, taller than anything else in the city.

Up north Julia wrote, "Last Sunday, Fort Sumter was evacuated. . . . Virginia has seceded and *the war has begun.*"[25] In Rochester, as in Alexandria, pro-war fervor carried the day. Newly elected Republican mayor John Nash convened a public meeting to respond to Lincoln's call for troops. People spilled out of the Reynolds Arcade, where the post office and telegraph office served as the focal point of news, for what was claimed to be the "largest indoor gathering ever held." In addition to announcing Lincoln's call, Nash launched a campaign to raise money for the dependents of the men who would march off to war. A committee formed for the purpose collected more than $36,000 in pledges within two weeks. The formerly anti-confrontation *Rochester Union and Advertiser* proclaimed, "Everybody for war!" and started displaying war news in the middle of its front page. The rival *Democrat and American* proclaimed, "We are one."[26]

Satellite meetings sprang up. Julia's father and stepmother rode over to Mr. Hartwell's store in Avon on the afternoon of April 20. When they returned, they told Julia that "they could not get into the store for the crowd. . . . Cannons were fired, drums beating, and the flags flying & little gray [the Wilburs' horse] did not know what to make of it. Civil war is upon us."[27] Emotions ran high. When a man with relatives in Mississippi raised a Confederate flag, a group of men made him take it down, tore it up, distributed the pieces among themselves, then threatened they would destroy his house if he didn't raise a Union flag. Julia did not support that move but thought, "He had better keep still if he is not a friend of the North. We shall not hold still for *his relations* to fight us, or lynch us, or hang us, or tar & feather us."[28]

Rochester raised a regiment, led by Professor Isaac Quinby, hastily on leave from the eleven-year-old University of Rochester, where he taught calculus. Now Colonel Quinby had attended West Point and fought in the Mexican War, making him one of the more qualified in the city to lead a regiment. Like many early recruits on both sides, the troops of the Thirteenth New York Infantry left home with great fanfare, innocent of the bloodshed they would soon confront.

For Julia the personal and the political again intertwined. The day she mourned the three-year anniversary of the burial of her sister Sarah, the regiment, en route south, stopped at the depot in Avon, miles away from the farm, from where she could hear its music and cheering. Even before hostilities broke out, she welcomed the fight, and not just to preserve the Union. "Bloodshed must ensue or Slavery will triumph, I very much fear," she wrote.[29] Unlike most people, including President Lincoln, she saw the war from the start as a way to end slavery.

Yet bellicose thoughts in the abstract are one thing. Personal connections change the complexion of things. The first regiment of young men who left Rochester bound for Washington included no family members or close friends. News came from Michigan that Julia's brother-in-law Joseph Van Buskirk, husband to her youngest sister Mary, had volunteered for the Second Michigan Regiment. Suddenly, in all Julia's talk about welcoming war, one of her favorite sisters had a husband about to go to war. She supported his sense of duty but also thought "he might have waited until it becomes necessary for more men."[30]

Abstract talk also came down to reality in Alexandria. In anticipation of the vote to secede, the federal military made plans to head across the river to northern Virginia. The Confederates knew about this as well as anyone and positioned sentries along the roads that led from the three bridges across the Potomac.

On May 23 white men in Alexandria formally cast their vote for or against secession. The town that had supported remaining in the Union a few months earlier voted to leave it by a vote of 983 to 106, about two-thirds the total that had cast votes in the presidential election the previous November. By May many would-be voters had left with their families or joined the Confederate army. But John Ogden wrote his daughter, "That vote was a farce—Union men dared not vote," although he acknowledged they were a small minority in any event.[31] American voters did not cast secret ballots anywhere until the late 1800s; moreover, Virginians voice-voted in public, a system known as *viva voce*.

In the very early morning on the day after the referendum to secede, a Michigan regiment led by Col. Orlando Willcox marched across the Long Bridge (location of the current Fourteenth Street Bridge) toward Alexandria. At the same time, the Eleventh New York Voluntary Infantry Regiment—called the Zouaves because of the soldiers' elaborate North African–inspired uniforms—boated across the river, led by Colonel Ellsworth, a personal favorite of the Lincolns. Knowing they were outnumbered, almost all of the Old Dominion Rifles, Mt. Vernon Rifles, and other local militias left and joined up with the Confederate army further south, leaving Alexandria open to occupation.

The Zouaves disembarked. Most headed west to occupy the railroad depot and telegraph office, per their orders. Ellsworth saw James Jackson's flag above the Marshall House and veered over to King Street. He couldn't resist—or maybe he already knew he would make the detour. Climbing to the top of the hotel with a small band (which included a New York reporter, a secretary, and a chaplain), he cut down the Confederate flag and descended the hotel stairs, the flag draped over his shoulder. Jackson came out of his room and killed Ellsworth with his shotgun. One of Ellsworth's men, Frank Brownell from Troy, killed Jackson. *Harper's Weekly* reported that Brownell telegraphed home, "FATHER—Colonel Ellsworth shot dead this morning. I killed his murderer."[32]

Within minutes North and South had their first heroes. In New York Julia Wilbur wrote five words in her pocket diary: "Col. Ellsworth killed in Alexandria." No further clarification of name or place was needed. In Virginia Judith McGuire, who had just fled Alexandria, wrote of Jackson, "He is the first martyr." An Alexandria clerk named Henry Whittington underscored the significance of the event from the Southern point of view. "The history of this flag will long be remembered by our people," he wrote in his diary, distinguishing "our" people as fellow Confederates, not U.S. citizens.[33]

Ellsworth's men brought their leader's body back across the Potomac, where it lay in state in the White House and Capitol before making its way north. The *New York Tribune*, among other papers, printed an oversized illustration of the late colonel front and center on page 1. Mourners ranged from everyday people (for example, eight babies baptized in just one church in Lancaster County, Pennsylvania, during the rest of 1861 bore some version of "Elmer" or "Ellsworth" or both in their names) to the Lincolns and members of the Cabinet.[34] The photographer Mathew Brady, who had fortuitously photographed Ellsworth in full Zouave garb a few days before, printed and sold copies by the thousands; he later posed Brownell with his weapon and a piece of the bloodstained flag.[35] Volunteer enlistments spiked across the North, spurred by a desire to avenge Ellsworth's demise.

Jackson's body lay at the Marshall House until the next afternoon, with Northern and Southern accounts differing as to the treatment of his family and his remains.[36] Finally the military allowed for removal of the body. The Fairfax Court House bell tolled as Jackson's body headed into Confederate territory, and mourners joined in a procession to the Jackson family's cemetery in the Washington suburb of McLean.[37]

As the Marshall House incident unfolded, the other New York and Michigan troops followed the original plan to march west, navigating their way to the railroad hub by following tracks. As they tore up the tracks and tried not to startle each other into friendly fire attack, they came upon a local militia that, in the confusion, had remained in town—coincidentally near the slave-trading company of Price, Birch & Company (formerly Franklin and Armfield) on Duke Street. The Union troops placed the captured Virginians inside the pen, where they came upon an elderly black man chained to the floor, left by the slave traders when they fled. They released the man, unfortunately unnamed through history, who traveled with the Michigan regiment as a cook throughout the war.

At dawn on May 25 Colonel Willcox sent a telegram to Washington: "Alexandria is ours. One company, Captain Ball, mounted, thirty-five men and thirty-five horses [captured]. I regret to say Colonel Ellsworth has been shot by a person in a house."[38] The people of Alexandria watched as troops streamed into their city. "Officers and men are busy in seeking and occupying quarters throughout the city," wrote Henry Whittington in his diary.[39] They found vacated homes, aided by a few locals who acted either through political conviction or expediency. Later Union men appropriated buildings to their liking even if the residents hadn't left. When the city council refused to furnish shelter and food for the military's horses, Willcox declared martial law. The town's two newspapers, the *Gazette* and the *Sentinel*, suspended publication rather than announce the declaration. Two Michigan soldiers entered the empty *Gazette* office, used the printing press to make the announcement, and then looted the premises. The press suspension was even reported in Rochester, in an article that also noted "the people of Alexandria are in a great state of agitation and terror."[40] The *Sentinel* ceased, but Edgar Snowden, the *Gazette* publisher, returned to publish his family's newspaper, with some notable hiccups, throughout the war.

For the locals martial law meant a curfew, the presence of hordes of Union troops, and, most significant of all, the need to swear an oath of allegiance to the United States to transact many once routine activities. Those who neither left nor took the oath found their livelihoods sharply reduced.

From one week to the next, life in Alexandria had completely changed.

CHAPTER SIX

"My Way Seems Clear to Go"

In the spring and early summer of 1861 most people assumed the war would end quickly, with each side predicting its own successful outcome. The Rochester regiment went off in a burst of glory, some of its members worrying they would arrive too late for battlefield glory. Alexandria residents left for an expected brief hiatus, leaving pictures on their walls and knickknacks in their parlors. Some also left slaves in their homes, assuming they would remain and guard the silver. All were proven wrong on all counts.

Julia Wilbur began to emerge from her grief over separation from her niece Freda to follow news of the war and to otherwise reengage with the world around her. In May 1861, during one of her more frequent trips up to Rochester, she met John Brown Jr., who the press incorrectly rumored was organizing African Americans to fight in western Virginia. Susan B. Anthony, Lucy Colman, and Rosetta Douglass, among other abolitionists, also sat listening to Brown that day. All joined in discussion about what the war would do for slavery. Someone, perhaps Brown himself, related that Charles Sumner, the ardent anti-slavery senator from Massachusetts, argued against a swift outcome in order to eradicate slavery; according to Brown's account, Sumner thought "the North must be castigated severely . . . before there will be a general anti-slavery feeling sufficient to make cause with the slave."[1] He and others, including Julia, feared the war would end swiftly, with slavery intact.

If Sumner wished for castigation, then the Battle of Bull Run served him well. At the end of July the Confederates defeated the ill-prepared Union troops on a hot Sunday afternoon twenty-five miles from Washington. "We learned this a.m. that a terrible battle has been fought at Bull's Run. . . . Little else is talked about now, so many are anxious to hear from friends. The Rochester regiment was one that suffered most & Avon boys were in that," Julia wrote.[2] In fact, the Thirteenth New York Infantry sustained so many losses that it became known as the Bloody Thirteenth. A Confederate soldier captured Albert Ely, Rochester's congressman, who had journeyed out to the Virginia countryside with other civilians to view the anticipated Union rout. Reportedly confronted with the soldier's cry, "You white-livered Yankee, you're just the cuss I have been looking for," Ely remained imprisoned in Richmond until released in an exchange at Christmastime.[3] Another Rochester civilian, who had accompanied Ely to view the battle and was also captured, died in the prison.

Julia's brother-in-law Joseph Van Buskirk fought at Bull Run with his Michigan regiment. His wife Mary and their daughter Minnie were in Rush at the time. The rest of the family tried to hide the news from Mary until they knew Joseph's fate. A few days later Mary heard from Joseph, safe but dispirited. Mary shared his letter, which described how the confusion of battle turned to a chaotic aftermath. "His regiment was . . . the last to leave the field. . . . All they had to eat on that day was 2 or 3 crackers. After the fight they marched 35 miles in 12 hrs. in the rain without blankets, & then slept in a barn on the hay without supper," Julia wrote.[4] Exhausted, they made it to Arlington Heights, one of many places in and near Alexandria where the regiment camped—places Julia would see for herself in the future.

Mary had come to Rush from Michigan that summer to seek comfort and company while her husband fought. But tense relations within the Wilbur household contributed to, rather than alleviated, her anxiety. "Nobody tries to make it pleasant for Mary," said Julia, blaming the rest of the family, especially her stepmother Laura, who "is disposed to join Henry & Ann in their efforts to make it uncomfortable for Mary & myself."[5] Things came to a head when Julia complained to her father; apparently Laura did the same, leaving Stephen in the middle. They reached a truce, however fragile. Julia lamented the absence of their biological mother because it meant Mary could not stay there indefinitely.

In late August Julia and Mary, with Minnie, headed to Somerset to stay with their older sisters before Mary and Minnie returned to Michigan. Julia saw mother and daughter off on the train. She then spent a few hours on her own in nearby Niagara Falls, admiring the "fairy scene" of the water pouring over the falls and catching the light in its spray. She looked over at Clifton House on the Canadian side and stopped into the International Hotel on the U.S. side, grand hotels built to accommodate tourists who visited, according to one travel guide of the time, "the most stupendous cataract on the face of the globe."[6] The hotel staff reported slow business without the customary Southern tourists who before the war had escaped the heat and traveled north each summer. One visitor attached himself to Julia: a stray piglet, which followed her as she walked the grounds and watched avidly as she ate her lunch. "When I stopped, the pig stopped. When I went on the pig went on. . . . At last I went up the steps of a saloon & through it & piggy could not follow."[7] It felt good to have a pleasant excursion, including the encounter with the hopeful pig, after taking leave of her sister and niece.

Julia passed several more weeks in Somerset and joined in a several-day family excursion to visit Forts Niagara and Mississauga on either side of the U.S.-Canadian border. Julia savored trips like this throughout her life—a group of friends or family visiting sites of interest and collecting relics and plant specimens. Figuring out how to make off with a four-pound cannon ball as a souvenir highlighted this adventure. The forts were quiet, Niagara tended by "an old man in the faded uniform of an ordnance Sergeant" and his family. A few months later U.S. troops occupied Niagara out of fear that Great Britain would support the Confederacy and enter the country via Canada.[8]

While in Somerset, Julia continued to tussle with her brother-in-law Alfred about the war, noting, "We had some sharp words. He lays all the troubles to Abolitionists. Doesn't blame the South at all." Yet despite their political differences (when she enclosed a letter to him in an envelope with a preprinted anti-slavery message, he declared it should not be allowed to go through the mail), they seem to have gotten along reasonably well. Unlike her own brother Henry, she found Alfred a "well-meaning person," especially as he related to the people around him.[9]

On her way home to Rush, Julia stopped in Rochester and commemorated Fast Day—September 26, 1861. Requested by Congress after the Bull Run fiasco, the president's proclamation called for a day of humiliation, fasting, and prayer. Julia did not record if she refrained from food or how greatly she felt humiliation, but she, Charlotte, and a friend fanned out to different churches throughout the city, reporting back on the sermons they heard. Julia returned unimpressed from hers, as the minister barely spoke out against slavery. Across the North ministers preached sermons with such titles as "The Valley of Decision" and "Comfort in Tribulation," many printed into pamphlets for permanent appreciation.[10]

When Julia arrived home that night, after seven weeks away, she found sister-in-law Ann and stepmother Laura sick. "On father's account I wish I had been at home, but on all other accounts I am glad that I was away," she decided. Housework resumed: "Yesterday & today I have washed & ironed & made pickles & cleaned some & worked in garden & am now very tired."[11] She noted another anniversary since her last contact with Freda (eighty-two weeks) but was busy enough not to dwell on it.

Many letters awaited her, including mail from Joseph from the army. She liked reading his eyewitness views of the war to supplement news accounts. War progress and household chores continually intermingle in her writing—the generals, the battles, the outcomes, and the casualties, combined with the routine of everyday life. A typical entry: "A battle in Western Virginia, our loss said to be 600 & the rebels 1500. Gen. Wise was made to run. Did housework & finished a dress for Florence."[12]

Julia did not get much involved in, or at least did not write about, organized efforts to provide supplies to the troops. On both sides of the conflict, women sewed, collected lint for bandages, darned socks, and otherwise contributed to the war cause from home. As the Ladies' Hospital Relief Association of Rochester, begun in early 1862, stated, "We must perform some *tangible duty*. For this we have but a limited range. We cannot go to the battle field, nor, with few exceptions, serve in the distant hospitals; but nearly all can aid our soldiers in some way."[13] Instead Julia began to dream of performing her "tangible duty" closer to the action. On Thanksgiving Day

1861, again back in Rochester, she watched a regiment of what she estimated as eight or nine hundred men board trains to head south. She couldn't help notice the women who slipped bottles of liquor into the pockets of their departing loved ones, some so drunk that "they were dragged on to the cars." But she realized, "These rough-looking men take leave of their friends, wives & sisters clinging to them till the last minute . . . & many probably took their last look of each other then."[14]

Looking at the throngs in the hundreds, Julia tried to imagine what seventy thousand men would look like—the number that, a week earlier, had marched in General McClellan's Grand Review in Baileys Crossroads, Virginia (now a Washington suburb, then a rural hamlet). And she realized, "How I would like to go to Washington & see those warlike preparations, the men, the munitions of war, the fortifications & all that pertains to the field."[15] Consciously or not, she set the wheels in motion, staying with Lucy Colman and making contact with members of the Rochester Ladies' Anti-Slavery Society.

Julia wanted to earn her own money again. Yet she wrote off teaching, her clearest option. When she visited one of her former schools, she thought it looked good, but she could muster no energy to return to the classroom. She also concluded she could not make enough to support herself with sewing and rejected taking on the work of a servant. While considering these options, on New Year's Day 1862 she realized, "I begin to think it will not do to wait some for anything to turn up, but I must turn up something myself."[16]

One thing she did quietly, apparently without the rest of the family's knowledge: she sent out feelers about becoming involved in efforts to assist African American refugees in the South.

On May 23, 1861, the day Union troops marched into Alexandria, three enslaved black men sought refuge at Fort Monroe, the largest fort in the nation at the time. On a peninsula that jutted into Chesapeake Bay, it remained under the control of 4,500 Union troops despite Virginia's vote to secede. How should Gen. Benjamin Butler, the newly arrived commander, handle these men? The Fugitive Slave Act of 1850, which required the return of escaped slaves to their owners, was officially the law of the land, and Butler was not known for his abolitionist sympathies. Although not a pleasant way to refer to human beings, he identified the three men as contraband property belonging to the enemy and thus did not have to return them in wartime. Moreover, before they had come into Monroe, their master had required them to build fortifications; if returned, Butler reasoned, they would continue to aid the Confederate cause.

Word spread about this route to freedom. Within days several score of people showed up at Fort Monroe—not just male laborers, but also women, children, and the elderly; by July, almost a thousand had entered. Many more fled into other Union-occupied areas, from Louisiana to Washington, an estimated five hundred thousand by 1865, almost half of whom worked for the military in some capacity.[17] Early in the war no official policy came from Washington about what the military should do, so individual commanders responded as they saw fit. On the southeastern coast, for example, Gen. David Hunter ordered the abolition of slavery in the territory he took over (an order that Lincoln revoked). In contrast, Gen. Henry Halleck ordered the removal of what he saw as fugitives from his camps in Missouri.

Some blacks did not move but found themselves in Union-held territory, most notably when the U.S. military seized the islands off South Carolina. More than ten thousand African Americans remained on plantations that white slaveholding families left. Until the Emancipation Proclamation on January 1, 1863, all these people, whether fleeing or left behind, held an ill-defined identity—not liberated but also not under the dominion of the slavemasters. As Julia would learn when she talked to refugees in Alexandria, flight was fraught with danger, especially for women with small children or the less physically strong. True, the Union might have advanced to territory just a few miles away, but slave catchers, Confederate troops, and/or rough, inhospitable terrain often lay between. Unlike pieces of property, the people who fled, both male and female, had to make conscious, difficult choices. No wonder the term "contraband" felt both inaccurate and insulting.[18] "When slaves are referred to, they must be called persons held to service or labor," said Frederick Douglass in January 1862, noting that "contraband" was a term "that [would]

73

apply better to a pistol than a person."[19] In some quarters "contraband" gave way to the term "freedman"—not perfect but certainly a more human-oriented word that carried over after the war with the creation of the Freedmen's Bureau.

In addition to the immediate needs of food and shelter, education was a top priority for children and adults. On September 1, 1861, Mary Chase opened a school for blacks in Alexandria, an outlawed practice punishable by whipping or imprisonment just a few months before.[20] Further south near Norfolk, Mary Peake (a black woman who had lived for about a decade in Alexandria as a young girl) had already operated a small clandestine school. At Fort Monroe she did so openly.

Northern relief and missionary societies got into the act, beginning with a request from a chaplain at Fort Monroe to acquaintances in New York. In response the American Missionary Society sent Rev. Lewis Lockwood to Virginia, terming his endeavor to assist the freedmen "a new field of missionary labor."[21] Edward Pierce, a U.S. Treasury agent who observed the activity at Fort Monroe, suggested something similar in the Union-occupied South Carolina Sea Islands. Pierce tried to organize continued cultivation of cotton by the blacks under the Treasury Department (given the crop's potential contribution to federal coffers). He offered Northern relief societies the opportunity to deal with other aspects of life, especially education, in what became known as the Port Royal Experiment.

At the end of 1861 Julia wrote to Lockwood offering her services; according to her diary in January 1862, "A letter from Rev. L. C. L. has been received in reply to mine." Things didn't work out—"shall not go to Fortress Monroe at present," she recorded a few weeks later.[22] She also wrote to Rev. William Channing, a Unitarian minister who had lived in Rochester in the 1850s, about going to Port Royal. He was more receptive than Lockwood, and with at least a semi-offer in hand, Julia spoke to her father about it. Stephen called the idea "a wild calculation."[23] He did not outright forbid her, but he questioned her ability to handle the conditions and laid on what we would see as a guilt trip about the need for her to help in the household. She may also have needed money from him in order to go, as many relief agents needed to pay their own way. As she negotiated with her father, she learned that Channing's group had gathered as many teachers as it needed, and the boat to Port Royal from New York literally sailed without her. But the idea was planted. Her time would come.

As Julia considered her next step, a twenty-four-year-old close friend of the family named Julia Winans died after a long illness, possibly from the effects of a spider bite. The same doctor who had tended Sarah Bigelow cared for the young girl, assuring her family that "she would get better until the p.m. she died." Needless to say, based on the experience with her sister back in 1858, Julia commented, "I have not a particle of confidence in Dr. N." But some consolation came in Winans's death: "As she lay on her death couch, she looked as if sleeping & there was nothing there of the gloom & repulsiveness of death. . . . She is safe now from harm & temptation."[24] With family and friends to watch over her, in her own home, Winans's death epitomized the so-called Good Death romanticized in Victorian times. As historian Drew Gilpin Faust has pointed out, it was the lack of a "good death" that so alarmed people when they sent their loved ones into battle, where they might die anonymously and alone.[25]

Henry and Ann moved to a vacant dwelling on the Wilbur property. Their move provided great relief. Somehow they had commandeered the best room in the house, locking it when away even for an hour or so. They made guests, including and maybe especially relatives, feel unwelcome. They left for days at a time without any advance word. "How unnaturally we have lived for nearly two years. But I think it will be more pleasant now," Julia hoped.[26] She cleaned out the room the couple had occupied and went again into the front parlor Ann had usurped. As strange as it seems that Stephen had allowed Henry and Ann not only to move in, but also to control the environment, who can say what happens inside families? Perhaps he needed Henry's labor enough to make allowances. Perhaps he and the others acceded to Ann's demands to avoid further conflict; at one point, Julia noted Ann had had "another" tantrum, so they must have occurred frequently.[27]

In April 1862 Mary asked Julia to come to Michigan. By then Mary had given birth to a second child, a boy named Stewart. At first

Julia did not know how to afford the trip and asked her sister-in-law Charlotte if she had any money to spare (she did not). While Southerners suffered disproportionate economic losses over the course of the war, everyone seemed to feel pinched at this time. A cousin from Quincy, Illinois, canceled a trip to visit New York when a bank failure resulted in the loss of her savings. Joseph didn't receive military pay for many months, so Mary was scraping by. Julia read a report from New York City that hundreds of enlistees' wives, armed with sticks and clubs, had stormed City Hall seeking the $4 per week promised them when their primary wage earners went off to war. But Joseph eventually received his back pay, the New York women received satisfaction from their claims, and Julia's relative managed to travel east and return to Quincy.

Possibly with help from her father, Julia pulled the money together to spend the summer of 1862 in Michigan. In addition to Mary, her sister Ella lived in Detroit with her husband, a physician. Her brother William Penn eked out a living in the village of Dundee. As the Wilburs illustrated, upstate New York had a strong connection with Michigan in the mid-nineteenth century, with many New York migrants (referred to as "yorkers") and location names cropping up in the newer state. In 1860 Rochester was the eighteenth largest and Detroit was the nineteenth largest city in the United States, and both benefited economically from their location near the Great Lakes.

With a cousin, Julia traveled by train across southern Canada to Windsor, where her brother-in-law met her to ferry her back to Detroit. He introduced her to a soldier taken prisoner at Bull Run and released two weeks earlier, a Sergeant Edwards. He was part of the Michigan regiment (commanded by Col. Orlando Willcox) that had invaded Alexandria in May 1861. This invasion subjected the captured Michigan men, including Willcox, to particularly harsh treatment in prisons in South Carolina and Virginia for almost a year. A huge rally in Detroit welcomed Willcox, promoted to brigadier general, when he returned to Michigan in August 1862. Although deluged by rain, Julia joined "the tide [that] set toward the foot of Woodward Avenue where Gen. W. was to land"; she "never saw so many folks together before."[28] In his memoirs Willcox modestly recalled, "The good people of Detroit, and some other parts of Michigan, always so partial towards my poor desserts, gave me what was described in the newspapers as an enthusiastic public reception."[29] Less than a month later Willcox led a division that fought at Antietam; Sergeant Edwards, now promoted to captain, also shipped out with a newly formed regiment.

Julia enjoyed the activity of Detroit, Ann Arbor, and other locations where friends and family lived, but her brother's home in Dundee proved a shock. William Penn, then thirty-six, "looks like an old man. He is quite thin, his front teeth are decayed & he looks broken down." His wife Henrietta, missing her front teeth entirely, also looked much more bedraggled than when she lived in New York just three years earlier. Their three-year-old daughter Florence reminded Julia of Freda: "a beautiful & interesting child. She resembles Freda more than any other child I know. Could not help having a crying spell when I saw her." They lived an isolated life, renting a farm and having a hard time with it. The mail came to town infrequently; William Penn did not subscribe to any newspapers. The Methodist Meeting House was unpainted, with a dirt floor, and "seats greasy & daubed with bread & butter." Julia stayed out the week, but compared to life in Dundee, "it seems to me now that I have at home every comfort & luxury that is desired." So one unexpected benefit of the trip was to make her appreciate her advantages back home.[30]

Julia went on to Pine Run, near Flint, to stay with Mary and her children. She settled into their routine of visits, housework, and reading, occasionally babysitting to give Mary a break. She saw firsthand the stress of reading news about battles in the papers but not knowing how they had affected a loved one. Often Joseph's letters reported everything was fine, but in the meantime his regiment had gone into combat again. In July, in the midst of weather too hot to sew, they read about large losses along the James River in Virginia, where they believed Joseph to be. After almost three weeks, "No letter from Joe yet. We have reason now to apprehend evil."[31] Finally Mary had word he was safe, although worn down. His unit's cook lost all his utensils, and each man had to cook his "bit of pork, hard bread and coffee" on his own. He lost his knapsack in another retreat, but at least they knew he had escaped danger this time around. Along with a friend whose son fought in the same regiment, the women dried fruit to send. "With the fruit, Mrs. B. & Mary send a basin to stew it in & two teaspoons, & order not to get to fighting & spill their huckleberries, blackberries &c."[32] Given that military-issued rations contained no fruit and only "desiccated vegetables," the two men surely treasured food packages from home when they were lucky enough to receive them. (More than six weeks later, Joseph still had not.) Meanwhile, as Julia recorded, the press reported that General McClellan's officers had requisitioned 174 cases of claret, 46 cases of blackberry brandy, 5 cases of sherry, 52 cases of French brandy, 46 cases of champagne, and 46 cases of whiskey. She asked rhetorically, "Isn't this a shameful fact?"[33]

Julia returned to New York in early September but took her time returning to the farm in Rush. She stopped in Somerset, visiting her older sisters and their families, after which she went on to Rochester. She learned Charlotte's husband, Lewis Griffin, had enlisted in the Eighth Cavalry, as had a nephew (the son of abolitionist-hating Alfred), so she had further family connections going to the front.

While in Michigan, Julia had learned the Rochester Ladies' Anti-Slavery Society "want a teacher to go South & are inquiring for me."[34] In Rochester she followed up with Anna Barnes, the woman who had replaced her as the RLASS secretary. She talked with an acquaintance who had traveled to hospitals in Washington and northern Virginia (possibly the wife of a surgeon), perhaps gathering more information about what such an endeavor would entail.

The RLASS inquiry morphed over the next few weeks—first that she would join the group in Port Royal, then that she instead would go to Washington on her own. How did this bold request come about? The organization in 1862 ran a healthy surplus, so it had the money to support a relief agent.[35] Perhaps Frederick Douglass put in a suggestion. The group also would have heard reports from Fort Monroe and Port Royal. A few weeks earlier the *Liberator* had published a vivid account of a trip Harriet Jacobs had taken to Washington "[to report] on the condition of the contrabands and what I have seen while among them."[36] In it she commented on seeing white women relief workers in Washington.

Looking back at the decision the following year, Anna Barnes wrote, "In former years we found opportunity to help a few [fugitive slaves] on their way to freedom. . . . A new field of labor opened to us, a field that three years ago we hardly dared to hope live long enough to labor in: comforting, cheering, advising, educating the *freed* men, women and children."[37] In a variation of what other women's groups undertook, including the Rochester organization's providing supplies to soldiers, the RLASS started to consider ways to accomplish a "tangible duty" to support the Union cause.

Without a record of its deliberations, we do not know how the RLASS decided to ask Julia to act on its behalf. (Although removed from active RLASS involvement, she had resumed contact with Anna and other women activists the previous year.) Maybe the group first asked others who refused the offer. Neither Anna Barnes nor Maria Porter, the long-time treasurer, was married at the time (Barnes was a widow, and Porter never married) and either one could conceivably have gone. Perhaps as the members discussed this course of action, they realized Julia embodied many of the traits needed: trained as a teacher, devoted to the cause, not hesitant to express her opinion. At age forty-seven, she was mature and without the encumbrances of husband and children. Probably too Barnes or someone else brought up her situation with Freda and the Bigelows.

The fact that the RLASS could pay Julia's way made a huge difference. While it is unclear if she and the group agreed upon a specific monthly salary beforehand, the RLASS account books show regular transmittal of money to "Miss Wilbur" over the next several years, and she often noted in her diary when she received funds via bank transfers from Rochester.

When Julia finally reached home, she found her father well, her stepmother sick, and the garden overgrown with weeds. No one had seen Freda over the summer. It must have been an anticlimactic return, to say the least. Her father still opposed the idea of her departure, but even without a clear assignment, she quietly prepared herself mentally and physically to extricate herself from Rush. Not having to ask her father for financial support undoubtedly took away one large obstacle. "Uncertain as to what I shall do or when I go. But I will keep on getting ready to go somewhere," she wrote at the end of September. Finally, on October 8, she learned "the Ladies' Society in R. want me to go to Washington as soon as I can."[38] She went up to Rochester to iron out some of the details. In addition to visiting with the RLASS women, Julia told activist Amy Post about the upcoming trip. A few years earlier Post and Wilbur had been on either side of the divide between the RLASS and the WNYASS, but wartime circumstances erased this schism. They corresponded over the next few years. Amy collected clothing and other items for the freedmen with whom Julia interacted.

Through October Julia made plans to go south, although with some regrets about leaving the farm, especially without Henry and Ann around causing trouble. She spruced up the family plot at the cemetery in Avon, knowing no one else would in her absence. She heard from Revilo's brother that Freda was thin and had been unwell over the summer. Sad as this made Julia feel, she continued to arrange to travel, realizing Freda remained beyond her reach. "I have a great deal to do & to think of in order to get ready for, probably, a long absence from home," she wrote. "I do not like to leave father to go so far away. If he is sick I would like to be here. Still, my way seems clear to go."[39]

If Julia had gone to Fort Monroe with Reverend Lockwood or to Port Royal with Reverend Channing, she would have fit into a male-led structure. It might have been easier, especially at first, if someone told her what to do and where to live. She would have had built-in friends and an already defined mission. Instead, armed with letters of introduction (in keeping with the custom of the time), she took charge of her own destiny. Her years obtaining her own teaching positions and boarding accommodations served her well. She had packed her trunks many times, tied up loose ends in one place to go on to another. Many women of her time had never lived away from their families.

When Julia left on the morning of October 22, 1862, she didn't report much of a farewell from her family. Hopefully her father and stepmother at least waved from the doorway. An Irish servant living with them at the time drove her to the rail depot.

With all the anxiety and apprehension, with the several years of false starts and grief over Freda, Julia reached Avon as a rainbow spanned the sky. "Was this bow of promise for me?" she asked. "I will accept the omen & go hopefully on my way."[40]

CHAPTER SEVEN

"What a Place I Have Found"

Perched in one of the steamboats that left from Washington across the Potomac to Alexandria, Julia Wilbur didn't know that she would see two dead bodies within the hour.

A thin light glimmered on the river the morning of October 28, 1862. The boat on which she sat with Rev. William Channing, now active in freedmen's issues in Washington, chugged alongside others that traveled back and forth between the nation's capital and the Union-occupied town. From the middle of the Potomac River, they could look behind them to see the Capitol, its dome under construction, the partially completed stump of the Washington Monument obelisk, and the Navy Yard. Ahead on the Virginia side, forts and encampments dotted the denuded hills. They spotted Robert E. Lee's Arlington House, not yet sealed to its fate as guardian of the Union dead. Alongside them might have sat businessmen trying to win the army's stream of contracts for everything from drumsticks to cannonballs, family members tending to loved ones in Alexandria's ever-increasing number of hospital beds, women smuggling alcohol under their skirts into officially dry Alexandria, and others headed across the river for affairs nefarious and not. Things were not always tranquil on the boats, on which they had each paid twenty-five cents to ride. Wilbur and Channing did not know, or did not speak of, the *James Guy*, the steamboat that had exploded just a few days earlier, killing a crew member.[1]

The boat landed near tons of supplies waiting for unloading and movement to the front and camps, as Alexandria had become one of the Union's main logistics centers. Waterfront warehouses that had once shipped tobacco and wheat out of Virginia now received and disbursed fuel, fodder, and much more. "Miniature mountains of hay and pyramids of oat bags, high up in the air, meet the gaze as one approaches the city from the river," observed a reporter from Philadelphia in early 1863. Others were less poetic as they described their first impressions. A young New York recruit wrote home, "I expected to find a nice Clean City, but found narrow Dirty streets and everything looking miserable."[2]

Three days before, Julia had arrived in Washington after a twenty-two-hour train journey from upstate New York, through Elmira, Harrisburg, and Baltimore. A fellow passenger named Frank Phelps, known as the Showman from Elmira, attached himself to her early in the trip so he could justify staying in the Ladies' Car. (Men could sit in this usually more comfortable car of the train only if they accompanied a woman.) "A Democrat, a negro hater, a goodnatured, generous offhand fellow, we discussed his calling & my own likewise," Julia said about him and his plans to entertain wartime Washington, his charm overcoming his politics. In the odd intimacy that characterizes long trips, they dozed next to each other, and "We had a regular battle of words. I shall not soon forget him although I was glad to be rid of him."[3] The train arrived hours later than scheduled, in part because it had to slow down past cars that had wrecked or derailed in earlier calamities, including one the night before. Because of the delays, she spent the day at Barnum's Hotel, one of the finest in Baltimore. Although the hotel flew Union flags from its roof, it had a reputation as a Southern-sympathizing establishment. While Julia sat in the drawing room waiting to head to the train station, a woman shared her book of portraits of Confederate generals.

Once Julia arrived in Washington, a colonel navigated her onto a horse-drawn omnibus to the Willard Hotel. At the Willard (then located next to its current site at Fourteenth and Pennsylvania) one could expect to meet old friends or at least acquaintances of acquaintances. The Lincolns stayed there in the days before moving into the White House. Author Nathaniel Hawthorne observed about the place, "You are mixed up here with office seekers, wire pullers, inventors, artists, poets, editors, Army correspondents, attaches of foreign journals, long-winded talkers, clerks, diplomatists, mail contractors, [and] railway directors."[4] As Julia wrote to Anna Barnes about her distinguished fellow guests, her sense of humor intact, "This morning at breakfast I was seated by a live Major & a still liver Colonel, yet I presumed to eat in their presence & before the meal was concluded I discovered scores of shoulder straps of all orders from Generals down to Lieutenants for Willards is where Shoulder straps most do congregate."[5] Julia met two sympathetic Quaker women from Philadelphia in the spacious public rooms. But she wanted to move on, both to begin to accomplish her purpose and to avoid the hotel rate.

Armed with her letters of introduction, Julia set out early the next day to offer her assistance on behalf of the RLASS. "After breakfast, went to seek my fortune, didn't find much," she said, getting her first lesson in how things worked in Washington.[6]

She started with George Baker, the treasurer of the National Freedman's Relief Association of the District of Columbia, a group created in April 1862 in recognition that "a new state of things exists in this community and important events seem to be rapidly approaching."[7] In the 1850s Baker edited a many-volume series of the works of William Seward, then governor of New York. Now that Seward was secretary of state, Baker, perhaps not coincidentally, had a job as a clerk in the State Department while he carried out his freedmen's duties. Baker sent Julia onward to his fellow association officers, who also maintained their philanthropic endeavors while receiving government paychecks. Walking from one man's office to another, she received cordial treatment but no firm assignment. Finally she reached John van Santvoord, the association's secretary, at the Patent Office (the same place where she herself would work within a decade, but she certainly had no inkling then). He saw before him a small, middle-aged, well-groomed woman, vouched for by common acquaintances. He would not have known anything about her past, about why she wanted to leave Rochester to start a new life. But he did see someone who said she was willing to be of service. And he took advantage of that with graciousness and flattery.

Julia was flattered enough to repeat van Santvoord's words in her diary and in letters: "Why, Miss Wilbur, it seems as if God had sent you here just at this time."[8] People needed her. Never overtly religious, she herself appealed to a higher being in a letter a week later. Although homesick and confused about what she should do, she wrote to Amy Post back in Rochester, "I have never undertaken anything before when it has seemed so very plain that the Lord has directed my life and will continue to do so."[9]

On her first day in Washington Julia also visited Camp Barker, newly repurposed for freedmen from barracks occupied by troops shipped out to southern Virginia for Gen. George McClellan's Peninsular Campaign. It was a raw encounter. She saw "from 5 to 20 in a room, some have fire & some have not, some are in old tents without floors, with old blankets & rags to tie on, & many are sick."[10] The government provided the very basics—shelter, such as it was, and rations and military guards. At the time, according to the *Evening Star*, 675 people lived there, mostly women, children, the elderly, and the infirm. Those who worked could draw rations and clothing, "while those at the camp sick and unable to work are furnished with rations only; having to rely altogether on charity for clothing."[11] The Freedman's Relief Association labored to provide this clothing and everything else, including medical care.

Instead of Julia's helping out at Camp Barker or elsewhere in Washington, as she had expected to do when in New York, the Freedman's officers proposed she go to Alexandria, where they said about five hundred African Americans (probably at least twice that number by then) lived "in worse shape than here in W[ashington]." The group had already appealed to Gen. James Wadsworth, the military governor of Washington, that it "found many contrabands in bad condition" across the river.[12] This new twist of location surprised her, but Julia did not object.

Van Santvoord's subsequent letter to introduce Julia to Wadsworth illustrates how good intentions often met bureaucratic boulders. Wadsworth was a wealthy Republican, also from New York; his family, in fact, had at one time owned much of the land south of Rochester, including the Wilburs' property. His fervent principles meant he often butted heads with those who did not live up to his standards, including General McClellan. He told Julia he "heartily" approved her mission and sent her on to Gen. Nathaniel Banks, then head of the Military District of Washington, ultimately to receive a message to give to Alexandria's military governor, Gen. John Slough. In the exchange of information among van Santvoord, Julia, the generals, and a passel of aides, she ended up with a limp message to give to Slough, signed only by a captain, that the commanding general wanted to "express his wish that Miss Wilbur may be made use of in any way, in your opinion, not inconsistent with the interests of the service."[13]

Julia didn't like the message. Instead of a rousing confirmation of her mission, she had a few weak words putting her in her place. After stewing about it, she went back to Wadsworth to see if he could change the wording, but he chose not to intervene with Banks's missive. (Within days Gen. Samuel Heintzelman had replaced Banks. Heintzelman, nicknamed "Sourdough," proved less sympathetic to the freedmen than Banks.) Julia had to take the note and, for the time being, do the best she could with it.

After their boat landed on that late October morning, Channing and Wilbur walked up King Street past grocers, oyster houses, and novelty houses that catered to the thousands of soldiers making their way through Alexandria. "Alex[andria] is an old dirty town," Julia thought, echoing the impressions of everybody who described it, but she thrilled to walk past the Marshall House, the scene of the Elmer Ellsworth–James Jackson encounter. She would soon learn to navigate the grid layout of the city, with east-west streets heading from the Potomac intersected by north-south streets parallel to the river.[14]

First stop: Alexandria Academy, a school once endowed by George Washington, about a half mile from the docks on Washington Street, the main north-south thoroughfare.[15] Confiscated by the military, the Old Schoolhouse, as it was known at the time, housed 150 blacks, mostly women and children, in two small rooms upstairs and one large room on the main floor. It had no furniture, bedding, or anything else at all to provide comfort.

Next door to the academy, in a once stately brick house labeled a hospital for contrabands but without a medical person in sight, the sick and dying lay on the floor. In one corner a mother sat holding her dead child, wrapped in a piece of ticking. Another dead child lay in the adjoining room.

Two dead children, soon to be buried in Penny Hill, the paupers' cemetery. No ceremony, no gravestone, no names to commemorate them. In theory Julia knew she had come to help in such situations—if not to prevent death, then at least to comfort those left behind. Eventually she could do so. She would soon know many people who died from diphtheria, typhoid, and other diseases, as well as those wounded in battle. Death would never become acceptable, but it would be common, as she witnessed funeral processions through Alexandria's streets to Penny Hill and the other cemeteries south of town. Later she would visit the new cemeteries built to handle the overflow of civilian and military deaths. For now she could just stare.

Stare and smell. With no adequate sanitation, clean clothes, or ventilation, people reeked. Young and old sat on the floor, some in rags, some less clothed still, barefoot, or even naked. Wilbur and Channing walked up Duke Street to the former slave pen, used to provide squalid housing to black refugees and jail cells for disorderly soldiers and civilians.

Julia also saw hopeful signs, in particular a school run by two African American ministers, Clem Robinson and G. W. Parker. Over the next few years at least fifteen schools of different sizes would operate for freed adults and children, in addition to this school and the small school opened by Mary Chase back in 1861.[16] Putting on her teacher hat, Julia commented, "It appears [to have done] as well as any white school would have done in such a crowded place."[17] Before taking the boat back to Washington, Wilbur and Channing climbed to the knolls west of the city, where Fort Ellsworth (named of course after the fallen hero of the Marshall House incident) and other fortifications and camps had taken over the landscape.

Julia returned to Washington from the day in Alexandria exhausted and no doubt emotionally spent. Although she had read accounts in the *Liberator* and other publications, corresponded with her brother-in-law, and heard other firsthand accounts, nothing prepared her for the sights, sounds, and smells she encountered. She returned to General Wadsworth's office the next day and reported what she had seen. Out of sincerity or a desire to get her out of his office, he sent her on to Secretary of War Edwin Stanton, who took a few minutes to see her. The secretary promised he would attend to things, although she already knew such people said one thing and did, or did not do, another.

By then Julia had moved out of the Willard to a room in a boarding house on E Street. While she firmed up her plan to move to Alexandria, she began what became a regular practice to tour historic buildings, just as sightseers do today. She went to the Capitol, White House, and the Washington Monument, then only an undignified block of stone "surrounded by shanteys & a cattle yard."[18] The Smithsonian, which had opened to the public seven years earlier, held curiosities that ranged from six Egyptian mummies to headdresses from the Fuji Islands.

And Julia saw the effects of war on those who fought it. With a new acquaintance named Mrs. Munson, she went to Harewood Hospital, one of the new military hospitals built to accommodate the ever-growing population of sick and wounded. "Hundreds of tents arranged in streets. . . . Each ward has a master, some tents look clean & comfortable, but many quite otherwise. 2000 or 3000 here," she described. Mrs. Munson solicited supplies from her home town of Albany, which she distributed with a special eye out for the New Yorkers among the patients. Julia spent time with a few patients from the Rochester area. "Although not acquainted with me, they were glad to see me," as she represented at least some vestige of home.[19]

Reverend Channing apparently wanted to do all he could to ensure Julia settled in Alexandria, as he came back with her for a second visit a few days later. They stopped in to see Capt. John C. Wyman, the provost marshal responsible for contraband affairs among his myriad of order-keeping duties, to tell him of Julia's plans and receive his sanction. In the stream of men who occupied the provost marshal position, they were lucky Wyman had charge at that time. A Republican from Massachusetts, he was known as sympathetic to the abolitionist cause. Wyman wrote a note that authorized Julia to act as a "visitor, adviser & instructor" and declared her eligible for

government-provided food rations. She also met Rev. Albert Gladwin, a white Baptist minister from Connecticut "who is doing all
he can by way of assisting, in schools, taking care of the sick, etc."[20]
At this point Julia was pleased with her new acquaintances; soon
enough, Wyman's replacement proved less accepting of her activities and Gladwin emerged as a persistent nemesis.

Channing tried to recruit at least two other women to join Julia—
Massachusetts Quaker sisters named Lucy and Sarah Chase. On
November 4, the day before Julia moved to Alexandria, he wrote
them, "Miss Wilbur . . . would be very glad to have your assistance
& sympathy—if you see your way clear to maintenance here." Julia
may indeed have welcomed the company, especially in her lonely first
few weeks, but it is not clear if Channing consulted her to gauge her
receptivity. Perhaps his message to the Chases that they would have
to arrange their own funding, as "our Society has no means to do
more than they are already doing," dissuaded them.[21] Julia crossed
paths with the Chases over time, but they did not move to Alexandria, instead going to Craney Island, Virginia, under the auspices of
a group from Boston.

So when Julia moved to Alexandria, she came alone. She left
Washington at 10 a.m. on November 5 and sat with her baggage an
hour later in a rented room in the home of George Seaton, a builder
and well-established member of Alexandria's free black community.
Gladwin and other Northerners boarded there, but Seaton's home
was not Julia's first choice. Armed with a list of boarding addresses
and proprietors, she had knocked on many doors seeking a room.
The first house had no vacancies, nor did the second through fifth.
The Seaton house was well located on St. Asaph Street, near the Old
Schoolhouse, the docks, the offices of the military governor and the
provost marshal, and other places that would soon form part of her
daily rounds. When it was built ten years earlier, the *Gazette* included
it in an article about recent "Building Improvements," describing it as
"a large frame building corner St. Asaph and Wolfe for Geo Seaton—
built by him"—a noteworthy undertaking for an African American in
antebellum Alexandria.[22] But Julia thought the house dirty and was
already planning to move. Whether the Seatons' home was in fact

dirtier than any place else is not clear—as noted, Alexandria had a reputation for less than hygienic conditions. Perhaps she felt uncomfortable living with a black family at this point or simply harbored unrealistic expectations in regard to the amenities of a rented room.

"What a place I have found!" she wrote, now that she had time to reflect on her decision to move.[23] The day stretched before her—as did the week, the month, to some point in the future. She had no friends yet in this new place, and friends and family back home still assumed she had settled in Washington. In those first few days she wrote letters to them, but nothing came for her, despite her frequent stops at the post office on Prince Street to check. She was confused about her new role and homesick for the world she had left behind. She returned to mourning the loss of Freda and had bad dreams.

Nonetheless, Julia started to find her way around town. Initially she joined up with Gladwin or with two other men who boarded at the Seatons': Rev. J. W. Warwick, a colporter for the American Baptist Publication Society, and D. R. Whipple, though she never figured out under whose auspices he labored.[24] Whipple took it upon himself to go by the Old Schoolhouse every morning, then report at breakfast on how many people had died there the night before. At this point Julia saw the men doing what they could to help, although her views would change. Meanwhile, from them she tried to learn about the ways things worked, or didn't work, for the refugees.

She learned the passage to Alexandria for many was far bolder than her own. A woman who had been enslaved by former Virginia congressman Jeremiah Morton told her, "When Master heard the Unions was coming, he tried to get away all the women and children. Twas in the night." She told Julia she swooped up her three children and walked six miles through the woods to safety. (The congressman also declared that "before he would let one of his niggers be free, he would put them into a barn & burn them all up.") Another woman "did not wait for a bonnet or anything; she brought away 6 children, 3 of her own and 3 of her sister's who was dead."[25] As bad as conditions were in the sheds, shanties, and abandoned buildings in Alexandria, they and others chose to make the trip to freedom.

In addition to the losses among soldiers and refugees, Julia also witnessed death in the relatively well-off Seaton household, when fifteen-year-old Virginia died suddenly in mid-November. Out of her own unfamiliarity and ignorance, Julia wrote Anna Barnes that the mourning and burial of the young girl "was in the style of the most respectable white folks." She noted in her diary, "The ways of people are quite different from our ways. But I am getting used to them."[26]

From the first days of going from the Old Schoolhouse to shanties to sheds in alleyways, with conditions from bad to awful, Julia realized the lack of even barely adequate refugee housing. It had already snowed once in November 1862, rare for Alexandria but a warning about the upcoming winter weather. She wrote to friends and acquaintances in different parts of New York, asking for contributions of bedding and clothing for distribution, which would soon become a big part of her mission.

Two days after she moved to Alexandria, Julia wrote to President Lincoln. Her letter beseeched the president to expedite plans to build better shelters before winter. Even with all the faults of Camp Barker in Washington, she pushed for a similar setup in Alexandria.

"Will you permit me although a stranger to claim your attention for a moment?" she began her letter to the president. (Why not? Everyone else clamored for his attention.) He may not have made the connection, if he even read Julia's letter himself, but his wife had talked to him about freedmen's conditions a few days earlier. Mary Todd Lincoln related the difficulties that Elizabeth Keckley, her black seamstress and companion, had in assisting the "immense number of contrabands in W[ashington]" through her newly founded Contraband Relief Association—so, "dear husband," she had told Lincoln, she had given Keckley $200 to purchase bed coverings.[27]

Julia described in her letter what she had seen in her first days in Alexandria, then homed in on her request: "Could barracks be built for them [refugees] at once so that we could have them move together & physician & medical stores be provided for them, I think we can get supplies of clothing & bedding from the North & they can be made comparatively comfortable for the winter." Embellishing on what she had recently characterized as her weak letter of introduction, she assured the president that "Gen. Banks & Gen. Wadsworth have given me their sanction and approval as to act as matron visitor, adviser & instructor to these poor women & children. The Provost Marshal here is ready to help in any way he can." Of course Banks and Wadsworth hadn't exactly employed those words, although Wyman had described her as such when he authorized her rations. She apparently liked this description of her duties better than the earlier missive that she could simply be made use of in any way that didn't bother the powers that be.

From our vantage point, Julia misses the fact that "they" (African Americans) might well have different ideas of how to organize living arrangements or how "they" would want "to be made" comfortable. The attitude of white abolitionists toward African Americans was often patronizing, and Julia was not immune. Over time she did not totally shed condescension, especially when dealing with the poor and uneducated; her views often sound more class-bound than race-bound. Julia did not completely shed feelings of pity and, at times, superiority as she referred to "poor creatures" while still having trouble dealing with filth and odor. Yet she saw *people* in front of her—not just "contrabands," and certainly not the many epitaphs leveled at them, as offensive then as now. And more than almost any white person at the time, she socialized, worked, and prayed with black friends and colleagues for the rest of her life, beginning with her time in Alexandria.

Provost Marshal Wyman told her that her letter to the president had made its way to him, via Secretary of War Stanton and General Slough. "I hope it did not offend?" she asked. He told her it did not. She liked Wyman, and she trusted his intentions. (An opinion about Wyman depended on one's perspective: Virginia native Anne Frobel described him as "a most uncouth creature who sat all the time he talked with us, with his hat stuck on one side of his head and a cigar in his mouth.")[28]

Julia credited Wyman for the barracks' eventual construction and thought her letter to President Lincoln may have helped too. The barracks had been planned before that, however, even as debate about how much assistance to provide the refugees continued. General Heintzelman, in charge of the defenses of Washington, opposed new housing or doing much of anything, out of fear more people would come. "When they learn that the government will feed and shelter them, they will flock to Alexandria," he warned. Whether or not Julia's letter called attention to the matter, Secretary Stanton (or one of his aides) inquired about construction progress in December. On December 8 the Alexandria quartermaster reassured the War Department, "The buildings are now on course of construction and will be completed at an early date." A few days later he backpedaled, pointing out that when he received the construction order in late October "every available man in the Department was engaged and the supply of lumber exhausted," but "The work is now being pushed."[29]

Meanwhile, as African Americans struggled for some bit of roof and floor and Julia found a room to sleep in, Military Governor John Slough occupied two fine homes on St. Asaph Street, one for his family and one for his office. The McVeighs, a wealthy family who had left in 1861, owned both homes.[30] Gilt-framed portraits of the family stared down from the parlor walls. Julia noticed them when she called on the general for the first time in mid-November. Whether Slough did, or cared, is not recorded.

John Potts Slough took command of Alexandria on August 26, 1862, after a string of officers had occupied the position. The military needed someone not shy about bossing around potentially traitorous locals and drunk, disorderly soldiers. Troops with time on their hands between military campaigns discovered, and no doubt encouraged the proliferation of, bars and brothels. After the first New York and Michigan regiments moved into Alexandria in May 1861, the floodgates burst open. Thousands joined them, from Pennsylvania, Connecticut, Illinois, and elsewhere. Many had never gone beyond their home states, many never past their nearest town. They found different ways of adjusting to their new lives. A Pennsylvania chaplain recalled his regiment pitching tents on the property of a Mrs. Powell, "under the shadow of the fruit-trees in her orchard around her mansion. We were now 1070 strong; the men were large, robust, full of life."[31] The fruit trees didn't last very long amid these robust men. Beyond the city limits, where Union control was less firm, troops from both sides took what they needed, or wanted, from private property. One young girl reported seeing her family's forest, enough to provide them firewood "for hundreds of years," completely obliterated by Confederate troops, while a U.S. soldier observed Union troops committing "almost daily acts of high-handed robbery."[32] Crimes against people included robbery and assault. A Pennsylvania soldier was convicted of the attempted rape of a woman on Duke Street when he accosted her as she walked across a field; many other transgressions went unpunished.[33]

Slough, age thirty-three, was born and practiced law in Cincinnati. He was elected to the Ohio State Legislature in his twenties, but his colleagues expelled him in early 1857 for striking another legislator and refusing to apologize. After a stop in Kansas, Slough, his wife, and their children moved to Denver, founded as a gold-mining town in 1858. At the outbreak of the war, the newly organized Colorado Territory raised a Union regiment. Slough led a group of men from the regiment to pursue Confederates in the Battle of Glorieta Pass in New Mexico—a successful mission but in direct disobedience of orders to remain in fort. He resigned his Colorado commission and moved to Washington to see who might better appreciate his talents. Slough's wife, the former Belle McLean, also from Cincinnati, was the daughter of a former congressman and niece of a Supreme Court justice (one of two who dissented in the Dred Scott decision), so perhaps they had a Washington entree to smooth the way, or perhaps Slough was simply recognized as pugnacious. Secretary Stanton sent him to Harpers Ferry, notifying Brig. Gen. Rufus Saxton, "You will find him a bold and able assistant." Then, as if to hedge his bets about bold Slough, Stanton closed, "Keep us advised what happens."[34] Stanton next appointed Slough as military governor in Alexandria. Slough later recounted that the secretary of war had summoned him, told him "the town of Alexandria was beyond control," and sent him to "immediately assume command there and restore order" that very day—August 25, 1862.[35]

Immediately upon his arrival in Alexandria, Slough imposed a curfew for soldiers (9 p.m.), businesses (9:30 p.m.), and citizens (10:30

p.m.), and he prohibited alcohol. Patrols rounded up "straggling soldiers. . . . They could be counted by hundreds, and this motley crowd
were urged on at the point of the bayonet to their respective camps
without the city."[36] Mayhem did not totally disappear—one Michigan
officer wrote home in the spring of 1863 that he knew of seventy-five
houses of ill fame while on patrol duty in Alexandria: "Suffice to say
I never had so much fun in my life," he wrote once he had shipped
out.[37] But the Slough Reign had arrived, and it lasted through the
end of the war.

As November progressed, Julia acclimated herself. Letters finally
arrived at the post office, including ones from Anna Barnes of the
RLASS and sisters Frances and Mary, and they bolstered her spirits. One day she reported letters from "E. Wing & E. Wilbur & C.
Winans & A. Post & F. Douglass"—a bonanza reflecting her different identities as family member, friend, and abolitionist colleague.[38]

After two weeks Julia left the Seatons' to move to a boarding house
on the corner of Duke and Columbus Streets run by the Kimballs, a
Northern white family. Benjamin Kimball held one of the hundreds
of civilian jobs for the U.S. Military Rail Road. The huge house—
much larger than the Seatons', with forty rooms with an observa-
tory on top, large common space, and verandah outdoors—seemed
more familiar to Julia in many ways. The Hallowells, a prominent
Quaker family, had used it as a boarding school before the war; Julia
knew Hallowells in Rochester. In addition, the Kimballs ran rooming
houses in other places they had lived, and she knew a former boarder.
She moved as soon as space became available, even though it turned
out to be a small, noisy room over the kitchen for $7 a week ($650
per month in today's dollars). She unpacked her trunks for the first
time. Apparently she had planned on the Seatons' room as a temporary arrangement from the start and had not settled in.

An initial attempt to solicit clothing donations for blacks from
local white women proved unsuccessful, although Julia should not
have expected success, based both on predilection and the women's
own precarious finances. Instead she began in earnest to solicit donations of clothing from Rochester and other points north.

A postwar report identified Miss Julia Wilbur as the "first white woman who went to Alexandria to labor for the contrabands."[39] Certainly she would have stood out, especially when she walked alone down Alexandria's streets and alleys and into the homes of the refugees. When Wilbur started on her rounds, one thing became clear: everyone with an interest in freedmen affairs, whether because of job title, avarice, good-heartedness, or some combination, was male. She started trusting her own judgment, even when it meant questioning previous assumptions, such as her earlier positive opinion of Gladwin. "I don't like the way Mr. W and Mr. G speak to those women. They don't treat them as women," she wrote. "My delicacy, my fastidiousness must be laid aside." The women needed a woman, she concluded. She realized she could fill that role.[40]

Thanksgiving caught on in a piecemeal fashion in early America, with each state or city choosing, or not, to mark such a day and deciding upon the exact date. New York adopted an annual observance in 1817. In 1839 a contributor to the *Gazette* "rejoiced that Alexandria would observe the good old-fashioned custom prevalent in the Northern States." By the 1850s, however, the Northern connection made Virginia governor Henry Wise refuse to proclaim the holiday, which he deemed a "theatrical national claptrap."[41]

The previous Thanksgiving, in 1861, Julia had taken the train to Rochester to stay with her sister-in-law Charlotte, and there she had seen a regiment head out toward Washington. She imagined what the war entailed up close. A year later she had, in a fashion, joined those men.

On Thanksgiving 1862 public offices and some stores in Alexandria closed, while several churches stayed open for worship. Local resident Henry Whittington scoffed at the celebration, noting, "Our folks seem little inclined to follow [the] Yankee lead."[42] Convalescing soldiers in a few hospitals enjoyed special meals. In Washington freedmen were treated to special entertainment, which included an exhortation from Senator Samuel Pomeroy, a fervent advocate of colonization outside the U.S. for former slaves, "to emigrate and build up a nation of their own in another country."[43]

On that cold, bright morning Reverend Warwick showed up at the Kimballs' boarding house with an intriguing invitation. Julia, a newly made friend named Mrs. Winsor, and the two young Kimball daughters accompanied him to the Paroled Prisoners Camp for what turned out to be a short religious service for the men and a celebration for the officers and their guests. As pleasant as the afternoon was—and Julia enjoyed herself immensely, minus the wine and champagne of which the others partook—the disconnect between the events for the enlisted men versus those for the officers spoke volumes about why the early war effort floundered.

At that point in the war the two sides exchanged captured men. The men promised (gave their word or "parole") to remain off the battlefield until mutual agreement was reached to exchange them for soldiers similarly situated on the other side.[44] A small number were injured, but most waited in paroled prisoners camps to return to battle or receive a discharge from military service.

Commanding officer Lt. Col. Gabriel De Korponay, a Hungarian who taught the polka in Philadelphia before the war, warmly greeted the guests, "quite as sparkling as the champagne of which he drank so freely." He showed the visitors around the camp, complaining of his tiring job signing discharges for prisoners eligible for release. He did not sleep at the camp but rather in a hotel room in town. When Colonel De Korponay had taken command of the camp a month earlier, his "rules of good order at my camp" included that "intemperance [was] strictly forbidden among all officers and men," a rule he apparently chose to ignore for himself. He had a reputation as "a drunkard and unfit to lead" in an earlier incarnation in the Twenty-Eighth Pennsylvania regiment.[45]

The parolees stood in a square, several deep around, with Reverend Warwick atop a box in the middle. Julia thought she saw the men, even the rough, hard-looking ones, "reverently listening to the singing, praying and preaching." An avenue in the camp was christened Mrs. Belle Slough, in honor of the general's wife "& more cheers were given." De Korponay addressed the troops, acknowledging he couldn't do anything in particular to help them but urging them to behave themselves nonetheless.

The parolees returned to their tents while the officers and guests filled three tables in the officers' tent. The libations and comments flowed freely, especially once the Sloughs left. "Among these officers but little allusion was made to the object of the war, & no opinions were given. Their camp life was about all that seemed to interest them," Julia observed.

That afternoon, though, it was heady stuff. "I little thought one year ago at my quiet home . . . that I should spend the next Thanksgiving under Virginia skies, at the seat of war, & take my dinner in a company with officers of high rank." The freedmen may have huddled in their rooms around town, the enlisted men in their tents, but Julia had an experience to enjoy for an afternoon.

In the next days, it was back to reality. She went to get vaccinated against smallpox, but the doctor had no virus available to inoculate her.

Julia's first month in Alexandria coincided with a relatively quiet time militarily for the Army of the Potomac—to the consternation of the president. Lincoln's relationship with General McClellan was testy, with Lincoln pushing McClellan forward to battle and McClellan coming up with excuses not to engage his troops with the enemy. In early November Lincoln replaced McClellan with Gen. Ambrose Burnside. It was not a wise choice, as everyone else, including Burnside himself, recognized. Burnside understood the president's wish for the army to take the offensive, but his way of taking it resulted in disaster. After moving troops to Falmouth, about fifty miles south of Alexandria, he chose to advance to Richmond through Confederate-entrenched Fredericksburg.

News filtered up to Alexandria about terrible losses during the Battle of Fredericksburg, December 11–15, followed by the arrival of the casualties themselves. A few days later, "Looking down Duke Street, I saw ever so many soldiers coming"; these were the men healthy enough to walk on their own.[46] Ambulance after ambulance, stretcher after stretcher of the more gravely wounded followed. Earlier that morning Washington Street Hospital had just two beds filled. Within hours every bed was taken, with more men on the way.

Other women's memories about the Fredericksburg wounded echoed what Julia recorded. Mary Phinney Von Olnhausen, a nurse at Mansion House Hospital, recalled, "The whole street was full of ambulances, and the sick lay outside from nine in the morning till five in the evening. . . . They reached town last evening, lay in the [train] cars all night without blankets or food, were chucked into ambulances, lay about here all day, and tonight were put back into ambulances and carted off again," sent to Fairfax Seminary Hospital, about two miles outside of town. Across the river at Georgetown's Union Hospital, another nurse warned Louisa May Alcott, who had all of three days' experience behind her, to gird herself for the onslaught of wounded: "You will begin to see hospital life in earnest."[47]

Dealing with the post-Fredericksburg debacle occupied Alexandria's military leaders. "I do not like to make such calls when officers are busy," Julia acknowledged, but she went around to Provost Marshal Wyman and others to prod them to make progress on the freedmen's barracks and tend the sick. She also sought help to organize and distribute the clothing that had started to arrive. In addition to donations from her supporters in Rochester, boxes filled with clothing for men, women, and children came from Philadelphia. A woman from Homer, New York, wrote a collection was en route. A man visiting from Philadelphia gave her $1 for the cause, while Reverend Channing brought over a more substantial $20.

In mid-December Wyman let Julia use several rooms in a duplex on St. Asaph Street, and she started to clean and organize them. A few days before Christmas, however, fire gutted the place. The *Gazette* reported the fire "consumed the upper portion of the building and the roof and attic of the adjoining building owned and occupied by Mrs. Deborah Stabler." Julia described the duplex neighbor as a "virulent secesh." Stabler was an older widow and member of one of the few Quaker families who had not left the city or signed an oath of allegiance to the Union. The newspaper laid the blame on the Union side of the house: "The house in which the fire originated was taken by the Military authorities several months ago and used as a soldier's barracks for some time, but has been recently occupied as quarters for 'contrabands,' and was by the carelessness of some of these, set on fire."[48] Julia felt the firefighters could have suppressed the blaze but for the bad equipment ("water was frozen, hose was rotten"). More significant, she wrote, "The Union folks were quite willing to see this [Stabler's half] burn and the secesh having a spite against our half of the building, it stood a poor chance."[49] So both sides stood near and watched the fire progress.

Wyman did more than many officers would have done: he posted a guard to prevent looting and gave Julia the use of another building on the corner of Washington and Wolfe Streets. This place became her main center of activity for most of the rest of the war.

Julia Wilbur had come a long way. On New Year's Eve 1862 she walked over to the barracks, satisfied at that point with the construction's progress. She shared the anxiety of most anti-slavery people about whether the president would sign the Emancipation Proclamation on January 1 as promised, while also worrying about any backlash in the streets against blacks. She had suffered "an age of misery" since Freda had left three new years ago that very day, on New Year's Eve Day 1859. Yet she realized, "Time & distance has blunted the edge of my grief. . . . It may be for the best, for there is great work to do here."[50]

CHAPTER EIGHT

"Mrs. J and I May Carry Out Our Plans"

January 1, 1863: Would President Lincoln sign the Emancipation Proclamation as he had promised back in September? "I wish I knew what the Pres. is doing," Julia Wilbur wrote of Lincoln on New Year's Day, echoing others' anxiety that he would renege at the last minute. Finally news that he had signed the proclamation went out on the wires—Lincoln reportedly sat in the telegraph office near the White House while an operator keyed in the text. On January 2, newspapers, including the *Alexandria Gazette*, printed the full document.[1]

The document proclaimed people in areas of rebellion "forever free," leaving enslaved those in the pro-Union, slave-holding states of Delaware, Kentucky, Maryland, and Missouri and a number of smaller Union-held locations. In contrast to the simple majesty of some of Lincoln's other prose (at about seven hundred words, the proclamation is about three times longer than the Gettysburg Address), he fashioned a flat and legalistic statement, in part to withstand court challenges. Yet Julia commented with relief that "it is better than I feared," although she worried "fresh difficulties will attend it" if opponents tried to scuttle it. She picked up on one of the most controversial, and ultimately transforming, parts of the proclamation: black men "will be received into the armed service of the United States." Ultimately the involvement of the U.S. Colored Troops (USCT) not only materially helped the war effort, but also disproved those who doubted blacks' bravery and mettle in combat. And the presence of armed black regiments across enemy lines gave the Confederates conniptions. She delighted in the notion.

Beyond Julia's "rejoicing with fear and trembling" about the dissolution of slavery, the new year brought another welcome change. She had her first contact with the familiar since arriving in Alexandria a few months earlier. Her sister Frances and sister-in-law Charlotte came from Rochester; like many women, Charlotte visited her husband, encamped with his regiment near Washington over the winter. Julia took them around to sites in Washington and Alexandria—from the Marshall House, where Ellsworth had fallen ("We brought away a piece of wallpaper, just as any fools would have done"), to hospitals and an embalmer, and to the paroled prisoners' and other camps outside Alexandria.[2] In Washington they went to the Capitol and the White House. At the National Hotel on Pennsylvania Avenue, they spotted fellow guest Benjamin Butler, the general who had accepted black slaves as "contrabands" at Fort Monroe in 1861. Conditions in Alexandria distressed them, but Charlotte and Frances loved the excitement of Washington. They both returned several times to visit. Frances came to live in Washington in late 1864.

The women obtained passes to travel south to Falmouth, near the site of the Union rout at Fredericksburg that had filled Alexandria's hospitals a few weeks earlier. It was the first battlefront Julia had yet seen; better still, she also saw Michigan brother-in-law Joseph Van Buskirk. To get permission, they needed to talk up the family connection in addition to proving their allegiance to the Union. The military devoted much time and attention to the issuing of passes. A soldier once described the duties of himself and five other clerks in Washington as "deciding from the evidence" whether to grant passes or not; they issued passes at a rate of four or five hundred a day, while rejecting many requests.[3]

Joseph borrowed a horse-drawn ambulance to show them recent battle landmarks and the hills and ravines that had led to such a disastrous outcome for the Union, an outing, Julia said, that "gave us a realizing sense of the war." Joseph pointed out Confederate soldiers on picket duty on one end of a railroad bridge. "We were within speaking distance of the rebels," Julia said, noticing some wore confiscated Union-blue overcoats against the cold. They spent the night on a bed made of pine boughs in the log hut of the regiment's chaplain. After dark they saw both sides' campfires light up the horizon and heard bands across the landscape play music into the night.[4]

Julia returned to Alexandria to a surprise—a potential rival but ulti-mately an ally and lifelong friend. On January 14 Harriet Jacobs, sent by the New York Yearly Meeting of Friends, an influential Quaker group, sought Julia out. Jacobs came to Alexandria with some renown in abolitionist circles as the author of her experiences in slavery and her dramatic escape in the book *Incidents in the Life of a Slave Girl*, published in 1861. "Mrs. H. Jacobs . . . is sent by N.Y. Friends to be matron of the contrabands here, & they wish her to distribute the goods they send," Julia recorded in her diary.[5] (A "matron" usually referred to a woman working in a Union or Confederate hospital, though the term also broadly applied to women in other helping roles.) Julia worried how she and Harriet would coexist with their simi-lar missions; turf battles were as alive and well in the 1800s as today.

When Julia first arrived in Alexandria, she wrote her contacts in Rochester that given the needs, she wished another female agent could join her. Now help had arrived in an unexpected and not alto-gether welcome way. Harriet came with instructions from New York to keep records of the clothing and bedding she distributed and to sell items, rather than donate them, as much as possible. Julia had no such instructions from the RLASS or from her various donors. "I don't know how it strikes *thee* but it struck *me* very unpleasantly," Julia wrote to Anna Barnes in Rochester. "It seems almost like an insult to us."[6]

Julia possibly felt threatened by Harriet's relative celebrity and the clout of the New York society, which was well known, male-led, and much larger than the RLASS. Maybe she felt that just as she had established herself, she had to accommodate new routines and sys-tems. Perhaps too she recognized that Harriet, as a formerly enslaved black woman, could make a deeper connection with the people than a white abolitionist could hope to make. In the late 1840s they had met in person in Rochester, where tales of Harriet's escape from slavery circulated. More than a decade later, in 1861, Julia read *Inci-dents*, where she learned more about Harriet, just two years older but with such different experiences than hers.[7] All these points must have affected Julia's initial reaction to Harriet Jacobs suddenly join-ing her in Alexandria.

At age twelve, in Edenton, North Carolina, Harriet had been "bequeathed" by Margaret Horniblow, relatively benevolent as slaveholders went, to her niece Mary Norcom in an unsigned deathbed codicil to her will. Perhaps not coincidentally, little Mary's father, James, served as Margaret's attending physician and one of the witnesses to the will's new clause. James Norcom, a lecherous, controlling man in his late forties, sexually threatened Harriet as she grew into adolescence in his household. "I now entered on my fifteenth year—a sad epoch in the life of a slave girl," Jacobs recalled.[8] Harriet's parents, enslaved in different households, had both died. Her grandmother Molly, who bought her own freedom in 1828 and ran a thriving bakery shop, tried to protect Harriet as best she could, but her power was limited.

Harriet took a bold step: she chose sexual involvement with a young white attorney, Samuel Sawyer, whom she perceived as more sympathetic and, as part of one of Edenton's most elite families, a potential protector from Norcom. This decision became a complicated piece of her biography. While the rape of enslaved African American women by white men was a perverted but accepted part of the social fabric, she herself had chosen to become Sawyer's mistress as her best option. "It seems less degrading to give one's self, than to submit to compulsion," she wrote in *Incidents*. She knew the shock of this revelation, especially to mid-1800s sensibilities: "Pity me, and pardon me, O virtuous reader! You never know what it is to be a slave; to be entirely unprotected by law or custom; to have the laws reduce you to the condition of chattel."[9] She became pregnant twice, at ages sixteen and twenty. Although Sawyer did not emotionally engage with son Joseph or daughter Louisa, Harriet hoped he would eventually find a way to free them. Otherwise the Norcoms claimed ownership since the mother's status governed that of a child.

The most famous aspect of Jacobs's story of escape was her hiding out in her grandmother's storeroom attic for almost seven years. In 1835 Norcom banished her to his family's plantation outside of Edenton. When she learned her children would join her, to be "broke in" as slaves, "it nerved me to immediate action."[10] She slipped away from the plantation in the middle of the night. With the help of family and friends, she reached her grandmother's, where her uncle built what was expected as a temporary solution under the eaves. Norcom assumed she had left town. His ad for her capture offered a $100 reward and described her as "light mulatto, 21 years of age, about 5 feet 4 inches high, of a thick and corpulent habit, having on her head a thick covering of black hair that curls naturally, but which can easily be combed straight."[11]

Molly and the few insiders kept looking for ways for Harriet to escape. Year in and year out, through illness, discomfort, and boredom, with no end in sight, she remained in the attic while life in Edenton swirled twenty feet or so below her. For fear of accidental disclosure, the family did not tell her children that Harriet remained close by. During this time Sawyer did purchase the children and Harriet's brother John; John escaped slavery on a trip to New York with Sawyer, for whom he acted as a valet. Harriet welcomed the news for his sake but worried about the impact on her son and daughter.

The attic grew ever more imprisoning. Molly was aging and in constant danger of punishment for harboring a fugitive. Finally in 1842, six years and eleven months after Harriet had climbed into the attic, word came that a ship captain, for a price, would help her escape. She did not recount the details in *Incidents*. But she did recount her joy in breathing fresh air, walking on the ship's deck after years of being cooped up, and seeing the sun rise. At twenty-nine, ready to start a new life, Harriet met sympathetic blacks and whites in Philadelphia who guided her to New York. But they warned her not to speak of her relationship with Sawyer or risk losing people's support. For this reason and her fear that Norcom might still try to find her, she kept a low profile. She found a position as a baby nurse with the family of best-selling writer Nathaniel Parker Willis. His wife, Mary, shielded Harriet from the Norcoms, who did indeed hunt her. And after years of yearning, Harriet achieved her goal to reunite with her children up north, outside of the bonds of slavery.

Harriet's brother John moved to Rochester in the late 1840s, drawn by Frederick Douglass and other aspects of the city's reformist atmosphere. At John's urging Harriet enrolled daughter Louisa in the Young Ladies' Domestic Seminary, an integrated boarding school in

Clinton, New York. With her daughter in Clinton and her son a sea-man who shipped out for many long months, Harriet also moved to Rochester. When John traveled, she staffed the Anti-Slavery Reading Room. Julia and Harriet crossed paths in the room in 1849—perhaps other times as well in the eighteen months that Harriet lived with Amy and Isaac Post, with whom she became close friends.

After the passage of the Fugitive Slave Law of 1850, the Jacobses became more vulnerable. Harriet's brother decided to go to California, then Australia, in search of gold and away from slave catchers. Her son joined him, unfortunately disappearing from their lives when in Australia. Harriet returned to work for the Willises; by then Nathaniel had remarried after the death of his first wife. Cornelia Willis became Harriet's new employer and, ultimately, the person who masterminded her purchase when the Willises learned the Norcoms were again actively seeking her. Although Harriet protested the principle that she was a commodity for sale, Cornelia went ahead and paid $300 for her. Nathaniel did not seem to play a role or contribute any of the money. Although fond of Harriet, he tolerated slavery and wrote disparagingly about blacks.

In 1852 a new chapter opened in the life of Harriet Jacobs: legally she was a free woman.

A number of men, most notably Frederick Douglass, had published powerful personal narratives of their lives in slavery. Sojourner Truth's account of bondage in New York State appeared in 1850, although written in the third person. The firsthand experiences of enslaved women were mostly invisible. Now that Harriet did not fear recapture and her grandmother had died, she had the freedom to write what became *Incidents in the Life of a Slave Girl*. Writing in snatches between tasks in the Willis household, she finished her manuscript in 1857. Finding a publisher proved difficult. She did not ask well-connected Nathaniel Willis, given his views; an attempt, via Amy Post, to interest Harriet Beecher Stowe failed. A Boston publisher finally accepted the manuscript if Lydia Maria Child, a well-known abolitionist and author, wrote a preface. Child, who already knew Harriet's story, agreed and acted as the book's editor and agent. In 1861 *Incidents in the Life of a Slave Girl* came out under the author's pseudonym of Linda Brent, although the fact that Harriet had written the book was openly known.[12] Reviews were favorable, sales respectable but lower than hoped for amid the events of the time. Harriet actively promoted the book and spent her own money to purchase the printers' plates when the publisher went out of business.

Julia Wilbur read and admired the book in 1861, noting that "Linda" was "incidents in the life of *Harriet Jacobs*, a fugitive slave who was in Rochester about a year ago & where I became a little acquainted with her" (she mixed up her dates). As she mulled over the book, Julia took a small step toward recognizing similarities between Harriet and herself: "Harriet Jacobs has noble womanly feelings although her skin is not quite as white as mine."[13] "Not quite as white" may have referred to her recognition that women are the same under their skin color (not a commonly held belief by most white women of the time), as well as the reality of miscegenation, something that later pained Julia as she came in contact with people then termed "mulattos" in Alexandria and Washington.

Unlike Julia, Harriet knew firsthand the conditions awaiting her when she moved to Alexandria because she had visited the previous summer. As she promoted her book, she met with William Lloyd Garrison, who asked her to travel to Washington and the vicinity for his newspaper, the *Liberator*. The paper published her account "Life among the Contrabands" in September 1862. She relished the assignment, not only writing to inform readers about freedmen conditions, but also soliciting and distributing clothing, bedding, and other supplies. At a row of buildings near the Capitol with the inaccurately picturesque name of Duff Green's Row, she visited "men, women, and children, all huddled together, without any distinction or regard to age or sex," many of them ill.[14] Coincidentally the buildings had housed Abraham Lincoln during his one term as a congressman in the late 1840s. As contraband housing, they were expected to accommodate fifty people, but almost four hundred crowded in for lack of other options. In the article Jacobs expressed hope that conditions would improve. Camp Barker, the place Julia visited her first day in Washington, was one of the supposed improvements.

Among others Harriet connected with William Channing, the Unitarian minister who brought Julia to Alexandria a few months later. Like Julia later in the year, the first places in Alexandria that Harriet saw were the Old Schoolhouse and the slave pen. Harriet learned the first task of the day was to see who had died the night before, as Julia discovered a few months later. And as Julia also later reported, Harriet witnessed raw surroundings but also people's determination to leave enslavement: "This I thought the most wretched of all places. . . . What but the love of freedom could bring these old people hither?" While describing poverty and woeful conditions, Harriet made clear she did not just meet pitiable victims, but rather people who had bravely taken their fate into their own hands. She put in a plea for readers to take in an orphan or to support institutions that did so. Her own past perhaps sharpened her awareness of the vulnerability of a child without parents. She also argued that after a lifetime of slavery, people needed time and support to get on their feet—reflecting the debate about how much assistance to provide the recently enslaved. "Some of them have been so degraded by slavery . . . , they know little else than the handle of the hoe; the plough, the cotton-pod and the overseer's lash," she commented. "Have patience with them."[15]

Upon her return north, Harriet became a prime candidate to serve as a relief agent on behalf of the New York Yearly Meeting of Friends. William Cromwell and Benjamin Tatham from this influential Quaker group visited Washington and Union-held sites in Virginia in November 1862. The day before Julia spent Thanksgiving at the Paroled Prisoners Camp, she met the two men, who "wish to learn every thing in relation to the contrabands & are ready to help them."[16] She told them about the woeful condition of the approximately 1,200 refugees who had come to Alexandria to date. At the end of 1862, according to the Friends' report, "the Committee concluded to accept the services of Harriet Jacobs—herself formerly a slave—to act as their agent at Alexandria."[17] Around the same time, Harriet wrote her Rochester friend Amy Post of her plans to go to Washington the following month, telling Post she planned to stay for the winter.[18]

When Harriet showed up, Julia put a brave face on it to Barnes ("She can do these things much better than I can & I am glad she has come & we want just such a person here") as she continued to solicit what she saw as useful items—chemises, bonnets, aprons, tin cups, quilts. They were to share the Clothing Room that Provost Marshall Wyman allowed Wilbur to use in December. Suddenly, with Harriet's items and record-keeping responsibilities, Julia complained, "We cannot spread [the clothing] out & it is a great deal of work to look over a pile of things every time an article is wanted, & to keep account of every article which is given out would take the whole time of one person."[19]

There is no account of Jacobs's initial reaction to Wilbur, but it was likely not as fraught. The summer before in Washington, Harriet had made note of two white women undertaking relief efforts—the first she had seen; meeting Julia a few months later would have been less surprising, especially when the conditions required attention by one and all. Harriet had already established partnerships with white women, especially Amy Post and Lydia Child, and she had warm, although more formal, relations with Nathaniel Willis's wives. She also was soon preoccupied; like many new to the city, she became sick shortly after arriving, possibly with digestive or respiratory ailments, both common.[20] Julia looked in on Harriet often as she convalesced. Maybe it gave her breathing space to get used to her new colleague. By the time Harriet felt well enough to work at the end of January 1863, they had developed a firmer footing. Harriet became "Mrs. J" to Julia for the rest of their lives.

Julia Wilbur needed a fellow traveler. By early 1863 she knew not to expect sympathy from local Alexandrians, but her days of assuming that fellow Northerners would have the best interests of the freedpeople (or any person) in mind were also gone. Cases of graft and fraud made the newspapers regularly. In Alexandria the two New York men responsible for distributing food rations were often drunk and charged with siphoning off some of the bounty. Without going into detail, Julia alluded to "mean scamps . . . who wear eagles & stars . . . [who] make it their business to destroy the virtue of ignorant & unsuspecting colored women & girls." Her boarding house landlords had no sympathy with the cause. Mr. Kimball, she reported, "abhors" black people, using the far more pejorative term that he easily bandied about. When the infant of Emma, a black servant, died, Mrs. Kimball had the body taken away before the mother could view and mourn over her child and before a coffin that Julia had arranged could arrive, arguing "it was not pleasant for the boarders to have a dead body in the house." Rev. Albert Gladwin, whom Julia once looked upon with approval, also loomed as a real menace. Time and again she witnessed his meanness to the blacks under his care while buttering up white higher-ups and visitors. She worried items meant for the refugees went astray when sent through Gladwin, giving Amy Post specific instructions to send goods to "Miss Julia A. Wilbur, Cor. Washington & Wolfe Streets, Alexandria, Virginia." While she assured Post that things would arrive safely, she requested a list of the goods, their value, a duplicate receipt, and the approximate date the packages were sent.[21]

On January 19, 1863, the *Gazette* reported, with no further detail, "Prophecies are again current respecting the approaching end of the world." The prophecies proved unfounded, and life continued in its helter-skelter way in Alexandria. The hospitals remained full, the refugees froze, the camps held men awaiting their next confrontation with the enemy, and the locals seethed under Union occupation.

Julia's typical day covered several miles of walking and included time in the Clothing Room, stops to patients in a military hospital or two, and visits to freedpeople, whether at the Old Schoolhouse or their own smaller quarters. She made the barracks construction site part of her usual rounds. The plans called for three wooden buildings, each with two long rows of ten-by-twelve-foot rooms on the bottom floor and a large common area upstairs, reached by an outdoor stairway. Residents would stay in the rooms below during the day, she learned, then go outside to climb upstairs at night. Julia worked to convince Wyman to alter the plans and set up individual rooms upstairs, rather than the residents all sleeping together ("just as if they were cattle," as Julia described it).[22] One obstacle, as with any construction project, may have been the difference between communicating and acting on instructions. Provost Marshal Wyman, in his office on King Street, had responsibility for the eventual operation of the barracks; the Quartermaster Department, headquartered down near the wharves, was building them; and the site itself lay further west up Prince Street.

Wyman seemed amenable to the change of plan that Julia suggested but didn't do anything, so she went directly to the Quartermaster Department one afternoon. With the quartermaster general not there—perhaps an auspicious happenstance—she managed to have one of his underlings go with her to the site and give specific orders to the workmen about the second floor. Although Wyman found Julia's continual attempts to improve the contraband barracks trying (once snapping at her that he wished she would work as hard for *his* lodgings someday), Julia felt his heart was in the right place.

But in early February General Slough, Alexandria's take-charge military governor, announced Lt. Col. Henry Horatio Wells would replace Captain Wyman as provost marshal. Losing Wyman meant losing, if not an ardent supporter, at least someone sympathetic to Julia and the cause.

Julia heard the news with alarm. She did not know Slough's control tendencies had come into play to cause the change. The night before removing Wyman, Slough had returned from a trip to the logistics facilities at Aquia Creek (down the Potomac) and had come across inebriated citizens and soldiers "shouting & singing bacchanalian songs" in the streets. A few nights earlier, when "rudely assailed by unknown persons," he had chosen to react by drawing his pistol.[23] Slough came to Alexandria to keep order; he would have it. At a court of inquiry on Wyman's performance, Slough charged his former provost marshal with "relaxation of vigilance," particularly concerning his lack of enforcement of the no-liquor order.[24] Wyman countered the accusation. He cross-examined many of the witnesses brought by the court and called many of his own, both military and civilian. Although Julia wondered if his abolition-leaning sentiments played a role, the only mention of this aspect of Wyman's performance was a defense witness who noted the difficulty of Wyman's job "owing to the forces passing through—Contrabands and a thousand things occurring make it very hard."[25] The court cleared Wyman and he served until an honorable discharge in May 1865.

Cognizant of the fate of his predecessor, Provost Marshall Wells warned he would vigorously enforce the army's ban on "the sale or gift of spirituous, malt liquors or wines" in Alexandria. He succeeded all too well. He soon had to tell Slough, "The cellar in which I store confiscated liquors is full to overflowing"; after sending a portion of the spirits off to the hospitals for medicinal purposes, he asked for guidance for what to do with the rest.[26] Wells also hammered down on the oath of allegiance system, in which local residents needed to swear loyalty to the Union in order to obtain a pass to travel or maintain a business. He announced a change of policy: individual members of a family had to provide evidence of their loyalty, rather than the previous practice to issue a single pass to an entire household. Even people who wanted to fish in the Potomac had to take the oath of allegiance to obtain a permit to do so.[27]

While Julia favored actions to support temperance and control the secesh (the secessionist-leaning residents), she found Wells decidedly less sympathetic to her main concern, the conditions of freedpeople. Ever the optimist, Julia thought, "He may do well for these people & favor our plans. I will hope for the best."[28] Wells, coincidentally, was born in Rochester in 1823 and moved to Michigan, like many members of Julia's own family. Their first encounters were pleasant; perhaps they even chatted about places they knew in common.

Acrimonious relations soon kicked in. At the end of February Wells requested that Julia accompany Reverend Gladwin and Dr. John Bigelow, a Manhattan physician newly arrived to oversee refugees' health (no known relation to Julia's nemesis Revilo), to his office to discuss "moving the people and some other things." It is noteworthy he included a woman in such a meeting. Gladwin certainly took note and expressed his displeasure; as she related, "[He] says I am out of my sphere, & he does not like to see a woman wearing men's clothes."[29]

Once in Wells' office, the men joined in common cause about the barracks. They proposed charging rent of $5 per month, "making $1,700 per year for these rude barracks." Julia did not stay quiet in her "sphere," arguing surely that President Lincoln and Secretary of War Stanton did not intend such an action. She recorded Wells's reply: "It makes no difference to me what the Pres. or Sec. S. thought. I shall have the buildings rented." Wells also stated sixteen people would live in each room (about the size of a modern-day bedroom). Julia countered with a request to set a maximum of twelve. "I wish I could see the least spark of feeling about Col. Wells," she lamented. She did not. In retrospect it was not a good idea to anger Wells; he had power and a few months later used it to tamp down Julia and boost Gladwin.

By the time the barracks were ready in early March, the spartan accommodations consisted of berths in the upper rooms, while "the lower rooms were each furnished a stove, cupboard, table, and two benches."[30] Julia reported that Wells had agreed to reserve one room for unaccompanied young women as a security measure. The *Gazette* reported, "A number of frame tenements have been built by order of U.S. authorities, at the upper end of Prince Street, for use of the 'contrabands,' whither a considerable number of them recently scattered in different parts of the town, have migrated."[31] In fact, freedpeople who had the means to do so preferred to build, rent, or otherwise find their own lodging, however small. The barracks could provide shelter to just-arrived refugees, who continued to make their way behind Union lines, mostly from other parts of Virginia.

Relationships among humans often come down to inches and feet. On the Civil War battlefields men gave their lives to seize, or reseize, creeks, pastures, and bridges. Off the battlefield the struggles were less deadly, but in occupied Alexandria they could still get intense. As with the provost marshal's office, General Slough's quarters, and many other sites around Alexandria, the Union army had a method to acquire space—take over the city's unoccupied homes, warehouses, and other places or simply inform owners who did not sign oaths of allegiance that they needed to leave. Dr. Bigelow, whom Julia saw as too full of himself, told Wells he eyed a house on Washington Street that "would suit his purposes very well" as a dispensary.[32] Two days later Wells sent a note that read in total: "To the occupants of the House No. 41 Washington Street: You are hereby ordered to vacate the house No. 41 Washington Street this day as it will be used by Government for hospital purposes."[33]

But victors don't easily divide the spoils. The space Wyman gave to Julia for a clothing room after the December fire was one such example—half of a brick duplex on the corner of Washington and Wolfe Streets. It was coveted space, with separate north and south sides and three good-sized floors. First Gladwin tried to occupy it, even, at one point, moving in a bed. "I have told him, there is no room for his bed where our goods are," Julia pointed out, although he later succeeded in living there.[34] Then Dr. Bigelow, using the northern half for a hospital, asked for control of the southern half in case he needed it. Julia and Harriet stood up for their space. In addition to using space for their Clothing Room, they both ended up living there for a time. For all their complaining about Wells, he agreed the southern half of the building could remain under their control rather than go to Bigelow or Gladwin—not that the men didn't stop trying.

Working together, Julia and Harriet also successfully fought a more dangerous idea: to move healthy orphans into the Claremont Smallpox Hospital.

Everyone feared smallpox, even though it was not the most prevalent disease of the disease-ridden Civil War. Carried through the air or on infected bedding and clothing, however, it was debilitating, with visible signs of ravagement. It hit white and black, civilian and military, rich and poor. Even President Lincoln had the beginnings of a mild case when he gave the Gettysburg Address at the end of 1863.[35] Cramped, unsanitary living conditions exacerbated contagion among refugees. Vaccinations were available, but the supply unpredictable and not 100 percent effective. The fluid migration of the refugees, combined with little attention to their health needs, made inoculation even more of a hit-or-miss affair among African Americans. Over the winter and spring of 1862–63, "Of the contrabands, we think about 700 died of the disease," Julia reported.[36] She periodically got vaccinated and stayed clear of the worst infected places.

Subterfuge and smallpox went hand in hand. Julia hid her comings and goings from the Kimballs for fear they would kick her out of their boarding house if they knew she had contact with the disease. The free black family with whom Jacobs stayed when she first arrived told her they could not board her if she circulated among smallpox patients. In Washington, Jonathan Dennis Jr., who helped the New York Friends, wrote Julia he had five boxes of clothing sent to him for Alexandria, but she couldn't come around to retrieve them because his wife "is so nervous about small pox she is afraid to have people come to the house." (Not realizing Harriet and Julia had already connected, Dennis also asked her to see where "Hannah" Jacobs was living and "write me what thou thinks of it.")[37]

A "pest house" that opened in 1862 reached capacity, but many people tried to hide infected family members so they would not have to go there. Every day five or six bodies left the building for the graveyard. Slough decided to turn a confiscated estate south of Alexandria (called Clermont) into an "eruptive fever" hospital for civilians—black civilians, that is. Several Union regiments had used, and abused, the site since mid-1861; as a smallpox facility, it would have 150 beds. The main goal centered more on keeping the afflicted quarantined than on providing medical care and comfort. Initially Julia reported, "There was no resident physician; it was visited only about twice a week," resulting, she thought, in unnecessary suffering and death.[38] In fact, while freedmen's health care was lacking on many counts, no effective treatment existed for a smallpox case once contracted. A patient either made it through or not.

Such patient care was bad enough, but Julia and Harriet learned Dr. Bigelow had a proposal for handling the increasing number of refugee orphans in Alexandria: move them to Claremont (the spelling for the property post-confiscation). Even with their basic medical knowledge, they realized the folly of boarding healthy children with smallpox patients. Julia found it hard to believe that "such an idea could enter the head of a sane, Christian man."[39] And Harriet had made care for orphans a special mission.

On a rainy, muddy day in early March the women trudged to General Slough's headquarters to request a meeting. Two women—one black and one white, Harriet about four inches taller and more solid than Julia—visiting a general was not a regular occurrence. It "was really quite an undertaking for us; we are in such a state of nervous excitement," Julia recounted. Moreover, an African American woman spoke directly to Slough and not just through the white person, also unusual for the time. They found Slough "reserved and unapproachable," but he "listened to us quite as kindly as we expected." To bolster their case Harriet drew on her own experience; as Julia related to Anna Barnes, "When pleading for these children said she 'I have been a slave myself.'" Most likely no one had ever spoken those words to General Slough. He agreed that "Mrs. J and I may carry out our plans," Julia said, to place orphans in a room at the freedmen's barracks on Prince Street.[40]

Two days later Julia and Harriet gathered their courage again and sought an audience with Provost Marshal Wells, whom Julia found more intimidating than Slough. "I introduced Mrs. J & Col. Wells condescended to talk to us for a while," she told Barnes.[41] Despite their frequent disagreements, they had a successful meeting. Wells went along with their idea of a room for orphans with adults to look after them. Having Slough's approval in their pocket didn't hurt. Wells professed he did not mean to charge the most indigent for rent or fuelwood. And he agreed to another of their requests: to remove military guards from the barracks. Harriet and Julia had disagreed with the quartering of the men in the midst of the women and children. "We composed ourselves & agreed not to cry if we could help it," Julia recounted, the two women psyching each other up before the meeting and debriefing together afterward.[42]

They set up a room for the children in the barracks and hired women to watch over them while seeking more permanent solutions. Some refugee women expanded their families, even in their stretched circumstances. "In many cases, mothers who have five or six children of their own, without enough to feed and cover them, will readily receive these helpless little ones into their own poor hovels," Harriet wrote Lydia Child in a letter reprinted (as she probably expected) in the *Liberator*.[43] Eventually other options included sending children to an orphanage established in Washington and trying to find homes for them with sympathetic families.

Contributions came in from New York, Massachusetts, Pennsylvania, and even England. Julia received thirty-three "boxes, barrels, and bales of bedding, clothing &c." in the first months of 1863. The women tried to solicit the items that were most necessary given the weather and what they had on hand. When Julia learned Frederick Douglass had given Amy Post $50, she asked Amy to purchase shawls, woolen hoods, dresses; "Anything warm is acceptable now."[44] She wrote a sympathetic donor in Philadelphia for bedding and shoes rather than clothing. Drawers were "not much needed," but "I wish someone would send us bonnets."[45] Harriet distributed 2,620 pieces between January and early May—about one-third of which she sold.[46] The New York Yearly Meeting set up a workroom with four sewing machines to make 6,935 garments for Alexandria and other locations, with about twice that many also donated.

Julia and Harriet lobbied for clothes that a person, especially a woman, would want to wear. After a lifetime of coarse, unattractive clothing, a woman did not want to wear ugly clothes in freedom, they argued. "In some of her [Harriet]'s first boxes, there were skirts & sacks of gray cloth, the worst looking stuff I ever saw. Some wouldn't take it as a gift. She has told them not to send any more of that kind," Julia wrote, while also taking care to compliment the more pleasant items received.[47]

Harriet's instructions to sell clothing as much as possible reflected the ongoing debate about how much to give the refugees lest they become "dependent." While Northerners, including abolitionists, recognized the disastrous aftereffects of slavery, many had unrealistic expectations about how long it might take to achieve self-sufficiency. Even freedmen's supporters advocated charging rent for shelter and deducting money for rations out of black laborers' paychecks (worrying that people who had spent their lives in often backbreaking toil were prone to idleness), both during the war and afterward.[48] As it happens, many more people, both men and women, *would* have had more money for basic needs if they received the wages earned for work performed. The government and private employers lagged in payment. On several occasions Julia went around to local white women to try to wrest payments due black women for cleaning and other duties.

After her initial reluctance Julia warmed to the idea of selling clothing when possible to "teach them self-reliance" and especially to have the additional money to purchase other needed supplies. In February and March Julia reported giving away 942 items and selling 448, with receipts of $520 and expenditures of $257, including the purchase of wood, medicines, and items for the orphans. Although it took her an hour or two every evening to "post my accounts," she admitted to Barnes she wished she had kept track from the start.[49]

In December 1862 Julia had lamented, "There is not a woman in Alexandria now who sympathizes with me in my work."[50] She wrote her sister Frances (and probably others) that she needed help; she couldn't do it alone. Ironically Julia Griffiths Crofts, her old Rochester nemesis who had married and returned to England, weighed in, lobbying the RLASS to send a second agent to Alexandria, but specifically a black woman, perhaps Rosetta Douglass. In her usual blunt style Griffiths Crofts wrote Anna Barnes, "If you send a second teacher, *pray & find* a suitable colored woman—The New York 'friends' have sent the *right* person in Harriet Jacobs." Although she reassured Barnes, "I do *not* doubt Julia Wilbur's ability for the work," she clearly put more faith in Jacobs than the group's Rochester agent.[51]

But in Alexandria, with Jacobs in place, Julia felt she no longer needed anyone else from Rochester. Harriet had planned to remain only over the winter, but in March Julia wrote to Rochester that "Mrs. J says nothing more about going away," a development Julia welcomed. Even so, she observed, "Affairs are very much mixed here, & I find it difficult to make persons at a distance understand them; indeed, no one here pretends to understand them."[52] Julia Wilbur and Harriet Jacobs continued to seek ways to negotiate their space and battle indifference and prejudice. Together, they decided, they could make a difference. They did not always succeed.

CHAPTER NINE

"An Interfering and Troublesome Person"

Rev. Albert Gladwin greeted Julia Wilbur when she first arrived in Alexandria in the autumn of 1862. Her initial favorable impression of him included the mistaken belief he had lived there for a while. "Mr. Gladwin is a Baptist minister, he has been here some time," she wrote Amy Post in Rochester. "I don't know who supports him. . . . He is very active & I think does a great deal of good."[1]

Julia got the Baptist minister part right anyhow. Very soon her view of him soured. The antipathy was mutual. When they had to, especially in the presence of others, they maintained correct relations. Otherwise Julia worked to undermine him, and he did the same to her. Julia was prescient when she observed, "He has done a good deal among the contrabands & soldiers. But between the two stools, he may yet fall on the ground."[2] In 1863, however, his seat remained firmly planted.

Gladwin's biography remains sketchy, and no identifying photograph or detailed physical description has surfaced. He was white, born in Connecticut in 1816, about a year younger than Julia. The 1850 census shows an Albert Gladwin in Middlesex County, Connecticut, as a teacher in his midthirties living in a hotel. He entered the Baptist ministry in the 1850s. Baptists were a small denomination in Connecticut—one early minister estimated about 16,500 communicants in 1850 out of a total population of more than 370,000.[3] Earlier Connecticut Baptists had suffered as a religious minority.

In 1856 Gladwin "served the church faithfully" in Block Island, Rhode Island, about thirteen miles out in the Atlantic Ocean. In addition to preaching, he raised money to build the island's First Baptist Church. He received a vote of thanks and $250 in remuneration, but his tenure was controversial. One recollection, written in 1876, noted "bitter and blind opposition" to his endeavors; his proponents credited his success in building the church as "almost superhuman."[4] Over the next few years Gladwin bounced around in missionary work in New York, Ohio, and Minnesota, among other places.[5] The American Baptist Free Mission Society, one of many religious groups involved in freedmen relief efforts, sent him to Alexandria in October 1862. Thus he arrived after Harriet Jacobs had visited for the *Liberator* in August and before Julia Wilbur moved there in November.

Gladwin had the annoying habit of hogging the credit for deeds done by others. From the early days of Union control in Alexandria, African Americans had set up classes for children and adults. Yet Gladwin made a great show of *his* endeavors in education; most infuriating of all, his public relations efforts proved successful. He started taking meals at the Marshall House Hotel—still operating after the Ellsworth-Jackson incident—all the better to meet up with visiting VIPs; as Julia observed, "He seizes upon everybody that is the least inclined & takes them around & some of them go away with the impression that Mr. G is the most self sacrificing & humane & pious & benevolent man living."[6] A postwar description in an official government report characterized him as "a man of very limited education, but [who] understood very well how to appropriate to his purposes the intelligence of others."[7]

Gladwin got into the clothing act too. He solicited items directly, asking a group of Philadelphia women for "clothing for boys and girls of a larger size," as well as bed coverings and quilts. The clothing "will be faithfully distributed," he told them, with no mention of the distributors beyond himself.[8] The New York Friends, who had dispatched Harriet to Alexandria, sent their donations via Gladwin, to Julia's dismay. She, in turn, made appeals requesting donors to address items directly to her. Besides her pride, she had a practical reason. When Gladwin didn't pick up the items, no one else could, and they sat unopened.

Julia and Harriet probably would have put up with Gladwin's grandstanding if not for a more fatal failing: he bullied those he saw as beneath him.

Time after time Julia watched Gladwin mistreat the blacks supposedly under his care. He threatened to flog those whom he perceived as misbehaving, criticizing what he saw as her gullibility. "Oh Miss Wilbur," he told her, "if you had been on the plantation as much as I have & knew these people as well as I do, you would find there is no other way of getting around them." It's not clear where his "plantation" experience came in, if at all, but such is not the most comforting comment by the person responsible for bettering the refugees' lives. The women and Gladwin saw the same things through different eyes. One day Julia and Harriet "went into every room in housing near the R.R. & wharf" to gauge the conditions. Where they saw distress, Gladwin judged the same places as quite acceptable. "I wish Mr. G was obliged to live as these people do, until he would quit saying, 'they are all pretty comfortable,'" she observed.[9]

As Julia had learned in her meeting with the provost marshal, Gladwin favored charging rent for the freedmen barracks. Possibly he operated with the goal of looking for any way, realistic or not, to avoid the dependency charge levied against black refugees. Or he looked at the enterprise as a way to make money. Although Provost Marshal Wells grudgingly agreed the most indigent did not have to pay, Julia found Gladwin threatening to evict people or selecting as tenants the people who could pay versus those who could not. "Those people are wronged in various ways & come to us for aid," she said. "Mr. G is very hard with them."[10] At one point, she claimed, he refused help to people unless they "go home & wash their clothes," never mind they might not have another set of clothes to change into.[11] Meanwhile, he professed sympathy and self-sacrifice for the cause, a stance that she saw as "sanctimonious speech & long face."[12]

Julia knew Gladwin didn't like her in principle, opposed to the idea of a woman out of her "sphere." It turns out he didn't like her personally either. In January 1863 he met abolitionist sisters Lucy and Sarah Chase on a train north. In a letter to their family they related Gladwin's "whirlwind of complaints" about working in Alexandria, which included "Miss Wilbur, who pays six dollars a week for her board and does nothing because she's afraid of smallpox."[13] If he spoke about her like this to casual acquaintances on a train—fellow Quaker women no less—he was probably not exactly mincing words with his male colleagues back in Alexandria.

In March 1863 whites, mostly poor and foreign born, straggled in from Richmond on their way into Washington. The *Gazette* described "a long line of refugees (foreigners), among them women and children, from the South. . . . They attracted the attention of all on the street."[14] Julia walked alongside them for a few minutes and asked why they had left. One woman replied they could get nothing to eat; another said food was available but they couldn't afford it. To continue north they had to sign oaths of allegiance and explain why they had lived in the South—usually because of economic circumstance rather than political conviction.[15]

But the vast majority of refugees swirling into Alexandria were blacks, creating new lives for themselves beyond the immediate needs of food and shelter. At its annual meeting in April 1863, the National Freedman's Relief Association estimated Alexandria's freedmen population at three thousand.[16] For many the first priority upon arrival was to try to locate family members. One spring morning, when a group arrived from Warrenton, about fifty miles west, a woman connected with her daughter and grandchildren, another with her mother. "This is the first arrival I have seen. It has almost overcome me," Julia wrote as she witnessed their reunion. Yet it was not always happy. "Some are wild with joy, others grieving because they cannot find their friends among them."[17] One woman made it to Alexandria with her six children, only to learn the husband who had preceded them had died.

Weddings became regular occurrences. Many couples wanted to legalize their marriages, something forbidden under slavery, but a moralistic element also infused the proceedings. Reflecting a commonly held view, Julia wrote, "This evening went to Chapel. Rev. Wm. Evans married 4 couples. They have lived together under the laws which Slavery sanctions. But we tell them that Religion, Morality & the laws of the land must be respected by Free people & they are such now."[18] In April the county court "appointed and authorized" Rev. Gladwin to perform marriages in Alexandria, so he got into the act as well. (When Julia attended a ceremony at which he officiated, she commented, "He was almost as awkward as the parties themselves.")[19]

Periodically the *Gazette* reported on the baptisms of blacks in the "usual-baptizing place" south of town on the Potomac River. African American churches that had existed under the radar before the war or had to have a white minister in charge could now operate more openly. Several new churches formed. Deaths took place in great numbers, but births did too—children who would have been born into slavery months or even days earlier. Julia was honored when freedwoman Matilda Washington named her infant daughter Julia Wilbur Washington.

Julia's life at the Scott House, the boarding house on the corner of Duke and Columbus Streets operated by the Kimballs, continued through the spring of 1863. While she remained discreet about most of her activities, Julia entered into the comings and goings of the house, taking meals with other residents and sometimes spending evenings in the parlor. Boarders came and went, often the wives of officers, surgeons, or patients, with whom Julia became acquainted for the few weeks or so they stayed in Alexandria. Three Vermont women who had stayed in their husbands' encampment in Fairfax County had to skedaddle back to Scott House when the brigade got sudden orders to move out. The wife of an Ohio lieutenant expressed interest in Julia's work, one of the few people who did; her husband, calling his wife "a little black abolitionist," did not agree with what he considered her latest fancy but was glad she had something to pique her interest.[20]

The dog of a fellow boarder fell out a third-floor window and died. Its owner successfully requested permission to use an ambulance to take the body of the dog, named Rose, to a photographer, who took a picture of the dead pet on a little white pillow. More seriously, the Kimballs' daughter Nettie was thrown from a horse during a riding lesson. "She left the house with Mr. Whitby in high spirits, & in less than an hour, she was borne through the streets on a stretcher, her face covered with blood," Julia wrote.[21] She and others in the household took turns keeping bedside watch as Nettie slowly but fortunately recovered. Another young, pretty local woman, referred to as Miss P., soon joined Nettie in the sickroom, complaining of severe stomach pains. The young head clerk in the provost marshal's office became quite enamored as he took his turn tenderly caring for her, to the mirth of Julia and the rest of the caretakers, who suspected Miss P. of exaggerating her condition for the attention.

And at night, as Julia lay in her small room above the Kimballs' kitchen, she heard sounds of impending battle: "The heavy tread of armed men is heard in the streets. This has a solemn sound at night. It tells of haste & secrecy & the opening of the spring campaign."[22]

Throughout the war Alexandria's military population ebbed and flowed. During the winter and between major skirmishes, King and the city's other streets and alleys filled with idle soldiers. Peddlers, pie sellers, entertainers, and anyone else looking to eke out a living beckoned them, especially when the men drew their pay. Periodic rumors circulated about rebel raids. One day alone, Julia heard a rumor about ten thousand rebels near the city; the number ballooned to forty thousand rebels, then deflated to four thousand (none true). General Slough ordered precautions, including fortified earthworks, stockades, the removal of pieces of a bridge south of town, and protection of the U.S. military railroad headquarters. Black men usually carried out the labor.

A ring of forts around Washington, along with batteries and other fortifications, further turned the capital from a vulnerable location before the war into, according to various reports, one of the most heavily defended cities in the world at the time.[23] The Confederate Army never seriously threatened Washington or Alexandria. But guerrilla incursions worried people or inspired them, depending on their political leanings. The daring exploits of Capt. John Singleton Mosby and his Partisan Rangers, always evading capture, attracted the attention of the public in both the North and South. In March 1863 Mosby's men kidnapped a Union general while he lay in bed in the supposedly well-protected Fairfax Court House.

The military also spent large amounts of time enforcing the liquor prohibition. In spite, or perhaps because, of Wells's strict edict, people spent much time and energy finding ways to evade the ban. One of the most egregious was when the authorities stopped two children whose parents had sent them on their own on the boat between Washington and Alexandria to smuggle in alcohol. They candidly informed the authorities that they had done so on numerous occasions.[24]

Petty crime proliferated—chickens and vegetables from one woman's home, kegs of butter from a grocer, merchandise from a locksmith's and a jeweler's. An anonymous "citizen" complained in the *Gazette* about "collections of idle boys, infesting the streets, congregating in corners and in vacant lots, committing all sorts of depredations, cursing and swearing, breaking and destroying whatever they lay their hands on and generally violating the city ordinances." The mayor responded with a message to the miscreants: "Know, boys, this is all in violation of city laws, which you are liable to be punished for, and I know you would not like to be brought up before me with these charges against you."[25] Maybe the "idle boys" recognized the diminished power of the mayor's city government during military occupation. When elections were held for mayor, city council, and other posts during the war years, the vote tallies were a mere whisper of the prewar totals. In the municipal election of March 4, 1863, 101 people cast votes, versus more than 1,400 in the municipal election of 1859.

Slough, not the mayor, was the de facto head of Alexandria. In March 1863 his was one of several names brought before a Senate committee for promotion to brigadier general. On March 10 the *Gazette* reported the Senate Military Committee had commented on the lack of military experience of several of the nominees, including Slough. We can imagine his reaction when he read that disparagement in print for all to see. The very next day the paper carried a story detailing Slough's military experience in "hard fought battles" at Pigeon Ranch, New Mexico (leaving out his insubordination charge) and "skill and energy" when given a command at Harpers Ferry. The Senate confirmed his promotion on March 14. At the end of the month his men presented him with a ceremonial sword, belt, and sash. It is not clear if people donated willingly or figured it was in their best interests to do so. When the nomination was first announced, Col. Gabriel De Korponay (the officer who had invited Julia to Thanksgiving at the Paroled Prisoners Camp) confided to her he didn't think Slough would get his promotion "because he talks so much." At the sword-presenting celebration, guess who publicly lauded his superior? De Korponay, of course.[26]

From the outset the army made use of the former Franklin and Armfield slave pen on Duke Street, with its living quarters, prison, kitchen, and other facilities stretching over five acres, to house refugees and imprison civilians and soldiers. (The Bruin slave business, where the Edmonson sisters had remained back in 1848, was used as a courthouse and residence of the pro-Union sheriff.)

The provost marshal used the cells to lock up soldiers, mostly for drunk and disorderly conduct, but also in some cases for insubordination, desertion, or other crimes, using other facilities for more serious cases. "Disorderly soldiers & secesh are confined there now," Julia wrote back to Rochester, as were some detained freedmen and women. About eighty people were imprisoned at any given time, with an average prison term of about ten days, according to one estimate.[27] One of Slough's complaints against Captain Wyman when Slough removed him as provost marshal was that Wyman occasionally provided meat to the prisoners rather than the bread and water Slough ordered.

Julia had visited the slave pen back in October 1862, when she had come to Alexandria with Reverend Channing. "No description can give an adequate idea of the filth & misery here, in some rooms we could not stay a minute," she wrote after that first visit. But she kept returning and told her Rochester colleagues what she saw, realizing that bearing witness would solicit more aid. "If the folks in Rochester knew the state of things here in Alex., they would make an effort I am very sure to help them," she suggested to Amy Post after one visit.[28]

In late March 1863 on one of their rounds to the slave pen, Julia and Harriet happened upon "a sight and learned facts that make us sick at heart." They watched in horror while soldiers subjected an African American man to what was called a shower-bath punishment. The contraption sat outside by a public water pump. Soldiers stripped the man, then repeatedly doused him with frigid water. The soldiers holding the water hose or standing around didn't see anything wrong with it. "I never was more indignant, & gave these *noble*

1. Julia once described herself as "unattractive in appearance," but as this photo (taken in Rochester probably in the early 1860s) shows, she was well groomed and presentable. Source: Quaker & Special Collections, Haverford College.

2. The farmhouse where the Wilburs lived from 1828 to 1864 still stands in Rush. The current owner believes the second-story section on the right is the oldest part of the house. Julia's bedroom was upstairs, perhaps in this wing. Courtesy of Clara Mulligan.

3. When Julia taught in Rochester from 1844 to 1858, the city was a boomtown. Its location along the Erie Canal brought in new people and ideas every day, leading to an active social reform movement. This illustration is from 1853. Source: Rochester Public Library, Local History Division.

4. Frederick Douglass published the *North Star* from the Talman Building in downtown Rochester. The Rochester Ladies' Anti-Slavery Society provided financial support to the enterprise since subscriptions alone would not sustain it. Source: Rochester Public Library, Local History Division.

5. Julia Wilbur arrived in Alexandria in October 1862 near these wharves, where the Quartermaster Department shipped food, fuel, and other items in and out of the Union-occupied port. A quartermaster later recalled the first official telegram he received: "Send to the front three carloads of ice. Prepare to care for ten thousand wounded." Source: Library of Congress, Prints and Photographs Division, LC-DIG-ppmsca-34824.

6. (*opposite top*) This 1863 view of Alexandria from the Potomac River shows its grid layout. Julia Wilbur regularly made her rounds on these streets. Union camps were set up on the hills, about one mile west of the Potomac. Source: Charles Magnus, Library of Congress, Geography and Map Division, G3884.A3A3 1863.M32.

7. (*opposite bottom*) As a civilian woman, Julia had to learn how to deal with the provost marshal, responsible for freedmen's affairs among other order-keeping duties. She no doubt passed through these doors to his office on King Street. Source: Mathew Brady, Still Records Picture Division, Special Media Archives Services Division, National Archives.

8. (*above*) The War Department appointed John Slough as military governor to establish order amid chaos. Although known for his mercurial temper, he kept control from August 1862 to July 1865. Source: Library of Congress, Prints and Photographs Division, LC-DIG-cwpb-04625.

9. As one of her first self-appointed roles, Julia advocated for speedy completion of the freedmen's barracks on Prince Street. Source: Library of Congress, Prints and Photographs Division, LC-DIG-ppmsca-34821.

10. (*opposite top*) The Union Army took over this building in May 1861 to house refugees and use as a jail. It was formerly a thriving business to sell enslaved people farther south, and many Northerners wrote home about its still visible signage: "Price, Birch & Co.: Dealers in Slaves." Julia visited often and complained about conditions, especially when she witnessed a black man receiving a "shower-bath" punishment in 1863. Source: Library of Congress, Prints and Photographs Division, LC-USZ62-65306.

11. (*opposite bottom*) Most freedmen and women who could work did so, such as these men and boys working for the quartermaster in Alexandria. However, the government often dragged in paying wages. Source: Library of Congress, Prints and Photographs Division, LC-DIG-ppmsca-33620.

Coloured school at Alexandria Va 1864 taught by Harriet Jacobs & daughter agents of New York Friends

× H Jacobs an Ex Slave

12. Harriet Jacobs, Louisa Jacobs, and other teachers and students pose in front of the Jacobs Free School in early 1864. According to Jacobs's biographer, Harriet arranged for the photo to be distributed to garner support for the school and perhaps also wrote the original caption. Source: Robert Langmuir African American photograph collection, Stuart A. Rose Manuscript, Archives, and Rare Book Library, Emory University.

13. (*opposite*) In 1864 Julia wrote that she stood for a portrait in Washington wearing a dress and collar borrowed from a friend. Source: Quaker & Special Collections, Haverford College.

14. (*opposite top*) Julia and Harriet used this building near the corner of Washington and Wolfe Streets for their Clothing Room and (at times) living quarters. It is believed that Harriet and Louisa Jacobs and Julia Wilbur are standing between the two doors at the top of the stairs, possibly during a celebration to mark the Union victory on April 14, 1865. Source: Still Records Picture Division, Special Media Archives Services Division, National Archives.

15. (*opposite bottom*) The same building near the corner of Washington and Wolfe Streets, as it stands today. Courtesy of the author.

16. (*above*) Julia Wilbur kept pocket and larger diaries from 1844 to 1895. These pocket diary pages record a celebration on April 14 and shock with the news of Lincoln's assassination on April 15. Courtesy of the author, from original at Quaker & Special Collections, Haverford College.

17. When Julia arrived in Richmond on May 15, 1865, she witnessed the ruins after a fire set by departing Confederate troops had spread through the business district. Source: Still Records Picture Division, Special Media Archives Services Division, National Archives.

18. (*opposite top*) Julia collected what she called relics throughout her life, including these manacles from Richmond's City Jail in 1865. Source: Division of Rare and Manuscript Collections, Samuel J. May Anti-Slavery Collection, Cornell University Library.

19. (*opposite bottom*) Julia and her sister Mary characterized postwar Alexandria as so quiet that grass grew between the cobblestones. The statue of the Confederate soldier (facing south, away from Washington, and still standing today) was erected on Washington Street, the main north-south thoroughfare, shortly before this circa 1889 photo. Source: Green Family Collection, Alexandria Public Library, Local History/Special Collections.

20. Julia worked at the Patent Office from 1869 to 1895 (current-day Smithsonian National Portrait Gallery/American Art Museum). From 1874 to her death she rented a small house on Eighth Street nearby, since torn down. She was near or in this scene when she attended the procession for Rutherford Hayes's inauguration, March 4, 1889. Source: Library of Congress, Prints and Photographs Division, LC-USZ6-166.

men who seem to enjoy it a piece of my mind. I may be arrested but I can't help it. May God forgive them," Julia wrote.[29]

The shower-bath was one of an array of nineteenth-century punishments. In 1858 *Harper's Weekly*, then a new publication, made a stir when it reported on a case at Auburn Prison in New York in which a black convict died within minutes of the punishment; an illustration of it and other abusive punishments ran under the title "Torture and Homicide in an American State Prison."[30]

Bad enough that Julia and Harriet witnessed a man undergo the punishment. A guard told them that soldiers also stripped and showered African American women. To add insult to injury, he reassured them that only black women underwent the treatment; as he informed them, "Oh! we never shower white women." Harriet, Julia said, had to walk away because "she feared she would say something & be arrested."[31]

To Julia and Harriet such action seemed wrong on many counts. The punishment was bad enough; that men used it on women made it worse; and—perhaps most galling—the men inflicting it didn't even consider an African American female a "woman." Two days later Julia returned to the pen and managed to talk to Chloe Ann Mason, a black who had undergone the shower-bath for fighting with another woman. Chloe reported that while most of the men were told to "stand back," anyone could take a glance. "Her limbs were numb to her knees," Chloe told her, after which she remained locked up in a small room for five days. When Julia returned yet again, this time with two white female acquaintances, the lieutenant in charge got ruffled and refused them entry. He complained to Wells. Wells wrote a note to Julia, hand-delivered by a sergeant, to tell her to stop interfering. She responded she planned to take the matter further. As she wrote, "What would Michigan mothers think if they knew their sons were kept here to strip women & put them in a shower bath?"[32] Although she was assured the punishment was a rare, and now terminated, practice, she soon learned of other cases.

The Rochester Ladies' Anti-Slavery Society officially complained too, although it is not clear whether or how the women coordinated their efforts with Julia's. On March 31 Anna Barnes wrote to President Lincoln. After explaining to the president that the society supported Wilbur "to civilize and educate the contrabands" in Alexandria, Barnes wrote that Julia "tells of one thing which I believe you would not knowingly permit. At the 'Slave Pen,' not only colored men but colored women are stripped and put in the Shower-bath by our Union soldiers." She said she had learned about the practice through one of Julia's "weekly reports." Barnes put in a dig against Gladwin in her letter to the president—a "brutal man—smoother than butter, to superiors, he is harder than iron to the defenseless."[33] To be fair, there is no indication that Gladwin was directly involved with the slave pen's shower-bath, at least not on the occasion that Julia and Harriet witnessed.

At the same time Julia felt she "can endure Mr. G's course no longer" and went across to Washington to visit with John van Santvoord from the Freedman's Association. He proved a sympathetic ear. Presumably she unloaded not only about the shower-bath incident, but also about her continuing struggles with Wells and Gladwin and the whole situation in Alexandria. He suggested she report her complaints to Assistant Secretary of War Peter Watson and accompanied her to hand-deliver the letter. Watson had joined the War Department as Secretary Stanton's close friend and law partner. In writing Watson, they must have known he had Stanton's ear.

In a long letter dated April 1, 1863, Julia let out her frustration against many people, excepting former provost marshal Wyman (who may not have appreciated her praise under these circumstances) but including Colonel Wells, Dr. Bigelow, and especially Reverend Gladwin. "I am not alone in the opinion that he is fitted neither [in] education nor habit to fill the office of Superintendent, although his name is now before the Secretary of War for this purpose," she wrote. She closed with some flattery: "Wishing these people to receive the full benefit of the wise and generous provisions already made in their behalf [and] knowing of no other course to be taken, I have presumed to make this direct appeal to the Secretary of War."[34]

Barnes's and Wilbur's letters made their way to Slough for further investigation. Slough, in turn, turned them over to Wells. Julia did not fear running afoul of men in power. Still, without the experience of working the system, perhaps she did not totally think through the Byzantine intricacies involved. Maneuvering around the chain of command in the military had repercussions. In this case Slough and Wells basically investigated their own policies.

Wells wrote two responses, answering Barnes's charges on April 11 and Julia's the next day. In the first he reported he had found no undue cruelty or misdoing but promised not to use the shower-bath against women any longer. He strongly defended Gladwin for his accomplishments in teaching the contrabands to be "frugal, steady, and virtuous." He could not resist a dig: "Miss Wilbur seems to labor under the belief that the chief object is to make life easy and obtain for them [freedpeople] the largest possible grants from [the] Govt. I am compelled to say that while respecting Miss Wilbur's goodness of heart, and brood benevolence, I regard her as an interfering and troublesome person." He ended with a recommendation to name Gladwin as superintendent of contrabands, a position that carried authority and a monthly salary.[35]

In the second letter Wells took on Wilbur point by point for five long pages, detailing past meetings and conversations, extolling Gladwin, and professing his concern about the conditions of the refugees. "Miss Wilbur is entirely mistaken in the covert assumption which she makes that I am not interested in these people," he countered. He *was* interested in their plight, he stated, "but do not intend until so ordered, to be directed by her"—as if that would ever happen.[36]

In person Wells told Julia the letters from Anna Barnes to the president and Julia's to Watson had done him a great injustice. He said (one could imagine him positively hissing)—"It will be fatal to you, Miss Wilbur."[37]

Wells possibly knew she had written a letter to the secretary of war about one week before the shower-bath incident with more general complaints about Gladwin. In it she asked Stanton to remove Gladwin from working with the freedmen. Shockingly enough for the times, she added, "A month ago, I did think of asking for the position of Assistant Superintendent. . . . Although a woman I would like an appointment with a fair salary attached to it." "Assistant" was all she would dream of, although even that would have been unprecedented. She did not write about this request in her diary, but in the letter she spelled it out, stating, "There is much that I do that does not come with a man's province & perhaps it is quite as necessary & important as any work that is done & I could still do more were I invested with a little more authority."[38] Although this indirect request for employment went nowhere, it reflects her growing confidence in her role.

Worse than Julia's not receiving an official appointment, Slough forwarded Wells's report to Stanton with the recommendation to name Gladwin as superintendent. He added, "If the ladies referred to would have made known to me their cause of complaint, there would be no necessity on their part of troubling the President or War Department. It too often occurs that these ladies in their mistaken zeal act as if they were [to] usurp the whole power of the Military Governor."[39]

Gladwin either had propitious timing or, more likely, knew about the investigation. He formally petitioned Wells for appointment to the position as superintendent of contrabands. "I have labored diligently with my hands, and have also taught and preached to these poor people to the utmost of my ability and have not received anything for my services," he stated, noting this was the first time he had made a "formal application in writing" for an official commission. Wells wrote to Slough that Gladwin "has done a very large amount of labor more indeed than almost any other man could have done [no mention of what women had done], and it is but justice to him to say that he has been indefatigable, diligent, and judicious."[40]

In contrast Julia and Anna Barnes received perfunctory responses, short cover letters with the Wells and Slough correspondence enclosed. The War Department took no further action—with one significant exception. On May 6 one of Julia's acquaintances gave her some news "difficult to keep over night": Gladwin had received his official appointment as superintendent of contrabands. "I have nothing more to say," she replied.[41] For now Albert Gladwin had the upper hand.

CHAPTER TEN

"I Wish to . . . Fight It Through"

"Nice, refreshing ride, country looks very fine," Julia Wilbur said as she looked out at the gardens, fields, and rolling hills of rural New York in July 1863. Besides the fact it "never looked more flourishing than now," another difference caught her attention that she probably never would have observed before: "Black faces are few and far between & I miss them."[1] She had come home to spend the summer with her family, away from hot and humid Alexandria.

Julia had changed. Yes, she immersed herself in visits with family and friends, and in the lives of her siblings in particular, activities that had once occupied a good part of her time. She ferreted out information about her niece Freda and may have tried to see her but did not make the humiliating visits she used to attempt for even the briefest glimpse of the little girl. Her stepmother Laura did not welcome her or others into the Rush farmhouse, but Julia accepted that was how her father's wife operated. She had her feet in two worlds: Alexandria as a woman on her own, New York as a member of a large extended family.

She was tired, a condition she credited to the last two hot summer weeks she had spent in Alexandria and travel north. But in fact all of May and June in Virginia had been daunting, with a series of events and decisions to make.

When the news broke about Albert Gladwin's appointment as superintendent of contrabands in early May, he quickly let people know about his new official position. His salary became common knowledge—$100 per month, about the same as the salary of an army lieutenant at the time—and was retroactive to October 1862. Given the disastrous results when she had complained to the secretary of war, Julia had to calculate how to respond to the repeated injustices

Gladwin committed. Remain silent? Continue to speak out? Report only the most egregious cases? She and Harriet Jacobs considered the issue time and again. Gladwin threatened to "turn people out" of the barracks; as one example of many, he told a gullible, newly arrived group on a Saturday that "if they didn't pay their rent by Monday 10 a.m. they would be put on the cars & sent to Richmond." He sent at least one woman to the slave pen unjustifiably. He usurped church services and made them so unpleasant that "a guard was sent around to command their [freedpeople's] attendance at church" since no one wanted to go. Yet he managed to burnish his image. An article in the *Home Evangelist*, a missionary paper, described "Mr. A. Gladwin, of New York, devoting himself most assiduously to the work of benefiting, in every way, the contrabands." In his own report to the missionary society, Gladwin wrote, "My labors have been incessant from house to house, in looking after their sanitary condition, clothing, schooling, employment and pay, and funerals at the barracks built for their accommodation and elsewhere."[2] Infuriating babble, as Julia might say.

Of course we see Gladwin through Julia's eyes—hardly the most objective source. But she and Harriet started getting validation from other quarters. An article in the *New York Evening Post* praised "Mrs. Jacobs" and "Miss Wilbur" by name. "These two ladies have been energetically occupied in this self-sacrificing work," wrote journalist Ulysses Ward. He, however, hedged his bets, adding later in the article that "much credit, also seems due to Mr. Gladwin."[3] The *Anglo-African*, a New York–based weekly, pointed out that a portion of Gladwin's salary came out of the rent collected from freedmen, a situation that might well induce him "to turn the screws on the tenants."[4] And several physicians complained about him when he turned off the water at the barracks' public tap because the area had become soaked and puddled. As it turned out, the doctors would soon prepare their own case against the superintendent of contrabands.

The Emancipation Proclamation opened the U.S. Army to blacks, who already served in the navy. "War meetings," the term in vogue for the spirited sessions organized to encourage enlistments, took place in Alexandria, as they did in Washington and other cities to target African American volunteers. (Unlike the meaning of the term today, the "volunteer" label did not mean service for no pay but rather referred to regiments apart from the standing U.S. Army.) Julia attended several meetings and submitted an article about them to the *Rochester Democrat*; the paper published it on May 22 as "Correspondence," signed by J. A. W. She described her own contribution: an American flag she had sewn in 1862 and brought with her to Alexandria ended up hoisted on a makeshift flagpole "unfurled to the free breezes of heaven." Little did she know when she made it in her "quiet & secluded northern home" in April 1862 that "the Freed men & women of Va. would gather beneath its folds."[5] Her article extolled the meetings and reported they had resulted in several hundred volunteers for military service. She also wrote that twenty white men had applied to the military governor to command black troops, including some opposed in theory to black military service. She hinted strongly at their reason—to garner a promotion.

Shortly after the war meeting, Wilbur joined four Michigan women to travel west into Fairfax County; the women included the wife of a chaplain and her daughters and Julia Wheelock, a Michigan Relief Association agent stationed in Alexandria. The two Julias had become friendly. Wheelock, the younger of the two, did not write about working with freedpeople in a memoir she published after the war, but she wrote about helping Michigan soldiers in need, another cause close to Wilbur's heart. As with the trip to Falmouth earlier in the year, Wilbur relished the chance to get closer to the battlefront, extend good cheer to the troops, and collect souvenir relics. Although the Union occupied this part of Virginia, Confederate raids and sentiments were common, and the army kept a close eye on the female civilian visitors. The women slept two nights in Michigan camps and traveled the countryside during the day. Thirty men accompanied them to see the area around Bull Run. Wheelock later wrote that in addition to guarding the women, the soldiers sought the body of a Michigan colonel believed to have remained on the field after battle; this perhaps explained the size of the contingent. Wheelock's brother was critically wounded at Bull Run in 1861, so the occasion was deeply personal: "Upon this very field he fell; here for days he lay beneath the scorching rays of a Southern sun."[6] Amid wildflowers the women saw human bones, even skulls, protruding from mounds of earth.

"The Centerville pike is fine. There was beauty all around, but it was mingled with desolation & dead horses," Wilbur observed, devoting almost twenty diary pages to the short trip. A general told them rebel women often came around to ask for food, which he provided. Julia wrote she did not agree with the policy—"The women have been as bad as the men. . . . To feed them is to give aid & comfort to the enemy"—but she kept her view to herself. Meanwhile, in one officer's tent, she noticed "a marble topped center table, a large gilt-framed mirror & chairs brought from a house near Bull Run."[7]

As soon as she returned to Alexandria, Julia bade good-bye to Harriet Jacobs, who traveled north for a month. Like Julia, Harriet was mindful of the need to inform supporters of her experiences. She arranged to bring eight orphaned girls with her and to speak at the large annual meeting of the New England Anti-Slavery Society in Boston. The audience gave her a warm reception, and members agreed to provide homes for several of the girls on the spot. According to one account, "It was stated that she purposed coming again to Boston, in the course of the summer, with more of the orphan girls, for whom she desired to obtain homes."[8] While the idea of handling adoptions or foster care by looking for sympathetic benefactors from a public stage sounds unusual today, guaranteeing a secure future for the orphans was a serious concern. At least several times Julia and Harriet worried whether households that offered to take in orphans would essentially re-enslave them. Given the tales of the sad fate of many nineteenth-century orphans, both black and white, their fear was not unfounded.

The day after Harriet left Alexandria, Julia had to move. The Kimballs gave up their boarding house and left town, although they had warned Julia they would do so only ten days earlier. Perhaps their departure was not voluntary. As Julia wrote to Anna Barnes, the commissary managers (one of whom came from Rochester) were charged with diverting the rations of contrabands and selling them to Mr. Kimball and others. "Mr. Kimball pleads innocence & ignorance, but I don't see how it can succeed," Julia wrote; perhaps leaving was part of a deal he made with the provost marshal.[9] In any event Charles Page, the newly arrived Mansion House Hospital surgeon-in-charge, decided he wanted his family to occupy the home and, according to Julia's account, refused her request to stay in one of the rooms the family didn't need.

With no other options Julia settled into a room in the house on the corner of Washington and Wolfe Streets, the location of the Clothing Room. After at least one previous attempt, Gladwin took possession of another room. Julia pointedly installed a lock and bolt on her door, although she had to bear "the tramping of men through the hall to Mr. G's room."[10] She arranged to eat most of her meals at the Leslie House on South Fairfax Street.[11] She took advantage of Harriet's absence to reorganize their shared Clothing Room. "Went to Emma's & took a cup of tea & a piece of bread & butter," she wrote on one of her first days in Alexandria without Harriet, "then went to work in the Clothing Room, overhauled it thoroughly & cleaned it completely. Mrs. J's habits are not like mine, disorder worries me."[12] According to her account, like any two people sharing space, they had different levels of tolerance about clutter.

While never directly attacked, Alexandria felt the reverberations of war. Almost daily rumors of rebel raids circulated, adding to the anxiety level. One night, "It seemed as if bedlam had broken loose";[13] hundreds of wounded federal troops and Confederate prisoners arrived in darkness from Culpeper County. On other days Julia watched—and the newspapers reported—the movement of troops out of Alexandria headed into Maryland and Pennsylvania, soon to confront the enemy at Gettysburg. On June 9 huge booms and eruptions came from Fort Lyon (south of town) when cannon weaponry accidently exploded. Two dozen men died, and thousands of rounds of ammunition ignited in a horrific mess. President Lincoln and Secretary of War Stanton, who reportedly could hear the explosion in Washington, came to the fort to inspect the damage the next day.

Before leaving for New York for the summer, Julia removed her possessions from Alexandria, given the possibilities of a rebel invasion or appropriation of her space by Gladwin. Maybe she was not sure she would come back, although she knew the RLASS wanted her to return, and "I feel now that I wish to do so & fight it through."[14] Packing was an ambitious undertaking. She sent a trunk weighing one hundred pounds to Washington and an eighty-pounder to Avon, the nearest large town to the Wilbur farm. Much of the weight came from relics she had collected in her travels over the previous few months—not just small bits of wallpaper from the Marshall House or buttons from the Bull Run battlefield, but, among much else, a rifle from Fairfax County, flower pots from a visit to George Washington's Mount Vernon, and a bayonet given her by a Washington acquaintance who said it came from the Antietam battlefield.

An acquaintance named Mrs. Henry was headed to Brooklyn, and the two women decided to travel by ship rather than train. It took a few tries, given rumors of an attack on Washington and ships already booked with other passengers. On July 4 Julia took a tugboat (decorated for the holiday with flags, streamers, and boughs of greenery) from the Alexandria wharf to Georgetown. There she and Mrs. Henry boarded the steamer *Empire* for what the women joked would be their ocean voyage together. Any semblance of a sumptuous cruise went by the wayside almost immediately. Their small cabin was hot and stuffy, with no shade relief on deck. They traveled south to get north, down the Potomac to Norfolk, then up past Delaware and New Jersey on the Atlantic. Seasickness set in. "Looked out all day on the green restless ocean. Could not hold my head up. Nothing to eat or drink that would relish at all," she wrote. Because of fog, they docked an additional night at Sandy Hook on the north end of the New Jersey shore rather than remain at sea. Echoing the universal feeling of seasick sufferers, Julia marveled that "as soon as the boat stopped, I felt better," although she regretted the stop extended the trip an extra day.[15] When they landed in Staten Island the morning of July 7, they heard about the Union victory at Gettysburg. "Three cheers given," she reported, no doubt recalling the troop movements north from Alexandria the previous month. The *Empire* continued up the East River to the foot of Wall Street, where she parted ways with Mrs. Henry. She had her luggage brought to the Girard House (now the Cosmopolitan in trendy TriBeCa, then an establishment suitable for a lady traveler) and set out to explore the city for a day. First stop: the *National Anti-Slavery Standard* newspaper, a short walk away. Editor Oliver Johnson was in the office on Beekman Street, but "he showed no interest in my mission." He perked up at the mention of Harriet Jacobs because, he said, "he was much attached to her." Julia found his lack of interest in what she had done in Alexandria, beyond knowing Harriet, perplexing. "I felt hurt by his indifference, as we are engaged in the same cause," she noted.[16]

Julia walked around lower Manhattan, feeling claustrophobic after the wider spaces of Alexandria and Washington. A horse-drawn streetcar brought her three miles north to Central Park. The park was less than a decade old, built on swamps, bluffs, and the seized land of about 1,600 small farmers. Far from the population center downtown, Central Park in 1863 served as an elegant park for the well-to-do. Between 4 and 6 p.m. Julia watched as "a stream of elegant carriages came in from 5th Av. Such fast horses & splendidly dressed people, I never saw before. . . . What tremendous wealth exists in this city." On the way back downtown, she noticed the signs on some streetcars that read, "Colored People are allowed on these cars." Whites could travel on any car; blacks, only on those for which they received this sanction.

Less than a week after Julia left Manhattan, this combination of economic inequality and prejudice ignited five deadly days—the New York City Draft Riots. According to historian Edward Spann, "A large floating population of unattached males, many the habitués of the barrooms of the city," caused most of the violence.[17] These men were prime draft targets after passage of the Conscription Act of 1863. The act's provision that allowed men to avoid service by paying $300 or hiring a substitute exacerbated tensions between those who could afford to opt out and those who could not. Throug the week of July 13 mobs leveled their first assault at a draft office. They then targeted specific white men (for example, officers involved with the draft and editor Horace Greeley, attacking his *Tribune* office) but went after blacks wantonly. One group burned the Colored Orphan Asylum to the ground, attacking the most vulnerable of all. The mayor and governor ineffectually tried to stanch the chaos. The military, including a regiment just returned from Gettysburg, finally restored order. At Gettysburg they could not have expected their next engagement would involve quelling violence caused by fellow Northerners.

Meanwhile, Alexandria residents encountered a different type of upheaval. Before Julia left for New York, rumors circulated about a plan to expel "secesh" from the city suspected of helping the rebels. As Julia saw it, "There are not only foes without, but there are foes within in great numbers."[18] Confederate sympathizer Anne Frobel saw it a different way. "Any one who chooses to go to the yankee authorities and make an accusation against another, whether true or false, he is seized up and sent outside the lines, only allowed a few clothes," she wrote in her diary.[19] But Military Governor John Slough shared the same worry as Wilbur, not Frobel.

According to historian Diane Riker, Slough compiled a list of "disloyal people of Alexandria" and proposed expelling them.[20] His higher-ups approved the plan. Provost Marshal Wells communicated with the people on the list that they needed to prove their loyalty to the U.S. or "be sent by boat to City Point," the Union-held port south of Richmond. They should bring "personal baggage, not exceeding 100 pounds" to the wharf on July 6 for inspection (no "supplies, stores, or medicines, nor any letters, correspondence or writings of any kind whatever"), to leave the following morning at 9 o'clock. The order covered 243 individuals and families but preoccupied everyone in town, whether directly targeted or not. Over the next week word circulated that the order had been rescinded, then that it had not, then that it would be implemented later than originally planned.

As local resident Henry Whittington recorded in his diary, the rain fell in torrents when the affected residents reported with their bits of baggage. News of Confederate losses at Gettysburg and Vicksburg, Mississippi, could only further dampen spirits. "The past week has been one of painful excitement," the *Gazette* reported, "and the suspense and anxiety were increased by the contradictory rumors and reports that prevailed."[21] The *Gazette* editor himself, Edgar Snowden, was among those targeted and announced on July 8 the newspaper would cease publication. But *deus ex machina*: Secretary of War Stanton sent a last-minute telegram to countermand the order. Slough responded icily, "Sir, I have the honor to acknowledge the receipt of your telegraphic order countermanding former order upon subject of sending disloyal persons from Alexandria." He would obey it, but he didn't like it. The would-be deportees received a reprieve. But as Snowden pointed out when he resumed newspaper publication the next day, some families "lost very considerably" when forced to sell their household effects quickly.[22]

Up north Julia "read that order to send secesh from Alex was countermanded. Too bad."[23] Maybe she would have felt differently if she had witnessed the event personally and seen women and children on the wharf; maybe not.

As she headed from New York City to Rochester, Julia spent two weeks near Poughkeepsie visiting family and childhood friends. She read about the New York riots while there, recalling she had stood in front of City Hall a week earlier. "Negro hate at the bottom of it, but when a mob begins there is nothing too bad for them to do," she commented. She noted the contrast between the chaotic city and the quiet in Taghkanic, the rural hamlet where she stayed with uncles and aunts. Yet the war seeped into this remote area too. She heard about the military service of one person's son-in-law, another's son. Two uncles, perhaps because of their Quaker roots, opposed the war, and she found conversation with them delicate. People closely followed the news, much more so than when she had visited seven years earlier with her sister Sarah or back in her childhood. "Everybody is concerned more or less nearly with the war," she wrote.[24]

Julia's first glimpse of Rochester came at 4 a.m. on July 23. She went from the train station to her sister-in-law Charlotte's, letting herself in before the family arose. She visited with Anna Barnes on her first day back, recounting in person what she had written over the previous months. She arrived back in Rush in the early evening.

Julia's homecoming sounds understated at best, even though sisters Mary and Ella were visiting from Michigan. If a welcome-home dinner or any other celebration occurred, she did not record it. Instead,

"It is not the home it once was." Lamenting the loss of her mother and presence of a stepmother, she felt, "It is very evident that none of father's children are welcome here, except to make a *very short* visit." She spent the next few days sorting out what she had shipped home—including a "box of arms, projectiles, & relics"; plant cuttings culled from Mount Vernon and Christ Church; and other mementoes. Life settled into a routine of chores and visits, minor aches and pains. After more than two weeks home, she wrote, "It is 178 weeks since I have seen my darling Freda & I have no hopes of seeing her at present." She missed her, but the longing of the past had dissipated, at least as she recorded her feelings.[25]

From the battlefront they heard from brother-in-law Joseph Van Buskirk in Jackson, Mississippi, a "very hot & most miserable place."[26] A few weeks later he wrote from Nicholasville, Kentucky, to ask his wife to travel to him, as many wives did when their husbands were in camp. Maybe she would have gone if she felt more comfortable leaving her two children with their grandparents, but her stepmother's attitudes and father's eye condition precluded that possibility.

Rochester and the surrounding area had a draft quota to fill of 2,015 men. Although no riots accompanied the announcement, as they had in New York City, the excitement of May 1861, when men couldn't sign up fast enough, had long passed. Julia's nephew Theodore received word he had been drafted. The twenty-two-year-old son of her sister Angeline and brother-in-law Alfred had already served a three-month enlistment in 1862 and contracted the measles. This time he or his parents paid the $300 commutation fee to avoid the draft.[27] Alfred was the brother-in-law with whom Julia had always squabbled about politics. But maybe his aversion to his son's military service was more personal: according to a family history, three other of Alfred's children, brothers, died within six months of each other in 1842, leaving Theodore as his sole surviving child.

Almost immediately upon returning to Rush, Julia wrote Harriet Jacobs. She worried when she didn't hear back. Instead she received several letters from Gulielma Breed, a Washington friend, to ask if she would become matron of the National Colored Home, the orphanage that opened in June north of Georgetown on a confiscated estate. Although Julia had become very fond of Gulielma and her husband Daniel, she turned down the request. "I do not feel capable of filling such a place as it should be filled," she explained to Anna Barnes.[28] Perhaps Julia recognized her personality was not well suited to managing the institution. Perhaps she felt she could accomplish more in Alexandria than start anew at the home.

When mail finally came from Jacobs and other Alexandria contacts, they all agreed: "Mr. Gladwin is acting like a crazy man."[29] Dr. Shaw, a surgeon who worked under Dr. Bigelow, wrote her, "Things go badly in Alex. Mr. G behaves outrageously, Dr. B. is a nuisance." Harriet provided more detail, and Julia shared part of the letter with Anna. "Every night we have had a fresh arrival of refugees," Harriet wrote to Julia, describing how she hurried to the barracks each morning at 6 a.m. before Gladwin arrived. Gladwin wanted to eject people from the city, saying General Slough had ordered anyone who received rations to leave for newly established contraband housing at Arlington House. According to Harriet, several freedwomen gave up rations rather than move against their will. Matilda Washington (mother of baby Julia Wilbur Washington) took ill; "Poor Matilda in her delirium called constantly on Miss Wilbur & Mrs. Jacobs to take her babies," Harriet wrote Julia. She also reported Gladwin tried to occupy Julia's room and, when Harriet would not let him, spread out in the building's common areas. He moved a stove from the barracks for his own use—"& a man & a woman to wait on him & do his cooking." In addition to informing Julia about the status of things in the summer of 1863 under Alexandria's superintendent of contrabands, the letter shows how many refugees saw "Miss Wilbur & Mrs. Jacobs" as bulwarks against him.[30] What Jacobs did not tell her—or Julia did not report until she returned to Alexandria—was that Matilda (also known as Milly) and her daughter, Julia Wilbur Washington, did not recover. They died sometime during the summer of 1863.[31]

When Julia visited with family and Rochester abolitionist colleagues, she conducted "begging occasions" to fill a box of clothing and other items to send south. One such trip resulted in "9 bonnets, one bed quilt, and various things of less importance."[32] She appreciated their interest in what was happening in Alexandria, unlike the ho-hum reaction of New York City editor Johnson. She commiserated with Lucy Colman, whose teenage daughter had died the previous fall, perhaps encouraging her to come south. After all, Julia saw the effect a change of scenery had had on her own state of mind. (In 1864 Colman moved to Washington and became a combative, and short-lived, matron of the Colored Home, the position Mrs. Breed had offered Julia. It was Colman with whom Julia spent time after Lincoln's assassination.)

Julia spent the better part of a week writing a report for the RLASS to publish.[33] In public writing like this, both Julia and Harriet balanced pleas to show dire need with reassurances that the aid provided made a difference. Although Julia wrote she would like to "present to the Society a full and accurate account of the situation of these refugees in Alexandria for the past ten months," in fact she did not reveal everything. Her principal comment about Gladwin in more than thirteen pages of text was the following: "Rev. A. Gladwin had been sent out by the Free Mission Society of New York city, and he divided his time between the soldiers and the contrabands." She wrote about the schools, pointing out blacks ran most of them; the refugees' willingness to work, countering arguments to the contrary; the barracks; sickness; and the clothing operation. She wrote, "I am convinced the Government means to do right by these refugees from slavery, but persons employed to carry out its measures are often prejudiced against them and evidently have no desire to benefit or improve them." Even this charge, unattached to specific names or situations, was daring.

The RLASS agreed to continue to sponsor Julia, giving her the moral and financial support to return. The treasurer's report for 1863 lists two expenses related to Alexandria: $560 to contrabands at Alexandria and Kansas and $177.73 directly to the agent in Alexandria.

On September 21, 1863, Julia left New York to pick up life again in Alexandria. "Sorry to leave father & Mary & children but do not feel so bad about leaving as I did last fall," she wrote.[34] The trip back to Alexandria—on a train this time, so much for the ship experiment—

was very different from the first one a year earlier. Phebe Cornell, a friend and cousin, accompanied her, hoping to find relief-related work. This time Julia was the expert, navigating the changes of trains and the arrival in Washington. She brought Phebe to see the White House, tour freedpeople's housing at Camp Barker, and take tea at the Breeds', where they learned Mrs. Breed had found a matron for the home. Phebe must have felt as overwhelmed with first impressions as Julia had when she had first arrived.

At 4:30 p.m. on September 27, Julia was back at the Clothing Room on the corner of Washington and Wolfe Streets. Unable to find a position, Phebe returned to New York and rallied donations from there. For Julia the frustrations would return. The discomfort would persist. She would find people still poor and uncomfortable, subject to injustice. But, she decided, "it seemed really good to be in Alexandria, again."[35]

CHAPTER ELEVEN

"Will It Pay?"

In mid-December 1863 Amy Post traveled to Washington from Rochester and then crossed the Potomac to visit her friends Harriet Jacobs and Julia Wilbur. Post had pioneered the women's rights movement at Seneca Falls, sheltered fugitive slaves in her home, and risen above the condescending attitudes toward blacks of many white Northern abolitionists—but even she found Alexandria's conditions daunting. "After we got up the hill in Georgetown, there were some nice buildings and a grand view of the City and surroundings," she wrote her husband Isaac. "But Alexandria. Oh—horrid—I look back upon it and shudder. . . . I don't know how Julia & Harriet can stay their [*sic*]."[1]

Julia too had her own days wondering how she could stay in Alexandria, despite her wish to return. Was what she accomplished worth the personal discomfort, the constant scrambling for position, the injustice she witnessed? Her views on the subject wobbled mightily.

When Julia came back to Alexandria at the end of September, she moved back into the duplex on the corner of Washington and Wolfe Streets, the building that housed the Clothing Room and on which Dr. Bigelow, Reverend Gladwin, and others continually had designs. Her room held a bed, a chair without a back, and a box to use as a table. The government issued furniture, but an officer in the Quartermaster Department told her he didn't have anything available for her, neither in an initial nor follow-up requests. Julia couldn't help noticing that "officers receiving large salaries can have furnished houses in addition & have the best of everything." Similarly one evening, on the other side of their shared building, Dr. Bigelow and some guests feasted on stuffed shote and other delicacies, while he insisted on providing only cornbread and salt pork for his patients, despite receiving funds to purchase other food for them.[2]

But Julia realized her presence could make a difference. Sometimes with Harriet Jacobs or another companion but often alone, she made the rounds to freedmen's housing. Beyond the barracks, slave pen, and Old Schoolhouse, people settled into other neighborhoods, some existing and some new. In Hayti, Grantville, Newtown, and the Bottoms, among others, they occupied rooms in existing buildings or built small houses. Down a dark, narrow passageway, Julia found an infirm grandmother, her daughter, and her grandchildren in a cold and windowless room "no better than a shed." When she learned Dr. Bigelow would not go to her, Julia received permission for an ambulance to bring the woman to the hospital. The driver objected that the ambulance "was not for Colored ladies but for white ladies," but she told him, in so many words, to get over it.[3] She managed to get the woman to the hospital within a half hour after days of neglect.

Julia or Harriet often interceded to help newcomers in particular get rations or medicine from the government or provided items from their own stock. After he visited Alexandria, abolitionist Samuel May Jr. published a letter in the *National Anti-Slavery Standard* lauding "Mrs. Harriet Jacobs ['Linda'] and Miss J. A. Wilbur." He urged readers to send "donations of money, or clothing, etc." to either woman, "at the corner of Washington and Wolf streets, Alexandria, Va." While extolling the goal of self-sufficiency, May reminded readers of "the number of the aged, of the very young, the feeble, the sick, together with the fact of occasional neglect and injustice in the payment of their wages."[4] The Union Army employed hundreds of thousands of black workers throughout the occupied South in addition to soldiers, from nurses to laborers, laundresses to railroad workers. Wages, however, often came fitfully.

The women encountered many scrappy survivors. As one example, Julia met a Miss Griffin, who had escaped slavery from Lynchburg, where she had learned to read and sew. She forged a pass to get through Confederate areas and made her way to Alexandria, where she helped teach and lived in a new house. "I'll warrant sure she will *take care of herself,*" Julia wrote, glad of it. Harriet estimated freedmen built seven hundred "little cabins . . . containing two to four rooms" with their own resources in late 1863 and early 1864.[5]

Albert Gladwin continued to bedevil Julia and Harriet because of his mistreatment of the freedmen, though he bemoaned the mistreatment *he* faced. He successfully wormed out of another investigation into his behavior, this one brought on by Dr. Bigelow and two other physicians, Samuel Shaw and Shaw's son-in-law Joseph Graves. Their discontent had roiled for a time. The specific event that triggered action had occurred when Gladwin shut off the water tap at the freedmen's barracks. The physicians insisted he restore water to the residents. Shaw further reported comments he had heard about Gladwin, writing, with some exaggeration, "I have yet to meet with the first Colored man or woman in the barracks that does not sigh for the cruelties of slavery rather than enjoy the tender mercies of A. Gladwin."[6] Although Shaw shared his concerns with Julia before she left for New York, it is not clear she knew he planned to carry them forward.

The three doctors cosigned a letter to the National Freedman's Relief Association of Washington, laying out their dissatisfaction about Gladwin. In a separate letter Dr. Graves observed that a building for which Gladwin charged $18 in monthly rent had such a bad roof "it affords an excellent opportunity for its inmates to become astronomers."[7] The association took up the cause. Its officers wrote to Secretary of War Stanton with a numbered list of complaints about Mr. Gladwin:

(1) [He is] oppressive

(2) He lacks sympathy

(3) He lacks discretion

(4) He endeavors to govern by force and violence rather than by kindness and firmness

(5) He lacks to a great degree business tact and capacity and general intelligence becoming his place.[8]

Once again the War Department tasked Slough with investigating Gladwin; once again Gladwin escaped censure. Slough asked his provost marshal at the time, Capt. William Gwynne, to respond.

Gwynne reported the charges were unfounded and precipitated by the doctors' own quests for power (which, at least for Bigelow, may have been true). Gwynne couldn't resist a jab at Julia and Harriet in his written response: "Two women Mrs. Harriet Jacobs (colored) and Miss Julia Wilbur (White) have also been meddling . . . and endeavoring to sour the minds of the Negroes against their Superintendent." Gwynne said he "was told by the families that they got along first rate, that Mr. Gladwin treated them well, etc., although some weeks ago there was strong feeling against him, gotten up, no doubt by female 'busy bodies' and urged by some of the Medical Officers." He repeated the old saw that Gladwin's policy to charge rent "has resulted in learning them to be self-reliant."[9] To further counter the charges, the two former provost marshals, Wells and Wyman, wrote glowing letters of support. If Julia knew that Wyman, whom she had once considered her closest ally in Alexandria, had praised Gladwin as honest, untiring, and judicious, she probably would have been appalled.

When Slough sent the report to Washington, he added his own endorsement and further indignation about "intermeddling would-be philanthropists."[10] Two days later, on October 3, 1863, the War Department exonerated the superintendent. When she learned about the investigation before it concluded, Julia cynically predicted the outcome. She explained in a letter to Anna Barnes, "Complaints against Mr. Gladwin have been sent to the Sec. of War & referred, of course, to Gen. Slough, who is angry because they were not made to him first."[11]

Perhaps the physicians would have taken the matter further, but Graves contracted typhoid a week afterward, dying later in the month. Shaw arranged to have the body of his son-in-law sent north, then left Alexandria as well. Julia had become friendly with the two men, as well as with Graves's young wife, Harriet. Adding insult to injury, none other than Reverend Gladwin "with his long face & sanctimonious tones" officiated at a short service at Graves's deathbed.[12]

Missionaries, teachers, and other "intermeddling would-be philanthropists," as Slough characterized them, came into and out of Alexandria. After more than a year of service, Julia sometimes acted like a grizzled veteran. When one man came on behalf of the Home Mission Society to "labor" in Alexandria, she commented, "There may be more Missionaries than there are people, after a time." Hardly the case: the "contraband" population steadily increased throughout the war. Julia estimated the number at five thousand in 1864, noting others had estimated seven thousand. An unspecified number also entered Alexandria and left for Freedman's Village, Washington, and other locations. Whatever the precise figure, the numbers posed a continual challenge.[13]

When Julia met three young white women sent by groups in Philadelphia to teach in Washington, she couldn't believe their lack of preparation; one told her she did not know the purpose of a slave pen, to which Julia snapped, "I really didn't know how at this day to teach the A.B.C. of Abolition." She first dismissed a woman who came from Boston, pointedly forgetting her name, and scoffed at her idea to teach children drawing rather than what Julia saw as more practical or academic skills. But a week or so later Julia's diary attached a name to the woman—Mary Collier. They became friends, and Mary occupied one of the rooms in the Washington and Wolfe Streets duplex for a time. (When Collier died a year after the war, Wilbur eulogized her: "She was the second white woman who went there [Alexandria] to labor among Contrabands. She died at her post, literally from overwork. The poor miss her very much.")[14] Many people who spent time in Alexandria became lifelong friends, in addition to Harriet and Louisa Jacobs, such as the Beldings, the couple whom she informed about Lincoln's assassination.

In November 1863 John and Rachel Moore from Philadelphia came "to learn the state of the Contrabands." The Moores were connected with several Friends groups that had sent supplies to Alexandria. When Gladwin came upon them, he charged that Julia was "a meddlesome woman & the complaints against him had amounted to nothing"; further, he said, General Slough threatened to have Julia arrested and expelled from Alexandria if she kept meddling. Julia worried his tirade "will be misunderstood & misrepresented to my disadvantage" by the Moores, perhaps worrying future support from Philadelphia depended on making a favorable impression. As she tried to figure out what to do, John Moore reassured her, "Julia, I believe everything thee says." Abolitionists from Philadelphia were a respected and powerful group; the fact the Moores would not speak ill of her must have been a tremendous relief.[15]

As often occurred, Gladwin looked for a new way to pounce—although his next attempt almost backfired on him. One Friday afternoon about two weeks after the Moores' visit, a freedwoman named Lucy Lawson sought out Julia to tell her several rooms at the barracks in which she and Harriet taught sewing and housed elderly women (among other purposes) were being emptied, with Gladwin behind the upheaval. This time Julia did battle, albeit more diplomatically than in the past. After talking to Gladwin, who told her that "he, Mr. G, had the control of things now," she wrote to General Slough, "telling him what the rooms were used for & they met a necessity for which no other provision had been made." This time, "I am careful to be very respectful & kept a duplicate of the letter."[16] When she received a perfunctory response from one of Slough's aides, she hoped it was only because Slough hadn't yet seen the letter, as turned out to be the case.

Harriet, meanwhile, returned from a trip that included a productive meeting in New York City with the Women's National Loyal League, founded by Susan B. Anthony, Amy Post, and other women's rights leaders, to support the war. She garnered league support for a school she wanted to open, and she returned to Alexandria with daughter Louisa and a friend, Virginia Lawton, to serve as teachers.

No doubt Harriet tried to prepare the young women for conditions in Alexandria, but an immediate run-in with Gladwin was hardly an auspicious introduction. The next morning Harriet took Louisa with her to see Slough to tell him that Gladwin had turned her out of the barracks. (A far cry from a few months earlier, when Harriet and Julia had had to calm themselves down before sitting face to face with Slough to discuss the orphans.) As Harriet wrote to a friend, "I had longed for this hour that I might explain . . . to his superior in command [Slough] how unjust he [Gladwin] had been to these poor people."[17] Harriet must have described the encounter to Julia afterward, the women savoring the details.

According to Julia, Slough heard Harriet out and sent for Gladwin.

He ate breakfast and returned to find Gladwin had not yet showed up. (No word on whether he offered the Jacobs women anything to eat, but it is doubtful.) An orderly summoned Gladwin a second time. When Gladwin arrived, he told Slough he hadn't come earlier because "he supposed he wanted him to bring the money."

Slough set him straight: "You have no right to suppose anything when I send for you."

Gladwin: "Why, I could have rented these two rooms for $90."

Slough: "What business is it to you whether they rent for 10 cents or $90?"

Gladwin pursued another line of defense and reminded Slough that Julia and Harriet interfered with contraband affairs. Slough threatened Gladwin with a stint in the slave pen. (The women must have loved that.) Gladwin then conceded, "*She* [Harriet] could have a room at the Barracks, but Miss Wilbur could have none." Harriet inserted herself into the conversation to tell Slough that Julia had "but one small room."

Slough to Gladwin: "I told you distinctly not to turn Miss Wilbur out of that room."

When Gladwin threatened to quit if the women occupied the rooms, Slough offered to write the resignation letter for him: "You have threatened to do it several times before. You don't frighten anyone. There are others to be had to fill the place."[18]

Although Gladwin clearly got the short end of the exchange, only Harriet recouped her rooms at the barracks, not Julia. "I am sorry for the people, for this room had been very useful. I have no place for my sewing school," she wrote Anna Barnes. Still, she noted with some satisfaction, "I have not seen Mr. G today, but they say he looks quite crestfallen."[19]

Julia and Harriet now understood how intimately Slough immersed himself in freedmen's affairs, not so much out of concern for their conditions but to assert his authority. And while Gladwin maintained his position, he clearly had less job security or power than he claimed.

Like Harriet and Julia, Gladwin painted life favorably in public. In a letter in the *American Baptist* a few months later, he described "an interesting day for our mission in Alexandria," which included "our usual Sabbath-school exercises" and a Potomac River baptism with "eleven willing converts." He requested readers to send "all contributions of money, clothing, or hospital stores."[20]

Gladwin continued to boss people around, preach, and collect money not just for rent, but also to build a church. To Julia's dismay, his appeal had success. She had her own views about where freedpeople should direct their money, noting, with some superiority, "If these people were not so ignorant, I should be disgusted with them as much as they need clothing & bedding." She was particularly infuriated when a man from the Home Mission Society was "begging the Contrabands for his Mission, instead of the Mission Society helping the contrabands, as it should."[21] In her opinion they should not heed sermons "full of the vengeance of God, of death of hell & damnation," delivered by Gladwin and other ministers, black and white. Harkening back to her days in Rochester, Julia felt uncomfortable with overt displays of religiosity, another time complaining when a minister "wrought up the feelings of the audience to the groaning & shouting pitch."[22] She did not seem to appreciate that one person's method of praying, even though different from hers, was equally valid.

As for the raising of money for churches or other religious purposes, yes, some charlatans preyed on people's gullibility. But for the first time in their lives, many freedmen could *choose* to contribute to whichever church they wished. On Thanksgiving Day 1863, the *Gazette* reported the laying of a cornerstone of a new African church, with "a procession of negroes" marking the occasion. According to Julia, the "procession" reported in the paper without numbers or names had more than two thousand people honoring the new Bethel AME Church. While not very supportive about the affair, especially the taking up of another collection ("sorry to see the colored people imitate the foolishness of the white"), she conceded, "It was a grand time for them and the day was perfect," at least weatherwise.[23]

In 1862 Camp Barker opened in Washington, near current-day Fourteenth and U Streets NW, a supposed improvement from previous refugee housing on Capitol Hill. Its inadequacy proved obvious. Hastily constructed as a way station for army troops, it had bad water and poor ventilation. The proportion of older people, women, and children increased as the more "able-bodied" found housing elsewhere. When Julia's friend Dr. Daniel Breed became camp physician, hospital mortality declined, from one-half to one-fifth of the patients. Yet he was eased out of the position in a personality battle.[24]

The chief of the Quartermaster Department in Washington, Col. Elias Greene, proposed a solution: a new freedmen's camp at Arlington House, the home of Robert E. and Mary Custis Lee.[25] The property had ample room for gardens and farms, as well as a more healthful environment outside the city. The irony of the location could also not be ignored. The Union already occupied the property, where some lucky officers lived in the mansion, but it did not become an official cemetery until 1864.

The first freedpeople moved onto the site in May 1863, with the Quartermaster Department sharing responsibility with the American Missionary Association. A month later Julia, Harriet, and several others visited the "tents & huts . . . almost under the drippings of the lordly rebel mansion. Here is poetic justice, righteous retribution! & didn't I enjoy it!"[26] Many of this first group knew the place well—they had lived there enslaved by the Custis and Lee families and recounted their mistreatment. Eventually Freedman's Village, as its name suggests, featured a laid-out street pattern, small hospital, schools, churches, workshops, and farmland. Those who worked (a strongly encouraged activity) received $10 per month, half of which was deducted for a "contraband fund."[27]

Freedman's Village had a mixed reputation in Alexandria. Many people preferred to stay out of it, especially when they felt forced to move, even refusing rations or other aid to avoid doing so. Julia knew about this apprehension and did her part to keep people in Alexandria. But she called the official opening on December 3, 1863, a glorious day, mostly because "government officials of all grades, wise senators, eminent divines" celebrated the freedmen on General Lee's land. "I wish all the world could have seen & heard it," she wrote, and she commented on the "elegant ladies & splendid-looking men & well dressed contrabands."[28]

Julia then took sick. She attributed her illness, which included "neuralgic pains in my head & rheumatic in my right arm & hand, & shooting pain in all my limbs," along with fever and chills, to overexertion and cold rooms. Harriet and Louisa Jacobs ("Mrs. J is a natural nurse, & I seldom meet a stranger I like so well as Louisa") and Lucy Lawson, the woman who had warned her about the barracks eviction, tended to her.[29] Several days later she recovered to welcome Amy Post, followed by a delegation from the New York Yearly Meeting of Friends, the group that sponsored Harriet's work.

Julia and Harriet made the most of the few hours their friend Amy spent in Alexandria. They took her to the barracks, schools, and other facilities. Gladwin came upon them as they toured rooms in a dark, leaky building near the wharves, and Amy expressed indignation the government charged rent for it. When Julia wrote about the encounter, she commented, "Of course he was angry & called us (Mrs. J & I) meddlers." It was this whirlwind tour that caused Post to shudder about Alexandria in her letter home. In addition to wondering how Julia and Harriet could withstand it, she wrote her husband, "If Mr. Gladwin is removed, as the committee hope[s], it will be better no doubt."[30]

Another attempt to remove Reverend Gladwin by a "committee"? When Harriet had traveled to New York the previous month, she must have shared her frustrations with her sponsors. According to a New York Friends report, "It was believed that a special visit to the hospitals and camps of Refugees at Washington, Alexandria, Norfolk, Yorktown, etc. would be of service." The three-man delegation judged some of the dwellings in Alexandria "favorable," others "extremely wretched," and expressed satisfaction with Harriet and Louisa. But they wrote, "There were many serious complaints against the Superintendent, Gladwin, who appeared to the Committee very unsuitable for the position he occupied." They reiterated the common complaint: "Harsh and tyrannical to the people under his charge, but fawning and obsequious to those in authority, he appeared to the Committee undeserving of confidence."[31]

Although not directly accountable to the New York Friends, Julia prepared for the visit, taking Mary Collier with her to inventory the worst dwellings. "I am going to arrange all the items & give them to Benjamin Tatham [the Friends' representative who also came in late 1862] when he comes," she wrote Barnes. The men spoke with Slough, but Gladwin again emerged with his job intact. Julia saw a few resulting improvements, such as windows and repairs. The visit, she concluded, "scared him a little & the people have reaped the benefit until he increases the rent on account of the improvements."[32]

As winter cold and darkness set in, perhaps combined with the letdown that Gladwin had escaped censure, Julia wrote, "Mrs. J has spoken very unkindly to me today. I can hardly think she knew what she was saying." She did not record the comment, but Louisa and Virginia were sick, probably adding to everyone's stress. Julia decided to spend a few days in Washington. On her return she complained, "I got back to my room about dusk. It looks more uncomfortable here than ever, now that I have been away 2 or 3 days & stopped in comfortable houses," admitting she was becoming "hard & cold & misanthropic."[33]

She rebounded. On New Year's Eve Day, at the launch of 1864, Julia marked the fourth anniversary of Freda's leaving her but did not dwell on the heartache. She spent New Year's Day with the Jacobses and Virginia Lawton, dining on turkey provided by one of the doctors. The Emancipation Proclamation was one year old. "Great deeds have been done for freedom. 50,000 colored soldiers in the field," she wrote. (The number in the Union Army reached 180,000 by war's end, 10 percent of the total.) She learned that Reverend Channing, the Unitarian minister who had first introduced her to Alexandria, received the honor of becoming chaplain of the U.S. House of Representatives. And she recognized the delicious irony when she walked to the slave pen the next day to distribute anti-slavery tracts sent from Rochester by Lucy Colman. "Distributing F. Douglass' speeches & Chas. Sumner's speeches in a Slave Pen in Alex Va.! Three years ago, who have would have thought this possible?"[34] Not only that, but three years earlier, would she have thought possible that she herself would be distributing those tracts?

As 1864 dawned Julia and Harriet took around another visitor, an abolitionist from Boston. They walked from one neighborhood to another (Julia and Harriet becoming quite expert at these "freedpeople tours") with a stop at Christ Church, where George Washington had worshipped. "Sat in W's pew & Mr. P [their visitor] lent me a knife to cut 3 buttons or tufts from the cushions. Those were about all there was left, & I thought I might as well have them as any body," she said.[35] The buttons' whereabouts, like most of her bountiful collection, are unknown.

Julia's sister-in-law Charlotte returned to Washington, as she had a year earlier, this time with her teenage daughter Mary Julia. They showed little interest in Alexandria, refusing to enter the barracks or most anyplace else except a dining room for lunch, much preferring to sightsee in Washington. For many years Julia worried about Mary Julia, described as good looking and spoiled. "She seems to enjoy nothing but dress & frivolous company," Julia said. The girl's favorite sight at the Smithsonian: the stuffed birds, which, she said, "would be so beautiful to wear on a bonnet." Julia was further appalled when Mary Julia proposed going to the theater, unchaperoned, with a man she had just met—and her mother allowed it. The women attended one of the many public receptions at the White House. "The President wore no gloves today & walked around as usual. Mrs. Lincoln was dressed in black velvet, trimmed with white, in very good taste. She looked flushed & a little excited."[36]

In early January 1864 Harriet's dream came true: a school run by blacks, for blacks, that did not charge tuition. Since 1861 permutations had operated—schools run by blacks that charged a small fee, schools that were free but run by whites. Construction had begun after she had gone to New York to raise money and bring back Louisa and Virginia Lawton. When the effort stalled, several white missionaries swooped in to "help" but also to attempt to lead it. At a probably emotionally charged meeting, the school trustees had to decide the direction of the school: that is, as Harriet wrote in a letter to Lydia Maria Child, "whether the white teachers or the colored teachers should be superintendents." To her satisfaction, the trustees decided Louisa and Virginia should run the school. "These people, born and bred in slavery, had always been so accustomed to look upon the white race as their natural superiors and masters, that we had some doubts whether they could easily throw off the habit," Harriet wrote. "The fact of their giving preference to colored teachers, as managers of the establishment, seemed to us to indicate that even their brief possession of freedom had begun to inspire them with respect for their race."[37] Harriet's letter didn't name names, but according to Julia, "Dr. B[igelow] wishes to control the house . . . & have white men manage it. Mr. Gladwin would like to get the control of the house & put ministers & teachers there after his own heart."[38]

With control came the requirement to raise additional money. Harriet organized a fair that collected $150. According to historian Jean Fagan Yellin, the fair was significant because Alexandria's free black community participated. In March 1863 the *Christian Recorder* had reported on the formation of the "First Female Contraband Aid Society" in Alexandria, and possibly this group joined in the fair preparations. Unlike in Washington, where Elizabeth Keckley and other free blacks operated a relief effort, Alexandria's organization did not have as high a profile. Individuals with the means provided assistance, but some black laborers, paid poorly and often late, resented the assumption by whites that their race automatically required them to provide financial support to the freedmen.[39]

The Jacobs Free School opened on January 11, 1864, with about eighty pupils. An opening celebration for parents and children featured singing, apples, cakes, and candies. Enrollments increased. While "the task of regulating them is by no means an easy one," Louisa praised the students' generous spirit, desire to learn, and progress.[40]

The successful opening of the school notwithstanding, the New York Friends still worried about Alexandria operations. They returned and again spoke with General Slough. Well-connected men, they also prompted Congress to launch an investigation into affairs in Alexandria.

With balance-of-power issues among the branches of federal government rife then as now, Congress had created the Joint Committee on the Conduct of War in 1861 to investigate how the Lincoln administration was handling the war effort. In 1864 Congress passed a resolution for the committee to "inquire into the military administration of affairs in Alexandria, and especially its system of military police there established."[41] Coincidentally committee member Zachariah Chandler, a Republican senator from Detroit, had been among the first to occupy the city, when he accompanied the Michigan regiment into Alexandria in May 1861.

Committee members took testimony from Slough, the current and former provost marshals, and other officials. According to the investigation, "Perhaps $10,000 have been expended during General Slough's administration for cleaning streets, repairing King Street (under contract to the lowest bidder), paying the superintendent of contrabands, detectives, and incidental expenses of the offices of military governor and provost marshal." About the slave pen: "The condition of the jail and slave-pen has been much improved under the administration of General Slough." The committee reported on a single incident in which a woman was subjected to the shower-bath, "a prostitute, a negro woman . . . [who] lunged at the guards and the judge with a billet of wood." The report to the full Congress concluded, "Your committee would say that, so far as they have been able to ascertain, the administration of General Slough has been characterized by energy, discretion, and a careful regard for the peace and good order of the community over which he was appointed, and deserves, as it has received, the commendation of the military and civil authorities of our government."[42]

Julia probably expected these conclusions given the piece of the investigation she had witnessed one afternoon at the barracks. "While I was there, 8 or 9 gentlemen appeared in the yard. I only knew Gladwin, Owen [Eliphalet Owen, Gladwin's assistant], & Gen. Slough. *Some* of them *looked* into the rooms. But Mr. G seemed about one foot taller than usual."[43] They made no reported effort to interview Julia or any of the residents.

Some intrigue ensued. Whether from a legitimate source or simply invented, the *New York Times'* Washington correspondent reported the committee "was not charmed with General Slough's government of contrabands." The *Gazette* printed an excerpt of the *Times* article. On February 23, no doubt demanded by the military governor, the *Gazette* retracted the story, directly under its masthead and entitled "False Statement."[44]

Conditions at the slave pen had slightly improved, as the congressional committee stated, but abuses in both the military and civilian justice systems continued. At the slave pen a new officer took command who, Julia noted, "does not swear & kick them about as Barnelo did," referring to the lieutenant in charge at the time of the shower-bath incident the previous year.[45] But a black woman received thirty-nine lashes for falsely accusing a man (presumably white) of murdering a soldier. The woman, Mahala Grady, remained locked in the slave pen for three weeks. Julia and Mary Collier visited her several times. When the authorities released her, "Miss C. . . . found a place for her & we hope she will do well."[46]

The day of the anniversary of her sister Sarah's death, April 19, 1864, Julia wrote of two cases of violence against black women by white men. The women involved were free blacks who already lived in Alexandria. In the first case the Merricks, mother and daughter, interceded when they saw a white man beating some black youngsters. The man, John Young, turned his violence against them, had them arrested, and had them brought before the mayor, who served as magistrate for these types of cases. The daughter, Jane, appeared at the mayor's office; her mother was too hurt to come. The mayor, according to Julia, told the young woman she couldn't speak on her own behalf because "the law does not allow colored persons to say anything in court." He said he would let the matter rest since Young had already hurt them, but "if he had not done so, they would have to be punished by stripes."[47]

The Youngs had a tough time with independent black women. In a second, separate case, a nephew in the family had verbally abused Mary Chase, the woman who started Alexandria's first school for blacks in 1861. According to Julia, Mary "had a broom in her hand & she struck him & told the Mayor that she would do it again if the boy called her such a name, or anyone else insulted her."[48] The mayor warned her he could have punished her with stripes but instead fined her $1.50.

Neither the Grady, Merrick, nor Chase cases was found in the *Gazette* or official documents, so they cannot be verified, although the details sound plausible. The Merricks and Mary Chase (free blacks) and several John Youngs (white) lived in Alexandria in 1859. The experiences stuck with Julia; in addition to her diary, she described them in some detail in a report to the RLASS many months later. They proved her point: "Colored people are still treated like slaves in Alexandria, and the slave laws of the State are still enforced."[49]

As she made her way around town, Julia hoped her RLASS colleagues continued to support her efforts. Although Rochester women, including Amy Post and Julia's friends and family, visited Alexandria, she never mentioned hosting Anna Barnes or other RLASS officers. Some discussion about finances took place via mail, for Julia wrote Anna Barnes in early March 1864, "As to the salary, my friend, it does not bother me at all," although "I thought, with thyself, that they might be willing to increase the salary." The RLASS report published later that year reported $962.63 to the "Alexandria agency," but an unspecified part went for donated items and postage.[50] And the group continued to send clothing to distribute, as well as a shawl for Julia as a personal gift.

Always an avid reader, Julia did not indulge in novels in Alexandria—maybe she had enough plots and intrigue without them. Spending a few days in Washington, she borrowed a best seller of the day, *Hannah Thurston*, by Bayard Taylor. In the novel Hannah is a Quaker teacher in New York, an advocate of women's rights. When one of her friends said Hannah reminded her of Julia, Julia did not exactly disagree: "I only see it yet in our both being A. [anti] Slavery, Improving Woman's Rights, & a resolution to live in single blessedness." But as she read to the end of the book, she realized the heroine, rather than remaining in "single blessedness," married and modified her views to accommodate her husband. Julia noted, "Many of the characters are true to life. I have seen just such reformers, but I am not quite prepared to accept all the conclusions."[51] She no longer pursued any identification with Hannah Thurston.

"My room is well enough now for the purpose for which I use it," Julia wrote Barnes, though she gave up on additional furniture from the quartermaster. Would-be visitors knew to meet her elsewhere, she commented, given that in her room they would have to sit on her bed and see her clothes in plain sight. She hired a woman to do her washing once every four weeks (it is unclear what that meant for the day-to-day state of her clothing), but she did her own ironing and cleaning of common areas. "I have to do my part of cleaning halls, stairs, &c., & with Mr. Gladwin's men tramping through them, & our customers, too, a great deal of cleaning is required," she commented.[52] While she and Harriet would have liked a small sitting room, they resisted Gladwin's promise that if they moved over to the north side of the building, they could have more room. In the meantime Gladwin filled several rooms with his growing staff, both white and black.

At the end of April Julia's brother-in-law Joseph Van Buskirk stopped in Alexandria. After Falmouth, where Julia had visited him in January 1863, his regiment had moved south and west, typically not knowing where it was heading until well on the way. Over the months, he wrote from Newport News, Louisville, Vicksburg, Jackson, and Knoxville. He received a series of promotions, from fourth corporal in 1861 to first lieutenant in 1863 (eventually to captain), and in 1864 he commanded an ambulance corps.

As Joseph and Julia ate dinner together and visited, they probably caught up on family news, and he described the sights in the vicinity—the road from Annapolis to Washington, where men discarded thousands of blankets, waterlogged from an evening storm; forty thousand troops assembled three miles outside Alexandria, including black regiments and two companies of Indians with the First Michigan sharpshooters. His talk whetted her curiosity. The next day, as a perk of his position, he sent an ambulance into Alexandria, and seven women piled in: Julia, Harriet and Louisa Jacobs, Virginia Lawton, the Michigan relief agent Julia Wheelock, Mary Collier, and a newly arrived teacher named Sarah Evans. They drove out to the encampments he had described. "A day to be remembered," Julia wrote, made all the better surrounded by like-minded friends. "As we sat in the ambulance . . . regt. after regt. passed on one side of us in one direction, at the same time that others were passing on the other side in a different direction." The men each left with three days' rations of hard bread and meat and one extra shirt. "The poor fellows! They seem to know that it is better to laugh than cry."[53] As she said good-bye to Joseph, Julia must have wondered if she would be the last family member to see him alive.

A few days later the Twenty-Seventh Colored Infantry Regiment from Ohio marched through Alexandria. Julia quickly got up from the dinner table and followed it to the railroad depot. "There was a great crowd & they moved off with cheers & hurrahs," she wrote, although she worried the newer recruits did not look ready for battle. "This was a glorious first of May . . . to see these armed negroes passing through Alex. Virginia. We hear the remark on all sides, 'Well, bless the lord, I did not think I should live to see such a sight!'"[54]

The men joined Gen. Ulysses S. Grant in the Overland Campaign, the 1864 offensive that brought the war to an end the following year. President Lincoln thought Grant, successful out west, would press to victory where so many others had not. In Grant's first few months of command, in places like the Wilderness and Cold Harbor, however, both sides suffered unfathomable carnage—the Union higher in overall numbers, the Confederacy higher proportionately.

Many Union wounded made their way to hospitals, and cemeteries, in Alexandria. On Thursday, May 26, "wounded soldiers brought in last night." Friday: "6 ambulances passed here & they contained 11 coffins." Sunday: "More severe fighting. . . . All the wounded have been brought from Fredericksburg. On one boat coming up 5 died & on the wharf 5 died." Monday's visit to a hospital: "One mere boy with one arm shattered & the other one off. Entirely helpless." Through the week it went. On June 5, 1864: "Funeral procession was passing, 2 ambulances containing 4 coffins. . . . 18 were buried yesterday. I have asked myself for the first time, 'will it pay?' We must receive some great good to make it pay."[55]

CHAPTER TWELVE

"As Good a Spot as Could Be Obtained"

The 1860 city directory for Alexandria listed six physicians, nine druggists, and no hospitals. Yellow fever and cholera epidemics, malaria, measles, consumption, and a myriad of other, often unknown, afflictions affected Alexandrians, black and white. For those who did not pull through, burial grounds awaited; most such grounds, after an 1804 ordinance banning them from within the city limits, clustered south of town, as did Penny Hill, the paupers' field.

By the end of the Civil War Alexandria had thirty-two military hospitals with 6,500 beds and two new cemeteries, one for soldiers and one for freedpeople.[1]

As in Washington and elsewhere, the military first converted existing buildings for medical use, including schools, churches, and homes. A school on Washington Street became Alexandria's first hospital in July 1861. As the numbers of wounded and ill soldiers multiplied, the army had to set up new facilities fast and grow its medical capacity. Before the war the U.S. Army's medical system consisted of a colonel who oversaw a total of 114 surgeons and assistant surgeons. By the end a brigadier general oversaw the work of 12,155 surgeons, according to historian and physician Bonnie Dorwart. Many men not sick enough for hospitals persevered in camps or on the battlefield with fever, diarrhea, or other maladies for a good proportion of their military service.[2] Julia's brother-in-law Joseph Van Buskirk, for instance, often wrote of various afflictions, fortunately none critical.

Among the freedmen smallpox got most of the attention (the *Alexandria Gazette*, for example, periodically reported on "outbreaks among the contrabands in this place"), but diarrhea, respiratory ailments, and other diseases, many preventable or at least treatable when caught early, killed most of the people, the total number hard to calculate. In Alexandria alone about 2,500 freedpeople died.[3]

Before coming south, Julia Wilbur had probably never set foot in a hospital. Few people did. As happened when her sister and brother took ill and died, family members watched over patients at home, with doctors coming around as needed. People with no other option, especially if they had a contagious disease, entered an institution that was more of a final almshouse than a hospital from which to recover. A few days after arriving in Washington in 1862, Julia described with amazement Harewood Hospital, one of the first purpose-built hospital complexes of the Union Army. "Hundreds of tents arranged in streets. . . . Each ward has a master, some tents look clean & comfortable, but many quite otherwise. 2000 or 3000 here," she wrote.[4] (The hospital also had permanent wards in addition to tents.) Accompanying Mrs. Munson, the woman from Albany who distributed food and clothing to patients, Julia sought out New York boys. She didn't fully realize it at the time, but the visit began her practice of making regular rounds to hospitals in Washington and Alexandria.

The next facility Julia saw was the makeshift one in Alexandria for the contrabands, where an untrained medical volunteer "showed us the hospital. In the first room we entered were people & piles of rags."[5]

By September 1862 three military medical divisions operated in Alexandria, each with a large general hospital and a few smaller branches, usually confiscated buildings. Julia often visited these hospitals, looking especially for men from New York and Michigan. She oriented their family members who traveled south to help loved ones convalesce. At the end of December 1862 she came upon James Mears, a former student, wounded at Fredericksburg. She helped him write a letter to his sister, then welcomed her when she came to Alexandria. All seemed copacetic. But about six weeks later, Julia wrote that she "went to Grace Church Hospital & [was] surprised to learn that James Mears was dead & that his remains had been sent home this morning."[6]

So it went. Conditions ranged from acceptable to awful. "Every convenience & comfort is provided," Julia wrote one day after a visit to Mansion House Hospital, the city's finest hotel before the war. But at King Street Hospital nearby, amid an "awful stench," she provided mush and strawberries to patients in distress. As she observed, ward masters made a huge difference in the quality of life for the patients.[7]

West of town the army established a hospital at Fairfax Seminary (now the Virginia Theological Seminary), where, according to an account by a nurse after the war, patients ate food tailored to their afflictions and observed all major holidays. Michigan relief agent Julia Wheelock described it as "situated in a delightful place . . . commanding a fine view of the country for miles around." Most praised it, especially compared to the alternatives, although a Wisconsin private who was a doctor in civilian life found the medical care lacking.[8]

Anything was better than Camp Convalescent, set up for soldiers not well enough to fight but no longer needing hands-on hospital care. Its well-known nickname: Camp Misery. According to one account, "The convalescents, numbering nine or ten thousand, were lodged in the depth of a very severe winter, in wedge and Sibley tents, without floors, with no fires, or means of making any, amid deep mud or frozen clods. . . . The stragglers and deserters, and the new recruits, were even worse off than the convalescents." In contrast to her praise of Fairfax Seminary, Julia Wheelock wrote that when it rained at Camp Convalescent, men "were obliged to stand up all night to keep their clothing from being totally saturated"; on cold nights those without blankets "were compelled to walk to and fro the entire night to keep warm . . . and, when the sun was up, lie down and sleep beneath the cheering rays, and so prepare themselves for another night's tramp."[9]

One resident wrote home, "My greatest fear is for lice"—a well-founded fear. When seventy-five men were brought into Mansion House Hospital as patients, a nurse wrote, "We scarcely knew what to do with them, not on account of their sickness but they are literally eaten up with vermin." The first time Julia saw the camp, she called it "a forlorn looking place, & a dirty place, too. They must be neglected sadly."[10] She tried to help two Michigan men transfer out but without success.

The U.S. Sanitary Commission stepped in to remedy conditions.

The organization had begun in 1861 to supplement the army's medical services and to coordinate about seven thousand Northern communities' soldier aid societies into a more cohesive unit. The office in Washington dispatched Amy Bradley to Alexandria in December 1862. A Maine teacher who had gone to Costa Rica on a combination teaching/health-restoring stint in the 1850s, she was another of the single women for whom the Civil War gave new opportunities. She volunteered to assist a Maine regiment after Bull Run, then went on to offer her services to the Sanitary Commission. Bradley took on Camp Misery as a special relief agent and managed to clean up the mess. The biggest improvement: the entire camp was moved several miles away in 1863 and started anew.

Julia observed conditions for military patients without any attempt to fix the system beyond providing comfort to individual men. Not so with health care for the freedmen, where she, along with Harriet Jacobs, took on the roles of advocate and critic. They had already successfully averted the plan to place orphans at the smallpox hospital. From the southern side of the duplex at Washington and Wolfe Streets, they looked at Dr. Bigelow's operations in the northern side, not liking what they saw. "A woman died last night & I feel that she died from want of medical care, & nursing," Julia wrote in April 1863 as a typical entry. "It is a week since Dr. Bigelow has been to the hospital to see these people. Graves, a medical cadet [the young physician who later died in October 1863] looks in nearly every day, but does very little for them." According to Julia, Bigelow had a successful side practice treating local Alexandrians and took on preaching responsibilities as a devout man of faith. He also built freedmen housing to rent out.[11]

In November 1863 Julia wrote of plans for the building of a new hospital for black civilians and soldiers (actually non-whites, as Native American patients were treated there as well), near the slave pen on Duke Street. She said Dr. Bigelow opposed the new facility, possibly because if it went under military command, he would have less autonomy. She wrote Anna Barnes, "Dr. Hines [senior surgeon and health officer under General Slough] says it will be done in 2 weeks, but I know better than this!"[12]

No surprise; the hospital construction took closer to three months than two weeks. In the meantime a freedwoman named Patsey languished in the old one with consumption. Patsey shared a room with a nurse and a woman "having the worst of all diseases," smallpox. Julia worried that Patsey "dies by inches" and finally arranged for her separation from her infected roommate. "Patsey is comparatively comfortable & I feel greatly relieved & so do the nurses. . . . I thanked Dr. Bigelow but he should have done it first," she wrote.[13] It was too little, too late. Patsey died a few days later. Her little son would go to the Colored Orphans Home in Washington. Before he left, however, he reported Patsey's ghost had visited him.

Odd spirits surrounded everyone. Around the same time, Julia dreamt that Louisa Jacobs and Virginia Lawton had drowned; the next morning, all the more disturbing given her dream, she heard rumored (and false) tales about the doctors kidnapping them and other blacks for dissection. When Reverend Gladwin again coaxed Julia and Harriet to move into the almost vacant north side of the duplex, pointing out they would have more room, they agreed with each other that the spirits and bad memories of the place made living there impossible. "I should not care about going through those rooms alone to night & yet I claim to be as free from superstition as any body," she admitted.[14]

The new hospital was named L'Ouverture, for Toussaint L'Ouverture, who had led the struggle for independence for Haiti. With other hospitals in Alexandria mostly named for their location or for generals, it sounded daring to name a hospital for a Haitian revolutionary. Or maybe not. Haiti was one of the places to which Lincoln sanctioned moving former slaves, a failed policy called colonization. A few months later those who were sent returned to America in far worse shape than they had left. (And L'Ouverture, although his cause succeeded, was tricked by Napoleon, resulting in his death during imprisonment in 1803.)

"I went into the new Hospital. It is being made very nice, & as it should be," Julia wrote during the construction phase. "Two portable furnaces in each ward, & more rooms have been made. I am afraid the colored folks will not have it long if they go into it; it will be 'good enough for white folks,' & they will be put into it eventually."[15] But the hospital remained a non-white facility. As the number of USCT patients grew, the hospital became more military than civilian, but the first recorded patient was a seventy-year-old freedman admitted with bronchitis on February 2, 1864.

In keeping with the guidelines established by the quartermaster general for new hospitals, L'Ouverture occupied the equivalent of several city blocks. Long, well-ventilated patient wards, about sixty beds per ward, had the ability to quarantine as needed. The complex included a separate cookhouse, laundry room, and other facilities, including a dead house to keep bodies before their interment or shipment home. It could accommodate about seven hundred patients. A private residence became the office; it still stands, but the army dismantled the rest and sold the building materials after the war.

Acquiring supplies and niceties for patients, both in the old hospital and new, became a top priority. On one stop to the Sanitary Commission office in Washington, Julia secured a promise for supplies if she could return with an ambulance to pick them up. With Harriet and another woman, Julia returned a few days later and was pleased with the bounty: "15 lbs. sugar, 5 lbs. tea, 15 lbs. dried fruit, 2 doz. old sheets, 3 doz. old shirts, 1 doz. wrappers, 1 doz. slippers, 2 doz. hdkfs—had no crackers, nor fish, nor toast—but I am very glad to get so much." On another occasion, "Several colored ladies came in with lots of good things, a feast for them all." ("Ladies" probably referred to members of the free black community rather than freedwomen.) Julia installed curtains and blinds, funded by the Freedmen's Relief Association of Philadelphia, and pushed for paint and whitewashing. She winced when she learned eleven women from Freedman's Village had come to work at the hospital: "They do but little work, & have a bad influence on the men & boys."[16]

General Slough did not appoint Bigelow to head the hospital. Instead Edwin Bentley, a forty-year-old surgeon, took the helm of L'Ouverture. Bentley had first enlisted as a surgeon with a Connecticut artillery regiment. He had been in Alexandria since 1862 at different hospitals, but his and Julia's paths had not crossed. He was slender, with a long face and piercing eyes, the kind of decisive, nononsense man that Slough liked. Julia went back and forth in her opinion about him. Similar to Slough, Dr. Bentley liked to make sure people respected his position.

In one of their first meetings, Julia urged Bentley to appoint a matron who could keep a close eye on the non-medical aspects of the operation. He agreed but insisted, "First, she must be *black* & then she must be *pious*," as she recounted. Julia, it turns out, was thinking of her sister Frances for the job, who would not have met either criterion. Whether because of that disappointment or her own prejudice, Julia portrayed her reaction in an unflattering light: "I have not seen a colored woman here that approaches at all to what my idea of a matron should be." Given her relationship with Harriet and Louisa Jacobs, Virginia Lawton, and other black women she admired, this was an odd comment. Dr. Bentley did not take kindly to her protestation. "He was barely civil & nothing more. No cordiality, no friendliness of manner. What right had I to propose anything to *him*? How could I presume to make a suggestion to a Div. Surgeon, with the rank of Major?"[17]

Later that day Julia acknowledged, "I have been almost too sick & too tired to do anything. I have hurt Mrs. Jacobs' feelings"— possibly by relating her conversation with Dr. Bentley. In any event, when Harriet Jacobs returned from a short trip to Philadelphia, she brought with her an African American matron for L'Ouverture named Margaretta Hazzard. "I confess to a little disappointment, for I supposed Mrs. J knew that I expected Frances to have a place there," Julia wrote. "But if the women she has selected are only competent I will be satisfied."[18] For the rest of the war Julia and Harriet included L'Ouverture—along with the barracks, slave pen, Clothing Room, and other places around town—as one of "their" places to monitor.

Julia might not have known hospitals back home, but she knew cemeteries. According to historian Keith Eggener, Americans in the early 1800s built picturesque rural cemeteries with ornate markers rather than the smaller church-adjacent graveyards of times past. The Avon cemetery in New York, where Julia's family members lay, fit the description. She often visited, walking the meandering paths, tending to the family graves and generally gaining comfort and consolation.

A few weeks after arriving in Alexandria, Julia went to the cemetery area south of town. Then, as today, "it comprises several large squares. Each enclosed with streets between them." As she wandered around, she witnessed a white resident's funeral ("very elegant hacks & drivers with long black hat bands"), then a soldier's funeral. "A large space has been enclosed for a Soldiers burying ground, about 100 graves in a row. . . . Each with a head board with the name & no. of the Regt. except now & then one marked 'Unknown.' . . . 8 or 9 other graves were dug & ready."[19]

Undertakers did a brisk business preparing bodies for shipment north ("$30 to embalm, to enclose a body in box lined with zinc $18," Julia wrote after a visit to an embalming room). Many families could not afford this option, if they even learned of their loved ones' deaths. The military took over a four-acre site to build a burial ground for the soldiers who would remain "on Virginia soil" rather than return north. On September 12, 1863, the *Gazette* reported 1,000 had been buried there since January; on June 27, 1864, it reported that the cemetery had expanded to an adjoining piece of land. About 3,500 were buried there during and right after the war, and others were transported to Arlington.[20]

Nearby Penny Hill accommodated the remains of the poor, including deceased freedpeople. Without an image, we do not know exactly what it looked like, but Julia's descriptions made it sound far from idyllic. On one visit she saw that "the contrabands are literally packed away." On a later visit with Louisa Jacobs, she "talked with a grave digger, [who] says he has been told to put 3 or 4 into one grave. I intend to complain of the state of things here. It is disgraceful to have such a state of things exist." In contrast, "Then we went to the Soldiers' Burying Ground. A large number of workmen are employed here all the while to improve it & make it beautiful."[21]

But the freedmen would have a new resting place too. Slough appropriated property from attorney Francis L. Smith, a close associate of Robert E. Lee, on Washington Street. On March 4, 1864, the *Gazette* reported, "A grave yard for the burial of 'contrabands' who may die in this place has been laid off near the Catholic cemetery." Gladwin later told Slough burials began on March 7—starting with three boys under age three.[22]

In April 1864 Julia took around a visiting New York cousin to see the sights, including "the Contraband B[urying] Ground which is the most repulsive & heathenish looking place I ever saw." But change was coming: "No more are buried here now." The next day she went to the new site, with "65 graves there already. It is as good a spot as could be obtained but very wet now. Mr. G is spending all his energies on this now. He no doubt intends this as a monument to commemorate his reign, the reign of Albertus I."[23]

Ironically "Albertus I" left a legacy with the cemetery. He began a written record of deaths and other milestones known as the Gladwin Record.[24] Based on this record, 1,711 people (more than half of them children) were buried in the cemetery between 1864 and 1869. The Gladwin Record provides names, dates, and other identifying features at a time when many poor people, especially blacks, died anonymously. Although the graves were close together, each person had his or her own site (except for a few family members who died at the same time), unlike in the former cemetery, marked with army-supplied wooden headboards and army-supplied coffins.

Inevitably with the introduction of USCT into the Union Army, African American soldiers would be among the dead. Julia observed the burial of the first black soldier on May 5, 1864—"buried in the usual way in the new Burying Ground for Freedmen." In other words, Private John Cooley, from the Twenty-Seventh Colored Infantry Regiment from Ohio, lay among the civilian freedmen rather than his military comrades. "I think a distinct part of the Ground should be appropriated to the soldiers & the graves distinguished from others," Julia said, at the time not even thinking of inclusion in the Soldiers' Cemetery itself. "They should be honored in some way. But we can't make Mr. G see it."[25]

Julia presaged a feeling shared by the soldiers themselves and on which they acted at the end of 1864, as we will see. Perhaps Mr. G should have made this concession while he still could. It turned out that his longest-lasting accomplishment—the creation of the Freedmen's and Contraband's Cemetery and of the record of those buried there—proved his undoing.

CHAPTER THIRTEEN

"Things as Usual, Quite Unsettled"

As she had the previous year, Julia Wilbur went home to New York in the summer of 1864 to escape the worst of Alexandria's heat and revive her energy. She met other acquaintances at the depot in Washington, including the wife of General Slough, "all going in pursuit of health like myself to various places of former residence." But although she left "in pursuit of health," she instead took sick on the train. She managed to make her way back home to Rush, which she found "ruinous and desolate enough," and climbed upstairs to her old room. Four weeks later she felt well enough to emerge. Her diary during this time contains short entries, many barely legible with loose handwriting, mostly recording visits from the doctor, symptoms of chills and fever, and complaints about sleepless nights and suffocating heat. When she recovered (no definitive diagnosis but a bill from the doctor for $13.25), she had to confront three family matters she had pushed aside while in Alexandria and while she convalesced: a move, a marriage, and a (probable) divorce.[1]

First and most immediately, the move. In March 1864 Julia's father Stephen sold the farm he had tended for more than thirty years to a man who owned much of the property nearby.[2] Julia received a letter from an aunt with the news. Her reaction: "I have resolutely kept this from my mind today." She took the avoidance path again two weeks later: "To day at my home there has been an auction, I suppose. I have been too busy to think much about it." Instead she went to listen to the noted British abolitionist George Thompson speak at the U.S. Capitol, an event attended by President Lincoln and other luminaries.[3]

Stephen Wilbur bought a house in the neighboring village of East Avon. Perhaps it had sunk in that he could not count on Henry and

Ann, Julia's brother and sister-in-law who had caused so much trouble for Julia, to shoulder their share of the farming and other responsibilities. Although Julia complained the new house was "old & poor & out of repair," an 1872 map shows the outline of a good-sized home with one of the area's largest lots, suitable for a garden if not farming, and conveniently located on a main east-west road. The Baptist and Presbyterian churches, a shoemaker and other shops, and a tavern all lay a short walk from the house, as did some old family friends.[4] As for vexatious Henry and Ann, they possibly managed to stay in one of the houses on the old property for a time or had already left. Julia did not mention their participating in the move. They do not show up in the 1865 New York census; the federal census of 1870 lists them in Kalamazoo, Michigan.

On August 30 Julia organized the household's crockery, the first of multiple wagonloads needed to move three decades' worth of belongings. Over the next few days the family members went back and forth, about five miles or so, from Rush to the new house, with furniture, clothing, and other wares. Soon enough Julia "had fire in my stove & my room is quite pleasant" in the new house.[5] She brought a bookcase upstairs to display choice knickknacks in her room, no doubt including relics collected down south. But she realized the new house, unlike the old, would never offer her emotional sustenance. If anything, this place belonged to her stepmother.

Second, a marriage. Julia's niece Mary Julia wed, out of the blue. Mary Julia, nicknamed Sis, had a special place in her aunt's heart, with their name in common and Julia's affection for her brother Theodore and sister-in-law Charlotte. "Uncommonly beautiful & remarkably lovely withal," Julia had described Mary Julia back in 1849, when the girl was two years old. But for almost as long Julia had worried about the "danger of her being flattered & petted too much"; indeed a few years later, "Those pretty winning ways she once had are all gone."[6] And much as Julia loved Charlotte, she thought the mother indulged the daughter. Charlotte's successful business catering to the hair and wig needs of Rochester society also glorified what to Julia was the more frivolous side of life, but Mary Julia lapped it up.

On September 16, 1864, Mary Julia Wilbur, age seventeen, wed William Henry Milstead (known as Harry), age twenty-one, of Washington. The small ceremony took place at the St. Nicholas Hotel in New York City, one of the city's most luxurious establishments. Perhaps Mary Julia and Harry had met the previous January, when Charlotte and Mary Julia had visited Washington and the girl had mostly concerned herself with socializing and fashion. (Was he the stranger with whom she went to the theater unchaperoned?) "Well, I have nothing in particular to say," Julia wrote when she heard about the ceremony five days later, those few words saying quite a bit.[7] The newlyweds moved to Georgetown to live. Harry worked in the Treasury Department, having received a medical discharge for malaria in 1863, so Julia saw them fairly regularly. The couple had a son in 1865. But Julia's worries proved correct. By 1870 they lived apart, and grandmother Charlotte cared for their son back in Rochester. Both Mary Julia and Harry remarried.

Third, the divorce of Julia's sister Frances—couched with the word "probable" because no records have turned up to verify a legal proceeding. Nor does the word "divorce" appear in Julia's diaries, even as she worried about her sister's situation. Frances, four years younger than Julia, had married Abner Hartwell, a neighbor, in 1839, when both were twenty years old. When they lived on the Hartwell farm, Frances easily went back and forth between the two houses and was especially supportive when niece Freda left to reenter the Bigelow household at the end of 1859.

Hints of unhappiness, or perhaps more, lurked. Indeed mere unhappiness would not have been cause for divorce. New York State had one of the most rigid divorce laws in the nation, with adultery the only acceptable grounds until the 1960s (although people found ways around it, including divorcing in other, more lenient states). Frances had no children but planned to raise the infant that Sarah Bigelow left when she died in childbirth in 1859; the little girl died suddenly the following year. In late December 1860 "Abner has bought a farm in Hartland," Julia announced, with Frances sounding as sad as Julia about the prospect. In 1863 Julia noted, "Letter from Frances. She is full of trouble. How I pity her. I wish she could come here & work with me. It would be a relief to her, occupy her mind, & help her to forget herself." A few months later, "F. is in R[ochester]—No good news. Did I allow myself, I might be sick over what she writes about." Julia tried to find work for Frances in Alexandria or Washington, including the unsuccessful attempt to propose her as the L'Ouverture hospital matron. Now in New York, Julia had to deal with her sister's plight straight on since no one else, certainly not her father, did. A plan evolved that Frances would accompany Julia back south.[8]

So did Frances and Abner divorce, and if so, when? The 1860 federal census lists the couple as living with his parents. New York State conducted its own census every ten years from 1825 to 1875; in September 1865 both Julia and Frances were listed as living in East Avon with their father and stepmother. In 1880, according to the federal census, Frances lived in Washington and identified herself as divorced (although she identified herself as widowed by 1900). As another piece of the puzzle, on September 29, 1866, Abner married a Civil War widow and took responsibility for her young twin sons. Frances maintained friendly relations with Abner's sister, so the Hartwells did not ostracize her, nor did she avoid them. No matter the exact details, the bottom line was that Frances had ceased living with Abner around 1863 or 1864, and her separate life increasingly involved Julia.

"Things as usual, quite unsettled," she commented about the state of affairs in New York.[9] With convalescing, moving, and dealing with family and friends, Julia spent three months at home, much longer than she had expected. Unlike the year before, she left her possessions in Alexandria, presumably safely locked up, intending to return.

More than Julia's health and spirits sagged in the summer of 1864. Morale ebbed throughout the North. Song lyrics lamented loss and longed for an end to the suffering; the mournful "When This Cruel War Is Over" was the most popular sheet music of the year, with sales of more than five hundred thousand copies. In Rochester the Ladies' Hospital Relief Association, while still highlighting its prodigious activity to support Union soldiers, had to acknowledge, "Our own

Society is viewing now, with no little concern, a waning exchequer." Rochester's two small hospitals learned they would receive men from the front; the afternoon train of June 7, 1864, delivered 375 wounded soldiers from Virginia.[10]

The presidential election of 1864 loomed in the fall. With war weariness prevalent and former general George McClellan the Democratic opponent, Lincoln believed he could lose reelection. But General Sherman's capture of Atlanta in early September, along with other Union advances, bolstered the president's chances, and he won by a large margin.

As it had done in 1860, Julia's family mirrored the country. Joseph, her sister Mary's husband, supported Lincoln, like the overwhelming majority of Union soldiers. After three and a half years in the army, he mustered out in October, narrowly escaping an eleventh-hour calamity: "He was in the fight at Poplar Grove church [near Petersburg, Virginia] the 30th Sept. Had horse shot under him." After his discharge, Joseph traveled to Rochester, where Mary and their children joined him from Michigan. On October 20 he attended a mass meeting to support Lincoln. Brother-in-law Alfred, true to form, supported McClellan, who won narrowly in the city of Rochester. Julia's father, a Lincoln supporter, could not vote because he did not meet the four-month residency requirement when he moved to Avon.[11]

On October 23 Julia wrote, "I am impatient to get back to Alex. I feel that I ought to be there." Yet she tarried almost three more weeks, spending some of that time in Rochester with Amy Post, Anna Barnes, and others. One evening she visited William Hallowell, the son-in-law of the Posts with whom Julia briefly boarded in the 1850s. The big draw of the evening: Harriet Tubman. "H.T. is employed by the Army as a scout. Has been in S.C. [South Carolina] & Florida 3 yrs. & done good service," Julia noted. Tubman's legacy today centers on her deftness in helping slaves escape before the war, but she also dared the odds during it. In addition to serving as a nurse and all-round relief worker, she developed a spy network and reported directly to top-ranking officers in the region. (Her application for a postwar pension states she was "under direction of Edwin Stanton Secretary of War and of several generals.")[12] In 1864 Tubman was in

New York and New England to see her family and recuperate from her own illnesses. The RLASS had provided Tubman with some money for her Underground Railroad efforts in the 1850s, but it is not clear if Julia met Tubman before 1864 or just knew of her by reputation.

Freda, and preoccupations about her, remained present but in the background, a scab best not to pick. A few days before returning to Alexandria, Julia learned the girl was well but pale, quiet, and delicate looking. "Poor dear child!" she wrote. "It is a year since I have heard from her directly & I must go back to Alex. & not see her. But I am thankful to have heard from her."[13] She actually didn't hear *from* Freda, at least not directly, only second-hand through an acquaintance. Reunion lay in the future.

As she did each time she left, Julia worried about her father, "poor blind man that he is & with his children all at a distance from him," yet she also blamed him for marrying a woman none of them liked (or vice versa).[14] She gathered her trunks and boxes—and sister Frances— and arranged for a ride to the Avon depot.

Many things changed when she returned south.

CHAPTER FOURTEEN

"Flung My Flag to the Breeze"

A letter to Julia Wilbur in August 1864 contained the news that 250 soldiers had been brought to L'Ouverture Hospital. Other people echoed the news of the number of wounded USCT brought en masse to L'Ouverture from Petersburg. A young Christian Commission volunteer also referred to "two hundred & fifty" when he recorded the following in his diary: "I have today witnessed some of the most harrowing scenes which a terrible war can possibly furnish," describing patients' horrific injuries and their stoic valor. The patients came from the Battle of the Crater near Petersburg, where an ill-planned Union mine explosion created a huge chasm, a literal crater, that left thousands of soldiers open and vulnerable to Confederate attack.[1]

Although the first patients of the hospital complex on Duke Street were African American civilians, the balance tilted to the military as members of the USCT saw more combat. Within months, around Christmastime, the patients organized a successful protest to demand rights befitting their status as men taking up arms for their country. When they did, they accomplished something neither Julia, Harriet Jacobs, the freedmen's doctors, nor anyone else could: the end of Rev. Albert Gladwin as Alexandria's superintendent of contrabands. He left Alexandria in early 1865.

Very soon after she celebrated Gladwin's ouster, Julia left Alexandria too.

On August 1, 1864, L'Ouverture celebrated Emancipation Day, the end of legalized slavery in the British West Indies in 1834. For decades black communities in Northern U.S. cities, including Rochester, marked the occasion in hopes that slavery's end would someday be celebrated in the United States. The emancipation of blacks in the District of

Columbia in April 1862 and the president's Emancipation Proclamation on January 1, 1863, had since created domestic occasions, but
an August 1 event could certainly boost morale for the patients. Harriet and Louisa Jacobs organized a small ladies' committee, collected
money for a special meal, and arranged for a donated flag to present
to the hospital leaders. At the ceremony Harriet stood before the
assembled patients, staff, and other guests. A female speaker, especially an African American, was a rare sight.

As she presented the flag, Harriet addressed the soldiers: "Three
years ago this flag had no significance for you, we could not cherish
it as our emblem of freedom. . . . Soldiers, you have made it the symbol of freedom for the slave." The American flag belonged to blacks,
she stressed, as much as whites. Gladwin, never one to shy away from
public attention, served as a sort of master of ceremonies, but Harriet received the loudest vote of thanks.[2]

Back on her New York sickbed, Julia had felt her worst in early
August, and she did not write about the event. Hopefully Harriet
or another correspondent, perhaps L'Ouverture director Dr. Bentley
(she characterized his letter to her as "remarkably considerate and
kind"),[3] told her about it, as well another juicy bit of news. Gladwin
had requested a medical leave from Military Governor Slough on
August 5, stating he had been "suffering in my health for my continued cares and constant labor, for nearly a year without intermis-
sion." Leave granted, he recuperated in New York City. He and his
doctors wrote to Slough at least twice, in early and late September,
to extend his leave of absence to recover from pulmonary and liver
diseases, "the results of exposure and fatigue incident to his duties
in and around Alexandria."[4]

Gladwin arrived back in Alexandria, feisty as ever, a few weeks
before Julia did in early November. In fact, he had enough time again
to attempt to kick her out of the house on the corner of Washington and Wolfe Streets. Unbeknownst to her, a standoff had ensued
shortly before she returned. When she did, with her sister Frances in
tow, she "found the ladies in considerable excitement. I left the key
to my room with Miss Evans [teacher Sarah Evans], & Mr. Gladwin had demanded it of her & she was obliged to give it up." How-

ever, Evans, with Harriet Jacobs to back her up, refused Gladwin's order to move Julia's things out of her room, stalling the eviction. Julia appealed to Provost Marshal Wells and a captain who was acting on behalf of a traveling General Slough. Although they backed her with words, with Wells telling Gladwin "he had given him [Gladwin] no order to take the room," nothing changed. Julia trudged to four places in town to seek new lodgings, then finally had to ask Gladwin for a room on the north side of the duplex with the former hospital, a request she had earlier avoided. "He keeps saying he has control of both houses, but still will not say I can have a room. I really do not know what to do," Julia wrote. It is not clear what Frances did in all this, but she may have wondered what she had gotten herself into by leaving New York.[5]

Lo and behold, when Slough returned to town, "from that moment Mr. G was another man." Julia recorded his smarmy comments: "Why, yes, of course, you can have the room. Can I do anything for you?" Two corporals helped move her things from the north side of the house back to the south. A few days later she reported that he "is trying to make amends for his meanness by putting my room in repair. Has had plastering done, a lock put on the door, &c." Around the same time, Sarah Evans decided to move to Washington, possibly with this incident as the tipping point. "She will not stay here & be under Mr. G's control," Julia noted.[6] Gladwin didn't like her plan to leave. His biggest concern, according to Julia, was how he would look to Evans's circle of influential friends in Philadelphia.

Frances, after some looking, found a position teaching in a freedmen's school and a place to live in Washington, although Julia judged the room on Twelfth Street "a miserable place."[7] Frances and Sarah, combined with this newest tussle with Gladwin, may have started Julia thinking about moving across the river. For now, however, she settled into her routine in Alexandria to visit hospitals, welcome freedmen, and keep her eyes and ears open as she walked around town. The schools, including the Jacobs School, continued to flourish. Many freedmen were finding work and their own places to live, joining churches, and building new lives. Frederick Douglass visited Alexandria November 30 and December 1. He gave two well-attended lectures at Liberty Hall. "I am told there were even some secesh present," Julia commented, as they also were curious to see the country's most famous black man. She and Harriet accompanied him and a small delegation to the slave pen; Soldiers' Rest, a large camp built on the outskirts of Alexandria as a way station for troops in transit; and other spots. While their interracial group did not sit well with everyone they visited, "the white men there [at Soldiers' Rest] were very civil & deferential & some seemed amazed." They went on to L'Ouverture, where "the men who were able assembled in the dining room & Douglass spoke to them a few minutes, & they sang John Brown with a will."[8] Douglass was a guest at a dinner at the Magnolia House, "an honored guest at the social board," as Harriet Jacobs wrote, and she saw his status as a sign of the "rapid march of events."[9]

But hardship persisted. Winter came early and hard. Some days ice on the Potomac made boat traffic impossible. Clothes froze on the line instead of drying. Walking proved a windy challenge. On a particularly cold day in mid-December, a group of refugees came up by boat from Petersburg, having spent the night on board with no food or fuel. Gladwin pushed increasing numbers of vulnerable people like them out of Alexandria before they could understand what was happening, in this case sending them to Mason's Island in the Potomac River (part of an estate belonging to the prominent Virginia family, now Theodore Roosevelt Island National Memorial). Julia suggested a minor improvement to Gladwin that went nowhere: "There should be a receiving room in the barracks for such persons, where they could be warmed & fed & stay long enough to find their friends, before they are sent away."[10]

Christmas was quiet. Julia unpacked a clothing barrel received from up north and took tea with Harriet Jacobs. Calm broke the next day.

Although Julia occasionally remarked on some transgression at L'Ouverture—an ineffective matron, a cruel wardmaster, or the women from Freedman's Village who seemed (to her) an unwanted distraction—the hospital ran relatively well. There is no indication the doctors assigned to it had lesser skills than those assigned to white patients, and Dr. Bentley had a good reputation.

Chauncey Leonard, a Baptist minister from Washington commissioned as chaplain at the end of July 1864, was assigned to L'Ouverture, one of only fourteen black chaplains throughout the Union Army. The previous year, sponsored by the American Colonization Society, Leonard had traveled to Sierra Leone and Liberia to investigate settlement there by American blacks, a "solution" suggested by many (mostly whites, including President Lincoln) until reality proved its unsuitability.[11] He returned to America ill. Recovered, he arrived at L'Ouverture in time for the Emancipation Day celebration and offered a benediction. In addition to officiating at funerals and other religious duties, he taught reading and arithmetic, established a literary society, and lectured on topics that included his travels to Africa. He distributed voluminous amounts of religious tracts—eleven thousand religious papers from August through January, by his own reckoning—but recognized, a few months later, that the patients preferred the more secular books in the small library he set up.[12]

Through the chaplain's activities and many other efforts, L'Ouverture was developing into its own community, one that could take action.

Back in May Julia had commented on the lack of appropriate recognition for the burial of the first soldier at the contraband cemetery. At the end of December, when Gladwin sent two deceased soldiers to the "colored burying ground," she recorded the reaction at L'Ouverture: "Soldiers are indignant. I think Mr. G is in personal danger," she wrote on December 26. Perhaps resentment built over the summer and fall (Gladwin had had approximately 122 soldiers buried at Freedmen's Cemetery, known as the Colored Burying Ground, since May), or perhaps one or more new patients had come in and raised the issue to the fore. Why were USCT buried with civilians and not soldiers? The men took steps to change this practice. The next day, December 27, Julia noted, "This p.m. two colored soldiers were to be buried & Mr. G said if they went to the Military Burying Ground, he would have the escort arrested. The bodies went to the Colored Cemetery without an escort & Mr. G thinks he has triumphed."[13]

He did not. That same day Dr. Bentley received a communication from the patients. It contained more than a letter—it was a petition, more than six feet in length, and it read in part as follows:

> We the undersigned Convalescents of Louverture Hospital & its Branches and soldiers of the U.S. Army, learning that some dissatisfaction exists in relation to the burial of colored soldiers, and feeling deeply interested in a matter of so great importance to us, who are a part and parcel with the white soldiers in this great struggle against rebellion, do hereby express our views, and ask for a consideration of the same. . . .
>
> We are not contrabands, but solders of the U.S. Army. . . .
>
> As American citizens, we have a right to fight for the protection of her flag, that right is granted, and we are now sharing equally the dangers and hardships in this mighty contest and should shair [*sic*] the same privileges and rights of burial in every way with our fellow soldiers, who only differ from us in color.[14]

We do not know who composed the letter, which went on for several more paragraphs and included biblical verse from the Book of Ruth. Was it Chaplain Leonard or Rev. Leland Warring, a civilian minister, or perhaps a particularly eloquent patient? At the bottom of the text 446 men, organized by hospital ward, allowed their names to be included as co-signatories, a huge task that a group must have divvied up to accomplish so quickly.

Dr. Bentley wrote Quartermaster J. G. C. Lee about this development since the Quartermaster Department oversaw the military cemetery. The next day Lee wrote to Quartermaster General Montgomery Meigs in Washington for guidance, enclosing the petition, or the "memorial," as he called it. "I have recently learned that Mr. Gladwin, Superintendent of the Freedmen at this place, has caused interment of colored soldiers to be made at the contraband burying-ground," he wrote (recently learned by him but going on for more than six months). "This ground is not owned by the U.S., is not fenced, as I learn, nor is it taken care of, as the regular [military] cemetery is." Lee informed Meigs that he had earlier directed "the interment of colored men, as well as white, be made in the military cemetery, keeping them in a separate portion," but Gladwin still diverted the USCT dead to the civilian cemetery. (Gladwin may have received extra money per burial or simply wanted to assert his authority.) Lee closed by telling Meigs the obvious: "The feeling on the part of the colored soldiers is unanimous to be placed in the military cemetery and it seems just and right that they should be."[15]

Meanwhile, the mood roiled on the ground. Julia wrote, "The soldiers are furious & there is danger of a fight." When Harriet came across Gladwin picking up a headboard for another burial at Freedmen's, Julia wrote, "Mrs. J expressed her feelings in some very uncomplimentary remarks about white men who come here from the North and pretend to labor among the colored people. Mr. Gladwin & Mr. Owen [his white assistant] considered the remarks personal & were pale with rage." Her comments elicited a quick response from above: "About an hour afterwards Mrs. J received an order to appear at Gen. Slough's headquarters at 9 tomorrow morning. She feels quite disturbed, for she does not know what is coming, but no harm will come to her I am sure, good will come of it."[16]

True to Julia's prediction, Harriet reported encouraging news when she met with Slough on December 28. Slough told her, "Mr. G had misrepresented the matter to him, but now the Quartermaster's orders will be carried out & after this the colored soldiers would be buried in the Mil. ground & those buried in the Colored cemetery would be removed & furthermore he would discharge Mr. Gladwin today." Julia tempered her optimism about the cemetery policy with pessimism about Gladwin's fate: "Mrs. J is in high glee, but I do not regard the thing [Gladwin's discharge] as accomplished yet." Indeed on New Year's Eve Day, December 31, the day Julia usually spent contemplating the year gone by and ruing the anniversary of Freda's departure from her life, she noted, "Mr. Gladwin is yet in power & I fear he will not be removed after all."[17]

Because of the soldiers' action, 229 USCT soldiers were laid to rest at Soldiers' Cemetery (of about 3,500 gravesites in total), including a few of the very men who had signed the petition. This number includes 122 buried earlier in the civilian cemetery and re-interred to join their military brethren. Although in a segregated portion of what is now Alexandria National Cemetery, they have markers (first wooden but replaced with stone after the war, as were all markers), and their names and regiments are recorded in the cemetery register. If they had remained at Freedmen's Cemetery, they would have gone into posterity in unmarked graves.

January 1865 began another year of war. According to historian James Barber, the local white population greeted it in "quiet passivity."[18] The city had entirely altered from its prewar composition. The 1860 census showed Alexandria with about ten thousand whites and three thousand blacks. Rough estimates were that about two-thirds of the whites had left and about seven thousand black refugees had moved into the city. Add the fluctuating population of military and other Northerners who came into Alexandria, which peaked in the tens of thousands, to the mix. The white local population, in the majority in 1860, was decidedly outnumbered.

Beyond the demographic change, the secesh saw properties confiscated or sold at bargain rates to Northerners and Union-leaning locals for lack of tax payments (they couldn't pay if they left). In late 1864 Slough arrested Edgar Snowden (*Alexandria Gazette* publisher) and other prominent citizens in a scheme to protect Union trains and tracks against raids by Confederate colonel John Singleton Mosby and his men. As General Slough wrote to the War Department, "A small party of guerrillas have been operating in the vicinity of Burke's. . . . This can only be stopped in one way—that is, by placing on the trains prominent secessionists and captured guerrillas. I ask permission to arrest twenty of those in Alexandria, to be used in this manner; also the privilege of using the captured guerrillas here in the same way. Please answer."[19] Slough received permission and so plucked a few Alexandrians at a time to ride out and back on the trains, serving as a type of human shield for several months.

When Snowden resumed publication on January 3, 1865, he wrote he "appeals to the public for encouragement. . . . The same attention will be paid to truth and honorable journalism which characterized the 'Gazette' in its best days."[20] Fortunately for posterity the

Gazette published throughout most of the war, but Confederate-leaning Snowden walked a delicate balance in operating a newspaper under the watchful Union eye.

Julia and Frances went to the annual New Year's reception at the White House. They watched VIPS glide in before public entry at 1 p.m.: Cabinet members, military officers, and foreign dignitaries. Then all hell broke loose. "We were in the crowd & were pushed up the steps of the portico as far as the door," Julia described. "The breath was almost crushed out of us. . . . I shook hands with the President but hardly saw him. I merely felt his presence. . . . We paused a few moments in the East Room & then were pushed out of a window over a platform built for the purpose."[21] So much for a dignified White House reception.

Julia spent a few more days in Washington around New Year's. Among her stops she looked at a school and residence at 207 I Street set up by an acquaintance, James Miller McKim, for the Pennsylvania Freedmen's Relief Association. Frances instigated the idea that the sisters move into it together. While Julia commented on the failings of the establishment, she wrote, "House neither cleaned nor finished. . . . Nothing pleasant in the vicinity . . . [but] F. will be disappointed if I do not go."[22]

With these plans percolating, Julia continued her work in Alexandria. When she asked Gladwin for rations for a few families, Gladwin immediately agreed. "Oh yes, he will do what he can & whenever I know of suffering cases please report them to him," she reported.[23] He knew he walked on tenterhooks but probably did not know his removal was sealed. The day before, January 12, 1865, Capt. James I. Ferree, an Illinois minister who served at Fort Monroe and Camp Barker, had received a letter from the War Department. He was ordered "for assignment of duty as Superintendent of Contraband, at Alexandria, Virginia, in place of the Rev. Albert Gladwin."[24]

On January 15 one of the doctors told Julia the news. Someone else reported he had overheard the order read at Slough's headquarters. The next day Julia wrote, "Ventured to rejoice a little & flung my Flag to the breeze" (maybe the same flag used at the USCT

recruitment meeting the previous year).[25] Most of her friends did
not approve of her outburst, but one of the few white male teachers offered to display the flag from his room, which looked over the
street. Gladwin divined the meaning of the flag-waving and said he
was highly offended.

Gladwin's removal created fodder for conversation around town.
Freedwoman Lucy Lawson told Julia that "there is only one place
where he ought to go, that is to the Rip Raps"—the prison island
near Fort Monroe. Gladwin managed to hang on for a while. At the
end of January he still lived in the house, where he "seems to think he
will be reinstated in office. He dies hard & is bent, evidently, on making all the trouble he can," Julia wrote. Indeed one rumor had it that
General Slough was working behind the scenes on Gladwin's behalf.[26]

But on January 17 Captain Ferree showed up in Alexandria as
the new superintendent. Julia did not report any of his actions until
about a week later, when he visited some of the most squalid quarters near the wharves. Gladwin charged rent for these places, but
Ferree said he would stop the practice, as well as expand the provision of rations. "Capt. F. has been to Gen. Slough & told him what
he has seen," Julia wrote at the end of January. "The Gen. tells him
to correct all abuses & says the people shall have rations."[27] Maybe
Slough realized he had better make sure the freedmen situation was
under control now that the higher-ups had a better inkling of the
repercussions of dissatisfaction through the cemetery issue. As a fellow military man, Ferree may also have had at least slightly higher
standing with Slough than did Gladwin.

Even with the change of regime Julia decided to move into the
house on I Street in Washington. Why, especially with Gladwin on
his way out? Although she never wrote anything definitive, Frances certainly drew her there. Additionally, in her annual report to
the RLASS, she wrote, "There seemed to be so much greater need of
help there [in Washington] than in Alexandria," so she moved "with
the consent of your society."[28] Yet it seems she informed rather than
asked them about her decision.

Although Julia wrote Maria Porter, the RLASS treasurer, "I feel
really bad on leaving," some other, unspecified reason propelled her.

Maybe confidence in Ferree facilitated the switch. "There are so many teachers & missionaries in Alex. that things are getting mixed up," she wrote. She also alluded to an issue at the Washington and Wolfe Streets house but without details: "Although Gladwin is to leave & a regular nuisance is removed, yet with all the new arrangements that are to be made, it will not be pleasant to live in this house. I think I shall part on friendly terms with all the household but Gladwin. But there are many unpleasant things attached to my present way of living which I hope to get rid of by moving to W."[29]

On February 3, 1865, Julia took leave of the household—listing eleven people who bade her farewell from its doorstep, ranging from Harriet and Louisa Jacobs, to several doctors, to three freedwomen, to Captain Ferree. At the last minute Gladwin showed up to "shake hands & hoped I would have a good time in W. & I hoped he would have a good time wherever he was." She avoided last-minute sentimentality: "I do not wish ever to see him again." (She did.) Meanwhile, as his parting shot, Gladwin said the flag as a sign of rejoicing over his removal "made him feel worse than anything else."[30] But he also warned that General Slough would make sure Julia did not malign him in her reports or other communications.

In addition to the reasons to go *from* Alexandria, Julia welcomed the chance to move *to* Washington, her original plan back in 1862. By 1865 the capital had two streetcar lines. Pennsylvania Avenue and the adjoining streets were filled with tailors, photographers, caterers— dozens of businesses both legitimate and not. She always had made frequent trips to the Capitol, to the Smithsonian, and to performances and lectures, and she enjoyed spending time with Daniel and Gulielma Breed and other friends in Washington. Now she could more easily visit all these sights and people.

The accommodations themselves were not the draw. As she wrote Maria Porter, "The floor is so leaky that it cannot be cleaned often nor thoroughly, for it would spoil the wall below in the 'reception room.'" She asked the RLASS to send matting for the floor or allow her to buy some.[31] Including her and Frances, six women and one man occupied the residence, "almost too many for so small a house." The convenient location on I Street, she realized her first night, made for a lot of street noise. She had a new perspective of the quarters when she injured her foot. Every morning for a week Frances helped her hobble down to the reception room, where she reclined with her foot up, "leaving the front door unlocked & whenever there was a knock, I would call loudly 'Come, Come in, open the door.'" Visitors were frequent, whether for conversation or to obtain access to clothing or a soup kitchen run by the relief group. Most left the door ajar when they exited, so she had to get up to close it against the winter air.[32]

Julia recovered in time for President Lincoln's Second Inauguration on March 4. She and Frances joined the "stream of humanity" heading toward the Capitol, early enough to find a good place to view the procession and ceremony. Intrepid they were, standing in the rain for three hours before anything began. Just before the president spoke, Julia reported, the sun broke through. As for Lincoln's famous Second Inaugural Address ("with malice toward none, with charity for all"), she wrote she heard only two phrases: "the progress of our arms" and "with high hope for the future" from the opening paragraph of his speech.[33]

Using I Street as a base of operations, Julia distributed clothing and visited schools and housing in Washington, similar to her work in Alexandria. At the end of March she wrote in a letter for the *Pennsylvania Freedmen's Bulletin*, "Soon after Mrs. Hartwell [Frances] and myself came to 207 I St., the city was divided into districts, and agents or visitors appointed for each district. The part allotted to us includes nearly all west of 18th Street and the whole of Georgetown. We have made 322 visits." She further reported they had given out three hundred "tickets" people could exchange for "soup, wood, blankets, &c.," as well as 927 pieces of clothing. She stressed that "only a small proportion ever come the second time; but they seem disposed to try to help themselves."[34]

The Jacobses and other friends often came over to Washington, and vice versa. On one visit to Alexandria Julia observed "the streets were quite unlike the streets of W[ashington]. I was never so forcibly struck with the dullness of the place." To be fair, she visited on a particularly windy, rainy day when most people would have tried to remain indoors.[35]

Reflecting on her role as relief agent, Julia wrote in one of her RLASS reports, "It has been said that my only object is to see that the contrabands have an easy time, and in this light I have been *mis-represented* to the War Department. I believe as much as the next person in teaching these liberated slaves to rely upon themselves. But in doing this I would not turn a deaf ear to their necessities and ignore their rights entirely." She signed off as a "missionary-at-large, a woman-of-all-work."[36]

By early April no one got much work done in Washington or Alexandria. Events happened quickly; the mood grew buoyant.

On April 3 Julia wrote: "Richmond is taken! Petersburg is taken! People do not know how to act or to express their joy. The city has been gay this p.m. Ever so many guns were fired, & where all the Flags came from I am at a loss to know." She and Frances tried to conduct clothing business but finally acknowledged, "207 I St. is too contracted for such an occasion. We went out to expand & drink in the inspiration of the hour."[37]

On April 4 Julia wrote, "I never saw anything like it before." She walked by Secretary of State Seward's house across from the White House; "Every window was occupied by a flag just the size of the window"; at Supreme Court Justice Salmon Chase's home at Sixth and E Streets, "every window was hung with a variegated transparency." The War Department, State Department, Treasury, Capitol, Patent Office, and Post Office were all lit up and decorated. In contrast, she noted, "The secesh houses were purposely darkened, the occupants had retired like rats to their holes."[38]

In the midst of the excitement Julia and Frances had an unusual encounter with someone who served in the cavalry with Lewis Griffin, their sister-in-law Charlotte's current husband. The soldier was a she—"She wore a uniform, rode a horse, & carried a sword & carbine just like a man." Stranger still, Maria Lewis, a.k.a. George Harris, was African American, a former slave who had crossed Union lines and fought with the Eighth New York Cavalry in the Battle of Waynesboro. Julia and Frances helped Maria with clothes when she decided to shed her military persona to "return to womanly ways & occupations." Her firsthand accounts fascinated them. True, Julia had come closer to battlefields than most women but with appropriate protection and after the fact. As for Maria and her regiment, "from the 1st to the 25th of March they were almost constantly in the saddle."[39]

In the progression toward victory Julia wrote on April 9, "Another memorable day! Lee has surrendered the army of Northern VA to Gen. Grant. The news came to W. this evening." On April 10: "At an early hour we were awakened by the report of a heavy gun & this was followed by 199 others." (Julia judged the terms of surrender too easy, dampening some of her excitement.) And so on, until April 14, when she went over to Alexandria to join the celebrations there. "I wished to see a gala day in Alex.," she wrote, still having a soft spot for her home for more than two years, and was not disappointed. Led by General Slough (of course), the procession began at 3 p.m. with cavalry, infantry, and artillery troops. Surgeons on horseback and firemen with their engines followed. Black Quartermaster employees marched (she was disappointed not to see any USCT regiment), some on a makeshift float decorated with three banners that read "Sumter & War, Sumter & Peace, Lincoln & Freedom." "I never saw such a large crowd make less confusion & appear more happy than this," she wrote. At night about a dozen or so buildings were illuminated, but "whole squares are totally dark & I do not think *Union* folks take particular pains to darken their houses." Unfortunately a planned fireworks display was botched when all the rockets exploded at once.[40]

As Julia and her friends celebrated, John Wilkes Booth and his accomplices conspired. Events were already in motion. The next morning, April 15, came the news of the calamity that shattered the nation: the death of Abraham Lincoln.

3
After the War

CHAPTER FIFTEEN

"The Paraphernalia of War Is Fast Disappearing"

On the evening of May 16, 1865, six women disembarked at the wharves in Richmond, Virginia, including Julia Wilbur, Harriet Jacobs, Julia's sister Frances, and Harriet's daughter Louisa. Six weeks earlier Richmond had been the capital of the Confederacy. Now this group of black and white women arrived from Washington out of both concern and curiosity.

"Three minutes before 6 o'clock Louisa & I saw Richmond first. It shows well from a distance. The stars & stripes were floating from the Capitol & the tall spires pointed heavenward as if it always had been a loyal city," Julia wrote, overestimating the city's "loyal" aspect but aware of the special opportunity to see it so soon after the war.[1]

The women remained in Richmond for varying lengths of time. Julia ended up staying the longest, from mid-May to mid-June. She had instigated the trip; as she wrote Maria Porter, treasurer of the RLASS, "I have been thinking seriously of the following plan." Her plan, she explained, was to solicit clothing, especially from Philadelphia, before heading to Richmond. "There must be a great deal of destitution there & I know of no one else who has gone there for this purpose." While Julia asked for permission to use RLASS money for the trip, she presented a semi–fait accompli: "I would like to hear from you immediately on the receipt of this. But I shall go on with my plan unless I hear something from you to interdict it."[2]

Julia received permission to ship donated supplies to Richmond via the military quartermaster. She did not make any preparations about where she would stay, or for how long, or what she would actually do. No matter. Her experiences in Washington and Alexandria, bolstered by travel with kindred spirits, perhaps kept any apprehension at bay. When Julia first went to Alexandria in 1862, she depended on Rev. William Channing and other men to orient her. After three years of war she was a veteran, confident she and the other women could navigate unfamiliar terrain on their own.

On the first evening in Richmond, the white women stayed in the Spotswood Hotel, known for hosting Confederate VIPs throughout the war. Harriet and Louisa Jacobs, whose race precluded them from staying at the hotel, stayed with a black family. Julia and Frances moved out of the hotel a few days later and lodged with Nancy Carter, a free black woman who lived near the Capitol.

Military analysts debate Richmond's strategic importance during the Civil War, but as historian Nelson Lankford points out, after mid-1864, "Virginia's principal city once more became both object and symbol of the war."[3] Its "fall" made the end of the war feel imminent, as the celebrations in Washington illustrated. Like Washington, Richmond had grown and changed over the previous four years, from a placid town to a city thronged by soldiers, newly minted government officials, fortune seekers, and others. By 1865 food was hard to come by and expensive when found. Civilians, white and black, struggled. Union prisoners festered in Libby Prison, a former tobacco warehouse, and the misnamed Belle Isle in the James River. Confederate soldiers recuperated on the heights above the city in Chimborazo Hospital, one of the largest and most successful facilities on either side of the conflict. To boost manpower the Confederacy had recently, and reluctantly, begun to recruit blacks to serve in the military, and white residents recorded an unprecedented sight: armed black men drilling on Richmond's Capitol Square. Slavery continued, although most of the city's twelve slave traders had closed or retreated farther south.

Despite the turmoil, hardship, and a raft of rumors, the fall of Richmond shocked its residents, a miracle or a tragedy, depending on one's point of view. On April 2, a pleasant Sunday, Jefferson Davis hurriedly left morning worship at St. Paul's when a messenger came in with a note. Robert E. Lee warned that the army defenses would not hold and that "all preparations be made for leaving Richmond that night."[4]

As government officials hastily left, calm became chaos. An order to set fire to tobacco and other goods, to keep them from Union hands, went awry. The flames spread throughout the business district—not just the warehouses and their contents but also an arsenal, banks, newspaper offices, stores, and saloons—and set off large explosions throughout the night. A poorly executed plan to confiscate liquor resulted in its literally pouring out into the streets; drunk, desperate people looted what didn't burn. When the Union troops entered the city on April 3, they fought fires, not battles.

Judith McGuire, who back in 1861 had written about her departure from Alexandria, lived in Richmond at the time. She watched fatalistically as Confederate officials, and anyone else who could, evacuated. On April 3 she wrote in her diary, "We have passed through a fatal thirty-six hours. . . . We could do nothing; no one suggested anything to be done." When President Lincoln, already visiting General Grant's headquarters at City Point, came into Richmond on April 4, she commented, "Our people were in nothing rude or disrespectful; they only kept themselves away from a scene so painful."[5] Back in 1861 McGuire had prayed that war be averted and the Union preserved. She had gone from one family member's house to another since then. Four itinerant years had hardened her.

Not everyone shared McGuire's sadness. Nancy Carter told Julia, who wrote down Nancy's words: "When the Yankees came, I did not know what shape to put myself in. I was obliged to jump up I was so light." She described the amazing day when Abraham Lincoln walked the streets of Richmond, "leading his little boy [son Tad] by the hand. . . . Colored people beside themselves with joy, bowed & curtsied & threw up handkerchiefs & aprons & then says 'I'm glad to see you. I'm glad you come. We have been waiting for you.'"[6]

That open-hearted joy did not last long. By the time Julia and the rest of the group arrived in May, inequities had surfaced. Blacks needed passes, signed by whites, to circulate around town, and they were subject to a curfew. Reports of black harassment by Union soldiers abounded. As Julia heard from Nancy, "The people are mighty disencouraged. They say these Union soldiers must be rebels disguised in Federal uniform."[7]

The morning after Julia and the others arrived, the U.S. provost marshal said he would not give them a place to set up their supplies. The American Union Commission, a Northern relief agency that came to Richmond in April, provided space but expressed some skepticism about the endeavor. Some of the commission teachers said the blacks they encountered were "in a comfortable condition," with no need of donated clothing. "I felt quite sure there was another side to this story, and in my walks around the city I found children who did not go to school for want of decent clothes to wear," Julia later reported.[8]

The women visited places they had heard about, including "Jeff's house" (the home of Jefferson Davis), Libby Prison, and City Jail. Mrs. Carter and other local blacks, both formerly enslaved and free-born, accompanied the group. They too saw the insides of places they knew about only from afar. "The colored people of R who were with us had never been in a trader's jail before," Julia noted when they visited the most notorious of the traders, Richard Lumpkin. According to her, they were delighted to hear the Northern women, including Harriet, berate Lumpkin and hear him sputter excuses. At the end of the first exhausting day, the group stopped north of the city at the Alms House, which housed the most destitute, white and black. "I had seen & heard so much to day, that I could endure no more & we stayed but a short time. But I must come to this place again & see what can be done," Julia wrote. True to her word, she returned many times to set up a clothing room, push for better conditions, and complain about brutal treatment by several white guards.[9]

Around the city terrible cases of punishment against blacks became known—whippings, imprisonment, men hanged from their thumbs. The army men in charge allowed the mayor to resume his position, and, as Julia wrote, "It seemed as if the military and civilians combined to make the situation of the colored people intolerable."[10] A group of black community leaders developed a "statement of grievances." (Julia reported attending their first organizational meeting, along with Nancy Carter and Mrs. Jennings, a black teacher. If so, she may have been the only white person present.)[11] On June 10 more than three thousand people met at the First African Baptist Church and sent a delegation to Washington to meet with President Andrew

Johnson. As they stated, instead of acknowledgment of their loyalty throughout the conflict, Richmond blacks faced mistreatment and persecution. The protest bore fruit. The worst of the military miscreants found themselves assigned elsewhere. Their replacements had reputations as being fairer to blacks.

Transgressions against blacks did not end, but "I am ready to leave Richmond" to return to Washington, Julia wrote on June 14. Perhaps giving her group too much credit ("the presence of the Party that came here with me encouraged the colored people mightily"), she recognized they represented something Richmond had not seen before. Especially when Nancy Carter and others joined them, "We were black, white & colored & yet there was no earthquake. The world did not come to an end."[12]

Amid the new places and people in Richmond, Julia and Harriet encountered a familiar face. They learned that a Baptist missionary had set up a school across the river in the town of Manchester—and it was none other than their Alexandria nemesis, Albert Gladwin. Harriet and a few others went to see him for themselves. (Julia spent the day in Richmond arranging for clothing to go to the Alms House.) Discontent about his management style had already surfaced, and the visitors stoked it. "Our party made a statement about G's doings in Alex. & I do not think he will have smooth sailing after this in Manchester or R," Julia wrote with some satisfaction. Gladwin came into Richmond a few days later and sought out Julia at Mrs. Carter's. "How do you do, Miss Wilbur," he said. He extended his hand, friendly as could be, settling in for a chat. As she wrote, "Nobody but G would think of doing so, under the circumstances," and she sat as far away from him as possible. They never saw each other again, at least not that Julia recorded.[13]

After a month in Richmond, Julia returned to Washington. While away, she missed the Grand Review of the Armies. Over two full days in May, tens of thousands of victorious army troops marched from the Capitol to the White House, together one last time before disbanding. (The USCT were not included, variously interpreted either as a slight or the fact that the regiments remained on duty farther south.) But Julia witnessed another historic event: the military tribunal conducted for Mary Surratt and seven men for the assassination of Lincoln in June. "Thought I might as well see something of this important trial," she wrote. She distinguished between the "fine, noble-looking men that compose the court" and the "unconcerned" appearances of the defendants, excepting Surratt, whom Julia described hidden behind a veil and a fan. She sketched the courtroom layout in her diary, among just a handful of drawings in more than fifty years of diary keeping. She attended the stifling courtroom only one day, unlike, as the *Evening Star* reported, "many ladies, some of whom have been present nearly every day the trial has been in progress."[14]

Julia continued direct involvement with Reconstruction until 1869. In Washington she served as a "visiting agent" for the Freedmen's Bureau. Through this work, along with travel and other experiences, she realized the end of slavery did not solve the problems it had caused. Racism and inequality persisted. Illness and death reached horrific levels, exacerbated by malnutrition, lack of health care, and other causes.[15]

Before the war ended, Abraham Lincoln and other politicians tried to envision what would come after the dismantling of slavery. The term they used, "Reconstruction," reflected the need to somehow rebuild the South's economic and social systems. Historians debate Reconstruction's accomplishments, its failures, and even its span, although the period is generally defined from the Emancipation Proclamation in January 1863 to the withdrawal of federal troops from the old Confederacy in 1877.[16] President Lincoln died without fully explaining his ideas (if he had a full plan), but he signed the law to establish the Freedmen's Bureau in March 1865. The bureau's limited resources and lack of support, especially once Andrew Johnson assumed the presidency, thwarted achievement of the goal to aid in the transition from slavery to freedom.

The bureau became embroiled in the debate that swirled during the war about the extent to which the government should assist freedmen, so Julia became embroiled in it as well. In his first official circular Gen. O. O. Howard, the director of the bureau considered sympathetic to the cause, stressed, "The negro should understand that he is really free but on no account, if able to work, should he harbor the thought that the Government will support him in idleness."[17]

Many ambiguities stemmed from that statement and other policies, among them the definition of "able to work"; the choices available to the "able-bodied," including what type of work they would do, where, and for whom; and what to do for those *not* able to work. Julia and other women connected with the bureau had a different view of the role of the agency, and more broadly of aid to freedpeople, than did politicians, the military, and even fellow (male) reformers, as historian Carol Faulkner has pointed out.[18] The bureau, while it supported schools and hospitals, established housing, and launched sanitation projects, defined success as an increase in the number of people who worked and a decrease in the number of people who received assistance. In the agency's defense, dwindling funds and negative public views of aid to freedpeople, combined with the usual fears about dependency, factored into its decisions. Vicious reactions against the formerly enslaved continued; the bureau records include monthly lists of "murders and outrages."[19]

In Washington, headquarters of the bureau, the black population doubled between 1860 and 1867, mostly through migration into the city. Jobs and housing were scarce.[20] The bureau thought the solution was to induce blacks to leave, especially to fill the labor gap in the South. "It is better for those who go; it is better for those who remain," exhorted the assistant commissioner for Washington when he urged ministers of black churches to persuade their parishioners to move.[21] Land ownership, contained in the original legislation to set up the bureau, may have offered a stronger inducement, but it never came to fruition except in a few special cases. As Julia asked rhetorically, "Why would they want to go south?" When bureau officials urged people to move to Mississippi and Arkansas, she wrote, "These people were never in Arkansas. It is a thousand miles away. They think if they cannot be protected near W[ashington], they certainly will not be so far off."[22] Nonetheless, through the bureau, through private efforts, and on their own, thousands of former slaves were on the move in search of family members and opportunities throughout the country.

When Julia and many other agents urged freedpeople to leave, they suggested that they move north or west, offering domestic service (females) and other manual labor (males) to adults and older children. At least once, in the fall of 1866, she accompanied a group of nine adults and children to upstate New York, with the bureau paying transportation costs. Larger efforts also took place. Dozens of people at a time went to Hartford, New York, and other cities. Employee and employer expectations often did not match. In a report to the RLASS, Julia claimed that "many of these men and women would not be wanted at all in the North because they are entirely ignorant of our way of working." This supposed deficiency did not account for all the friction. Those with experience, she acknowledged, "frequently have aspirations to become something more than mere servants and laborers for others." And as many letters to the Freedmen's Bureau attest, employers above the Mason-Dixon line could exploit vulnerable workers as much as those in the South.[23]

To assist the majority of the poor who stayed, Congress appropriated special relief funds to the District on at least three occasions, intended for both races. Visiting agents like Julia went door to door, checking conditions and providing relief to those deemed destitute in the form of tickets to exchange for food, fuel, or other items. "The business is done systematically this winter," she explained to James McKim in early 1866. "Affairs have been well-arranged by the Freedmen's Bureau."[24] The bureau set up subdistricts. Assigned to the West End and Georgetown, Julia, like her colleagues, would show up at a home to pass judgment on its residents and contents. We can assume Julia was among the more sympathetic; she continually reported she gave out more assistance than her ticket allotment. But she also criticized people in her diaries and official reports, and sometimes to their faces, when conditions did not measure up to her standards of cleanliness. "Some of these people might do better," she wrote in her diary after going out on a winter afternoon. "I was vexed & scolded them soundly. . . . What I saw this p.m. was too much even for me, of whom it has been said that 'my only object is to make an easy time for these people.'"[25]

As in Alexandria during the war, the men in charge took umbrage at what they perceived as blacks' dependency and white women's gull-ibility, and they accused the women of leniency. They particularly targeted Josephine Griffing, an Ohio abolitionist who had pushed for the creation of the bureau in 1864. She moved to Washington with her family and was appointed a special adviser, dismissed, then reinstated—the bureau gave various reasons for her changes in sta-tus. Overall, the way one bureau official described it, Griffing and other women were unable "in their earnest desire to assist all who asked . . . to discriminate between poverty and actual suffering." The women "were congenitally unable of the exact discrimination and mental toughness required to administer relief efficiently," as histo-rian Robert Harrison recorded the male way of thinking.[26]

Julia recognized the need for stopgap measures, especially when employment prospects dimmed. One cold February morning, when she went around to the bureau office, she saw a crowd of men. "They tell me they wait there day after day for somebody to come & hire them & there is (I think) about one chance for 50 applicants," she wrote. An officer told her the men didn't work because they asked too much in wages, but she responded, "I do not know about all this. But I do know that some of these people I am acquainted with & they worked faithfully as long as work was to be had." In a report to the bureau she pointed out that the lack of work forced some people to request aid as a last resort: "They have been doing well & needed no help, but it is mortifying to ask for help now. They do it reluctantly. I think one half the persons relieved have been reduced to this neces-sity by want of work during the past two months," she noted. When she itemized the tickets she distributed (436, with "blankets" account-ing for more than one-fourth the total), she pointed out she distrib-uted many tickets to people who unsuccessfully sought work. In early 1867 she wrote, "$50 allowed each agent this month but I have given orders amounting to $207." A few days later she told Robert Reyburn, the medical officer in charge of the relief fund, "No use of my going to see people if I cannot help at all. He says to do the best you can."[27]

Prejudice also clouded the bureau's efforts. "This evening [I] was at a meeting of the Bureau Officers, Visiting Agents, & others," Julia wrote after one of many such meetings. "It pained me to hear so many slurs cast upon these people. They were not spoken of with proper respect. I am glad no colored persons were there to have their feelings hurt."[28] Of course she had identified an underlying problem with the bureau's outreach without fully realizing it: its almost entirely all-white composition.

Although bureau officials complained about the women, they needed them to supplement their small staff. Throughout the South agents had often impossibly large areas to cover. Moreover, outside organizations financially supported most of the agents, as the RLASS did Julia (according to her, the bureau paid the salary of only two out of twenty-two agents in Washington). These groups also provided much needed supplies and teachers in the South, and they helped find jobs for freedpeople traveling north.[29]

Perhaps worried about criticism from bureau men and more generally the anti-Reconstruction "Copperheads," Julia voiced objections in early 1867 about an independent job-placement effort by Griffing and Sojourner Truth in New York and Michigan. They advertised in local newspapers and worked with intermediaries, such as Isaac and Amy Post in Rochester. They accepted small amounts of money to defray expenses; Julia apparently felt the payments would tarnish the endeavor if word got out. According to two of Truth's biographers, Sojourner interpreted Julia's criticism as an attack on her integrity. She told Griffing, "Miss Wilber [*sic*] was a very near sighted woman. . . . The people all know I am not doing it for my benefit or profit and then for Miss Wilber to think that the Copperheads think that I am doing it for speculating . . ."[30] Julia did not record this incident in her diary, although throughout the years when she had contact with the already legendary Truth, she wrote about her in complimentary terms. Yet the incident illustrates the pressures in figuring out how to keep everyone financially afloat—not only the formerly enslaved, but also those who wanted to help out.

Julia and her sister Frances lived in the house on I Street operated by the Pennsylvania Association of Freedmen, then moved with the group to a house "a hundred times better" on Twentieth Street between K and L. Frances at various times taught sewing and served as principal of the association's industrial schools.[31] The relationship between them frayed for reasons unknown. They went their separate ways—or rather Frances did, although we see the problems only through Julia's eyes. "Frances is away a great deal and is but little company to me," she wrote, typical of many such instances. On Christmas she noted she was thinking about religion and charity, "For I dare say I am none too charitable (Frances says I am not)."[32] When they traveled to New York in the summer of 1867, Frances remained to help care for their father, although she moved back and forth between New York and Washington over the next few decades.

Despite these tribulations, Julia, in her early fifties, led a busy life socializing, following the news of the day, and attending lectures and other events in a version of her life in Rochester a decade or so earlier. She often went to Howard University, founded in 1867, for events and ceremonies. She became acquainted with Clara Barton and visited the studio of Vinnie Ream, a young attractive "sculptress" who caused a sensation when commissioned to create a bust of Lincoln for the Capitol. On a day in which she saw Ream and attended a meeting with Susan B. Anthony, she wrote, "My mind can hardly take in all the new things I see & hear." And that was before she witnessed something else marvelous. At the Treasury Department, "We were shown the calculating machine worked by a young woman. It adds, subtracts, multiplies & divides as fast as she can arrange the stops & turn a little crank. It is a wonderful machine."[33]

Beyond such celebrity acquaintances as Barton and Ream, Julia became friends with teachers and fellow relief agents: white women from similar backgrounds as hers, many of them younger than she. In addition, noteworthy for the day, her circle of friends included black women, such as Louisa Butler, the wife of Secretary of State Seward's valet; Eliza Anderson, wife of a minister; and Emma Newman. Most of these women were freeborn and educated, but Emma and her husband were former contrabands who had come to Alexandria in 1862, as Julia mentioned (numerous times through the years) in her diary. Their transition from slaves to property owners validated, to Julia, that such progress was possible for people who had "willing hands to work."[34]

Julia returned to Richmond, becoming friendly enough with the governor to stay with him and his wife. She also went several times to Fredericksburg, about halfway between Washington and Richmond. "What a scene of desolation Fredericksburg presents!" she wrote on her first visit in December 1865; most of the buildings were damaged or in total rubble. In the home of a local white woman, she noted, "Rich furniture but hardly a whole piece. Old & costly ornaments but broken & defaced. The lady herself in a faded black moiré antique [dress] was in keeping with the premises."[35] She returned to sites of former battlefields and encampments she had visited with her brother-in-law Joseph Van Buskirk three years earlier.

About one thousand freedpeople lived in Fredericksburg at the time. Julia observed, "[I] do not find the destitution I expected," but she witnessed dissension between the Freedmen's Bureau and the army quartermaster. During that first visit she talked with several blacks laboring under conditions akin to slavery. She stopped at a school run by two women from Poughkeepsie, New York. Lack of shoes was apparently an issue because when she returned to Washington in January, she wrote two letters to James McKim, two weeks apart, asking him to acquire "75 or 100 pairs for scholars from 7 to 15 or 18 years of age. This seems almost indispensable in order to keep the school going." Returning to Washington after another extended stay in Fredericksburg the following year, she embarked on what she termed a "political excursion." She sought out Freedmen's Bureau director Howard and "laid before him" what she saw, including black members of the Burial Corps receiving half the wages as whites and other blacks being kept ignorant of their rights.[36]

In May 1866 Julia went on another pilgrimage of sorts to West Virginia to see places connected with John Brown. A small group traveled by barge up the c&o Canal from Georgetown. As the barge meandered, Julia reread Brown's biography, written in 1860 by a highly sympathetic abolitionist, "to refresh my memory" of the Harpers Ferry raid and its aftermath.[37] The white locals did not have much interest in showing them where Brown was hanged, but a black man riding by on horseback pointed the way to the field in Charles Town. "He said he helped saw the lumber there to make the gallows & he helped take it away again," she wrote. They met George Sadler, the undertaker who brought Brown to his execution. He painted a sympathetic picture of Brown, whom he came to know in Brown's few months in jail. They met the mother-in-law of one of Brown's men. She gave them a spirited tour, then asked them to intercede on her behalf with Secretary Stanton for aid.[38]

After the trip Julia did not mention contacting Stanton. She did seek out Jeremiah Baldwin, whom Sadler had formerly enslaved. Sadler said he gave Baldwin and his five other "servants" $100 each and "he hears from them & they say they are very sorry they left him." Baldwin, working as a waiter at the Metropolitan Hotel in Washington, acknowledged the $100 and said Sadler "treated his slaves better than any body else in Charlestown but it is not quite a fact that they would like to go back & be slaves again."[39]

Harriet Jacobs remained in Alexandria until July 1865, when she felt "the time has come when I should go where labor is more needed." She wrote the New York society that had sent her there in 1863, "Your Society has done nobly by these people: you came to their aid in their greatest extremity." Poverty persisted, but also progress, and she claimed credit for her own and Julia's work, writing, "Julia Wilbur and myself were entirely alone the first year; since then, others have come into the field."[40]

Julia and Harriet sustained their friendship. Through correspondence Julia knew Harriet and Louisa spent time in Savannah teaching and unsuccessfully trying to set up an orphan asylum and that Harriet regained possession of her grandmother's home in Edenton. They saw each other at least once in the late 1860s. "Mrs. Jacobs came this evening to stay all night," Julia wrote in October 1867. "Good visit with her."[41]

The women took the boat to Alexandria and revisited old haunts. Julia noted Harriet sat in the ladies' cabin—not a foregone conclusion for a black woman. Segregation in public transportation was frequently yet inconsistently carried out. Julia would have been conscious of the discrimination in any event, but it especially galled her when it affected her friends. For example, going north in 1866, Julia came upon Virginia Lawton and her sister at the depot. (Lawton was the young black teacher whom Harriet Jacobs had brought to Alexandria back in 1864.) The conductor said the Lawtons could not ride in the ladies' car despite purchasing tickets. Julia recounted, "I asked, 'Why?' He said, 'You know the reason.' I said, 'No, I know no reason. We are friends and wish to ride together.'" After some back and forth, Julia created a scene when she "complained" to the conductor about the presence of a black nursemaid accompanying a white woman and her infant. A black servant was okay in the ladies' railcar; an independent black woman like Virginia Lawton was not. More infuriating, on the way back from Alexandria the day Julia went with Harriet, a drunk white woman in the ladies' cabin vomited profusely, creating a "revolting spectacle" and causing everyone, white and black, to exit for fresh air. As Julia observed, "If a colored woman had been in that cabin in that condition, what a hue & cry would have been raised."[42]

To Julia and many others President Johnson's appeasement of former Confederates and harshness against blacks legitimized racism. In October 1865 Julia visited the White House when a USCT regiment was presented. She interpreted Johnson's words to the men to be "virtuous, industrious, & patient & intelligent" as "in other words, if you will be submissive & work for us as formerly, & be very humble, we will let you stay in this country."[43] She continued to attend White House receptions, positioning herself, as if Johnson would notice, in such a way as not to shake his hand going or coming.

Johnson and the Republican-controlled Congress battled back and forth. Attending congressional debates became a spectator sport. Congress extended the Freedmen's Bureau, the president vetoed it, the veto failed to be overturned (although it succeeded a second time around). Congress passed a civil rights bill, the president vetoed it, and Congress overturned the veto. And so on. When Republicans picked up more seats in the midterm election of 1866, friction between the president and Congress sharpened.

Johnson's impeachment trial came down to a power struggle that played itself out as a personnel matter. Congress passed the Tenure of Office Act, which required Senate approval if the president wanted to fire a Cabinet member. In defiance Johnson fired Secretary of War Edwin Stanton. Stanton remained in office—that is, he literally locked himself in. The House of Representatives charged Johnson with impeachment on March 2, 1868, and the Senate began its deliberations several days later.

Visitors needed much-in-demand tickets to attend the impeachment sessions. Julia brazenly asked contacts whom she barely knew for tickets. When New York Senator Roscoe Conkling gave her one, she wrote—facetiously but hopefully—"I shall surely vote for Roscoe Conkling (when I get a chance) (that is)." (Parenthetical wishes aside, the powerful senator opposed women's suffrage.) Another day Julia interrupted Senator Charles Sumner at breakfast, but he said he reserved his tickets for people from his state of Massachusetts. After weeks of following the trial, she couldn't wangle a ticket on the day the Senate voted but stood in the Capitol Rotunda with "hundreds of others" and learned of Johnson's acquittal by one vote. Her reaction: "Heartsick & disgusted with the great Impeachment farce. I hastened away to the more important task of getting material for a bonnet."[44]

What about Alexandria during this time? In 1865 more than seven thousand blacks constituted about 50 percent of the total population (compared with about three thousand, or 25 percent of the total population, in 1860). The increased number of blacks, the return of whites who had left during the war, and a bad economy for everyone did not augur well for harmonious relations, as a group of black leaders saw it. In April 1865 they presented a petition to President Johnson requesting that Alexandria remain under federal control rather than revert to local powers, "lest they suffer more from brutality of the white people around them."[45] Military Governor John Slough remained in place for a few months, no doubt chafing at the bit and ready for something new. He resigned in July 1865, telling the "Citizens of Alexandria and Soldiers of its Garrison" that he was headed out west, but "I shall ever remember with pleasurable emotions, my three years' sojourn in Alexandria."[46] Alexandria fell under the larger Defences South of the Potomac, commanded by H. H.

Wells, the former provost marshal who had criticized Julia's interference back in 1863.

"The paraphernalia of war is fast disappearing," Julia observed, as she witnessed the changes to many of the physical aspects of conflict. During one visit to Alexandria the absence of "Army wagons & ambulances & officers on horseback" struck her. Hospitals and other buildings were being dismantled or returned to their prewar purposes. "The houses are nearly all given up to their former owners," she wrote. Most personally to her own experience, "Teachers, doctors &c. have all been turned out of the houses on the Cor. of Washington & Wolfe"—the building where she had set up the Clothing Room and battled Albert Gladwin.[47]

On another visit she and a friend from Rochester went to the former slave pen. While the authorities sorted out what to do with it, a woman named Fanny Lee acted as caretaker. Formerly enslaved herself, Fanny said her brother had passed through the pen, either as a person traded or imprisoned. When Julia remarked she wished she had a souvenir, Fanny retrieved an axe and extracted several bolts out of a heavy double door. Julia reveled in the irony of the action. "When I first came to Alex. in '62, this slave pen was the terror of all the colored, as well as some of the whites," she wrote. "It did not occur to me then that I should ever see the bolts removed by a woman once a slave & that I should bring them away." An account book lying in a corner recorded the shower-bath punishment inflicted on four black men for a misdemeanor as late as 1865, and it brought the place back in all its indignity.[48]

L'Ouverture Hospital remained open until 1867, and Julia continued to check on, and occasionally try to intervene with, its operations. Over time most of the people she knew left Alexandria or died (as in the case of Mary Collier), so she had fewer connections with the city. But she kept returning, even riding in an "electric car" there almost thirty years later in 1893.

Julia maintained the custom she began in Alexandria of going north for part of each summer or early fall. As she had done during the war, she made time to visit her RLASS colleagues. While still supporting her efforts at the Freedmen's Bureau, the RLASS finances struggled after the war, a reflection of the difficulty that relief groups encountered as public sympathies moved on from the plight of former slaves. Julia experienced the challenge in raising money when she approached a wealthy Rochester businessman for a donation. He told her that he "can't afford it, taxes so high, [he] does so much for Rochester &c."[49]

In September 1865 Julia wrote, "Received $180 for 9 months services. This besides my expenses, which amounted to $235. All the society can afford to do." In August 1866 she wrote, "They wish me to go back & work another year among the freedpeople." But the line item for "donations and memberships" in the RLASS budget, more than $1,500 in 1863, fell below $70 in the years after 1865. (The group drew upon its diminishing reserves to support Julia.) In 1867 she reported to RLASS that she had accepted a job to teach sewing for the Pennsylvania Association of Freedmen "in order to lessen the expenses of your Society," as well as an offer from the Freedmen's Bureau to draw a salary of $30 a month. In the summer of 1868 Julia knew the RLASS "would like me to return to W[ashington] next fall & perhaps money can be raised for the purpose." But she acknowledged, "The funds of your Society are about exhausted, and without further contributions, you cannot longer sustain an agent."[50]

No, the RLASS could not sustain an agent. The organization that had begun with encouragement from Frederick Douglass wound down in 1868 after seventeen years. Many like-minded groups faced a similar fate. The Freedmen's Bureau budget was slashed in 1869, and Congress had it shuttered for good in 1872. When Julia appealed to O. O. Howard for continued work, he could only offer a letter of introduction on her behalf to seek employment elsewhere.

The writing was on the wall. To stay in Washington, Julia Wilbur, age fifty-four, needed a new job.

CHAPTER SIXTEEN

"That I Might Be There to See"

Julia Wilbur's first day as an office worker in Washington began as it did when she started teaching in Rochester twenty-five years earlier—with an examination. On July 1, 1869, she entered the grand building that housed the Patent Office (now the Smithsonian National Portrait Gallery/American Art Museum), "placed at a table with 28 printed questions before me to be answered," along with a sample letter to write and a timed test to see how fast she could copy a certain number of lines. "I was weak & trembling & could do nothing well," she wrote but performed sufficiently to get a position as a clerk.[1] She remained on the job for more than twenty-five years, until her death in 1895—with one major and many minor setbacks along the way.

The government's most famous early female clerk, Clara Barton, worked at the Patent Office for a few years beginning in 1854, when it employed fewer than sixty people. By the late 1860s patent applications had ballooned more than sixfold. The workforce grew as well, including, when Julia began, fifty-three "female copyists" tucked in six rooms in the basement. "The attendance," proclaimed the agency commissioner, "is nearly as good and the work is fully equal in quantity and quality" to their male counterparts.[2]

According to historian Cindy Sondik Aron, Julia, although older than average, typified the women who entered the federal bureaucracy from the Civil War until the end of the 1800s—middle class, white, and well educated for the time.[3] They needed money to support themselves and often other family members. The technology, the positions to which they and black men and women could aspire, and the civil service system have all changed over the years. Yet we would recognize many of Julia's trials and tribulations: complaints about the physical layout and room temperature (too cold, too hot);

new bosses with new ways of doing things; alliances and antipathies (i.e., office politics); and other realities of office life.

The best route to a federal job was to enlist influential people to intercede on one's behalf. Applicants wrote letters pleading their cases, rather than submitting résumés listing their accomplishments. Julia followed the pattern by asking Freedmen's Bureau director O. O. Howard and mayor of Washington Sayles Bowen to press her case with the secretary of the interior, who oversaw the Patent Office at the time. She succeeded in a quest that required persistence for both sexes but especially women. She hand-carried her letters to the offices of the secretary and other higher-ups. If one of the men she sought was busy or out, she waited hours or returned the next day. As she went back and forth one afternoon, she noted, "My new boots murdered my feet coming home. I put my feet in warm water immediately. They feel better, but I am so tired."[4]

Yet she almost jeopardized her chances of getting the job at all. Rather than appear like a woman who wouldn't make waves, she did something extraordinary while her application was under consideration: she tried to register to vote. The newspapers identified her by name. Mayor Bowen, himself an outspoken Republican destined to serve just one term in office, warned that her action could "kill her chances of getting a place."[5] The voting registration effort failed; the job quest did not.

Historian Kate Masur describes Washington at the time by drawing on a phrase from the influential radical Republican senator Charles Sumner: "an example for all the land."[6] In January 1867, months before Congress legislated black men's voting rights in the South and two years before it passed the Fifteenth Amendment granting universal black male suffrage, Congress passed a law that allowed black men to vote in local elections in Washington. On June 3, 1867, Julia wrote, "Long before 7 o'clock thousands of Negroes were at the polls ready for the work. . . . Every colored man that deposited a vote looked several inches taller as he walked away." Despite her happiness in witnessing the scene, she also noted, "I confess to feeling a little jealous . . . and I presume no convulsion of nature would have occurred, had white *women* and black *women* increased that line of voters."[7]

When Josephine Griffing, Julia's colleague at the Freedmen's Bureau, urged women in Washington to register to vote for the next round of municipal elections in 1869, Julia willingly volunteered. She recruited several friends, including Louisa Butler and Eliza Anderson, two of the black women with whom she often visited, and Sarah Evans, the white teacher she had first met in Alexandria. They gathered after dinner on April 22, along with two men, to develop a plan. Seven women signed a letter that read in part, "We know that it is unusual for those of our sex to make such a request. We do so because we believe ourselves entitled to the franchise."[8] Julia, Louisa, and another woman presented the letter to the election judges gathered that evening at a firehouse in the city's First Ward.

The *National Republican* reported, "The communication which was laid before the board on Thursday by Mrs. [*sic*] Julia Wilbur and other females, asking that they might be registered, was considered, and the board decided that this request could not be acceded to." The *New York Herald*, with its large circulation and anti-egalitarian views, fixed on the interracial nature of the attempt, entitling its article "Woman Suffrage in the District—Sable Sisters Demanding the Elective Franchise."[9]

The judges received them politely but without much reaction, and the group left—rather an anticlimax. But the women had publicly stated their case. They had joined the decades-long struggle for women to obtain the right to vote.

In May 1869, suffrage attempt notwithstanding, Julia received word from the patent commissioner that he would recommend hiring her to the secretary of the interior. (It's hard to fathom how the employment of low-level clerks received such high-level attention.) Almost as soon as she started, Julia complained about the conditions and her pay of about $700 per year—the standard rate for female clerks and $200 less than for most male clerks. She requested duties as a comparer rather than copyist, to do proofreading rather than writing, because her arm had started to ache. Several coworkers vexed her; supervisors seemed to lord their power over those under them. But she fell into a routine, sustaining a life outside office hours that included social visits, lectures, meetings, errands, and the like.

Julia tried several times to increase her salary. She heard after at least one unsuccessful attempt in the mid-1870s that "$900 is paid in preference for those who have families to support." It was probably true, but perhaps the powers-that-be used that reason to avoid a conversation about her performance. A Patent Office ledger at the time records her with the lukewarm "very fair," while many others had "good" and "excellent" attached to their names.[10]

Julia's stepmother died in 1870, reported to her in a letter from her sister Frances more than a week after the funeral. But when their father died two years later, Frances telegrammed and Julia immediately left for home, grateful to receive a month's paid leave. "Not wholly unexpected & yet it seems sudden," she wrote about his death, as he had seemed weaker every time she visited. His body remained in the parlor at home until as many siblings as possible could arrive. Julia "had the coffin opened twice. I put a pillow under his head & arranged the head & shoulders until it satisfied me better. It made no difference to the lifeless body, but it did make a difference to me."[11]

Rootless in Washington, Julia rented rooms in a series of homes, hoping the next place would overcome the deficiencies of the place before but always expressing disappointment. She lived in least ten places in five years. She didn't seem to inspect the places well before moving or didn't take into account the distance from the office. In a typical entry in 1872—two days after one move—she noted that "[I] think I cannot stay here. Dirty, bad smelling, no parlor, miserable fare, coarse, low-lived boarders. Breakfast late." When she moved to a supposed improvement, she complained, "Room hadn't been swept. . . . Did not sleep well. *Fidgetty on subject of chinches* [bedbugs]." By the first of the next month, she left that place too.[12]

Julia's nomadic life ended in late 1876. She rented a small house at 722 Eighth Street, near the Patent Office, where she remained for the rest of her life except for her annual trips north. The initial reason for moving to this house was momentous. Her niece Freda Bigelow had reentered her life two years earlier and came to live with her in Washington.

After fifteen years of counting the number of weeks since she had last had contact with the girl, bemoaning the anniversary of Freda's leaving each New Year's Eve, and gathering secondhand bits of intelligence about her, Julia heard from Freda in January 1874, a few months before the girl turned eighteen: "When I got home, I found a *letter* from my darling Freda B. The *first letter* & I believe it will not be the last from her. A nice, kind little letter & I answered it at once."[13] Freda's father, Revilo, must have decided to permit, or even encourage, the contact. By then he and his wife Nancy had two younger daughters. Maybe as Freda reached adulthood, he realized he could benefit from what he assumed correctly would be Julia's generous financial support of Freda. Freda inherited a small portion of Stephen Wilbur's estate as his granddaughter, so maybe Revilo had mellowed. It was not Freda who clamored for the reunion, as she barely remembered the Wilburs when she saw them.

Julia received mixed messages from Revilo and Freda. A much anticipated reunion in New York fell flat later in 1874; Julia complained about Freda's silence and passivity. They remained in contact, and somehow it was decided Freda would move to Washington. Julia went from a single person in a single room to part of a household that included her sister Frances, who had returned to Washington; Freda; and another niece, a daughter of older sister Elizabeth who had also moved south for a time. Julia and Frances, never-before parents in their late fifties, suddenly had charge of the comings and goings of two young women living in a city for the first time in their lives. "I see that Frances and I will have our hands full," Julia admitted.[14]

So Julia got her wish to reconnect with Freda—or did she? She worried Freda did not care for the family or the greater world around her, that she lacked curiosity and drive. But Freda had lost her mother at age two, lived with the Wilburs until her abrupt departure at three and a half, and then had grown up in a "blended family" of Bigelows, with no contact with her mother's side of the family. She was sickly and frail, with a spotty education (admittedly this described many nineteenth-century children). Julia had high hopes for how she could influence Freda, maybe too high. She enrolled her in a business college and took Freda around to her favorite places in Washington. But Freda disappointed her, at least in these first few years.

"A tall and good-looking girl, but her training has been neglected," Julia wrote. "Good & generally amicable like her mother whom she resembles in many respects. But sometimes like her father set in her way & unyielding." She expressed hope that Freda would at least stay in Washington until she could "teach or do something else to support herself when it becomes necessary."[15]

At the end of 1879 Freda took ill. Julia and Frances did not know what to do. Sanitariums were the cure of the day, and one of the most famous operated in Dansville, near Rochester. After consultation with Revilo, Freda entered the institution, her stay paid for by Julia. Letters from the doctor and from Freda herself refer to various conditions, such as dyspepsia and diseased lungs, although she may have had emotional problems as well. Julia despaired Freda would languish indefinitely. "She takes wine & eggs & has no water treatment. Has oil, acid & electric baths," Julia wrote about the array of remedies after more than six months. "She has so many ailments & suffers so much, she will be discouraged."[16] Julia even asked her acquaintance Clara Barton, who lived in Washington but was a periodic patient and owned a home in Dansville, to ferret out information from Freda's doctors.

Freda recovered, albeit with periodic bouts of illness, and returned to Washington in August 1881, although Julia and Freda never had the mother-daughter relationship Julia had once sought. About a year later Freda announced a plan to teach at the New York Juvenile Asylum, run by an acquaintance. "I have done all for her that I can," Julia wrote as she helped Freda pack to move to the institution in Washington Heights, above Manhattan.[17] After a rough start teaching a classroom of sixty boys, Freda acclimated, as did Julia without her. Out on her own Freda attended suffrage meetings and hosted Julia and other family members when they came to New York. Over the years she sent small money orders of five or ten dollars to Julia and especially to Frances, although Julia kept telling her not to.

Another welcome reunion in the 1870s came when Harriet Jacobs moved to Washington from Cambridge, Massachusetts. Julia and Harriet had seen each other after the Civil War, including their excursion to Alexandria together in 1867, and they corresponded. On November

1, 1877, Julia reported, "My dear old friend Mrs. Jacobs called at Office to see me!"[18] The women remained friends for the rest of their lives.

After four years of democratic self-government in Washington, in which black and white men elected a mayor and city council, Washington's white establishment grew uncomfortable with blacks' increasing political power. Congress restructured the government of the District of Columbia and in the process eliminated popular rule. Legislation in 1871 set up a governor and house of delegates for the District of Columbia (to encompass then separate Washington and Georgetown), although the real power rested with an appointed board of trade under Alexander Shepherd. Three years later Congress instituted a three-person commission it appointed, a system that remained in place until 1967.[19]

Large-scale public works projects accompanied the transition, including improved streets and sidewalks, dredging of the infamously filthy canals, and development of new parks and neighborhoods. "Within the past ten years, Washington has ceased to be a village," according to an article in *Century* in 1884. Although, sniffed the New York City–published influential magazine of the time, "whether it has yet become a city depends on the 'point of view.'"[20]

In the era characterized by Mark Twain as "the gilded age," money preoccupied everyone. Some grew fabulously wealthy, often through corrupt means, and ostentatiously displayed their wealth. While a small minority soared, others suffered. The Freedman's Savings and Trust Company, called the Freedman's Bank, got caught up in financial speculation and failed in 1874, as did banks and other businesses across the country. When Julia paid a social call to the Capitol Hill home of Frederick Douglass, who came on late in the bank's existence as president, she found him "sad & distressed. Poor & destitute men & women come to him constantly, hoping to hear favorable news of the bank."[21] Alas, all he could say was they may get some money back in a few years' time. Julia had money in the bank ($803.56, according to her own account) and eventually recovered a small portion, but many people, including former slaves finally able to acquire some savings, lost everything.

Julia regularly calculated what she called her accounts, trying to figure out how to stretch her salary. She supported Frances, who did not work when she returned to Washington, and, for many years, Freda. But she had other resources on which to draw in addition to her wages. Her father had bequeathed his house to Julia and Frances, his only two unmarried offspring at the time, and they sold it for $2,500. They owned small amounts of stock and later bought a house in Rochester to rent out, at the urging of a cousin who managed it for them—a decidedly mixed investment.

Julia also lent money when she could, a common practice of the time, according to Aron. Without credit cards or other ways to stretch money between paychecks, living beyond one's means or facing an unexpected expense often meant that one had to ask personal connections for a loan. Throughout these years Julia recorded visits by a wide range of coworkers and friends to "pay on their notes," a few dollars at a time. She earned interest, and the borrowers obtained cash to tide them over. No one seemed to question how these financial transactions might complicate relationships, especially when repayment was less than prompt.[22]

Julia managed to have enough money to travel to New York every year, often with side trips to Philadelphia, the Adirondacks in New York, Massachusetts, and other places. New York City became a regular stop, especially when her nieces Freda and Mary Julia moved there. Julia had first visited Philadelphia and the surrounding countryside back in 1864 to solicit clothing for freedmen, and she found it a welcome respite from Alexandria. She stayed in contact with several families she had first met then. In 1872 she stopped in Atlantic City, where some of these friends had a cottage. Dressed in a "gray tunic and Turkish trousers" and holding their hands, she entered the ocean for the first time in her life—"It was delightful, delicious. My first taste of salt water."[23]

In 1886 Julia faced her own financial crisis when she lost her job at the Patent Office. Rumors of dismissals flew after Grover Cleveland became the first Democrat elected to the presidency since before the Civil War. "The coming Democratic Administration will, perhaps, yes, probably change my way of living. I must contract expenses," she wrote at the end of 1884, six weeks after his election. In March 1885 Cleveland appointed Lucius Lamar, a former Confederate official, as secretary of the interior, an appointment designed to symbolize reconciliation between North and South. Julia slid through 1885: "6 dismissals today," she wrote in September, for example. "This makes us feel apprehensive, as we have no idea where it will strike next."[24]

"It" struck her on January 27, 1886, when she received a large envelope with a notice of her dismissal at the end of that month. Reported the *Evening Star* the next day, "There were fifteen employees of the Patent Office in the grades below the civil service rules discharged yesterday, to make room for applicants who are strongly recommended for office." First mentioned in the article: "Miss Julia A. Wilbur, New York," reported making $1,200 per year by then.[25] As a vestige of the patronage system, Julia remained identified with her home state, but this at least meant her home state congressman took interest.

A former supervisor with political connections named Emma Janes offered to work to reinstate Julia. Emma in turn enlisted Congressman Charles Baker from Rochester, who pressed Julia's case with Lamar and others. Weeks stretched to months, and relations with Emma grew awkward. (Emma, ironically, was one of the people who owed Julia money, in this case $100.) Julia and Frances considered renting out their front chamber, relieved when a talkative prospective tenant decided not to take it. Finally they decided to return to Rochester, where they could eke out a living and perhaps look to other family members for support. They gave notice to their Washington landlord and started to pack when Julia got word at the end of May that the reinstatement effort had succeeded.

Julia did not write about the arguments used to regain her job, and the personnel records were not found. But an article in the suffragist publication *Woman's Tribune* after her death included the following: "Never was there a more conscientious and efficient clerk, and, therefore, it was no violation of public good that led Secretary Lamar, when it was represented to him that she had nursed Confederate as well as Union soldiers to secure her reinstatement."[26] The idea that Julia would have ministered to Confederate soldiers is absurd, but maybe desperation caused her to accept that as her defense, if she knew at all that it formed part of the argument on her behalf. The country had changed in twenty years if nursing "secesh" eased the route back to the federal payroll.

For all she used to complain about the job, Julia felt greatly relieved to have it back. Julia and Frances hastily rerented the house on Eighth Street. When she returned to the Patent Building, she found her former desk occupied and accepted a transfer to another division, where she had to read aloud many hours a day. "It will be harder than my work *has been* but I mean to do it," she wrote.[27] Other dismissals did not have happy resolutions. Several friends left Washington, out of options.

Reconciliation between North and South, as illustrated by Secretary Lamar, was the order of the day. Civil War memoirs began to appear, including a book by Julia Wheelock, the Michigan relief agent who worked in Alexandria. When Julia read it, she reminisced and realized, "I would not like to part with my experience during the war."[28] But her trips to Alexandria became more those of a tourist than a former resident and relief worker. A snippet of diary written by her sister Mary recorded a trip from Michigan to Washington in 1881 that included a day in Alexandria. They visited the military cemetery, Christ Church, and the old slave pens "that we read about in the time of slavery," which sounded a long time ago rather than less than twenty years. Mary was not impressed with the place from which she had received letters from Julia during the war. Grass grew between the cobblestones on the streets, the sidewalks crumbled in disrepair, and she proclaimed she "would not live there if they would give me the whole city."[29]

Julia no longer engaged in active work to advance blacks' rights, although she maintained her cross-racial personal relationships. As she had done with abolitionist groups in the 1840s and 1850s, she became active in women's suffrage and other civic groups, not a leader but taking on roles behind the scenes.[30] She attempted to register to vote in her local ward in Washington's municipal election of 1869, as described above, and again in 1871, as part of a contingent of seventy women who went to City Hall.

In 1869 the suffrage movement split into two groups for two bitter decades. The female-only National Woman Suffrage Association (NWSA), led by Susan B. Anthony and Elizabeth Cady Stanton, pushed for immediate federal suffrage for women but regrettably took on a racist and classist tone, as its members watched with frustration when black and foreign-born men could vote when they still could not. The American Woman Suffrage Association (AWSA), led by Lucy Stone with both sexes as members, accepted the argument that black male suffrage should precede female suffrage and focused on obtaining the vote for women through state-level reform. During the split Julia cast her lot with the NWSA, perhaps because of her shared New York connection with Anthony and Stanton. She served on its committees at various times, and every year she attended its conventions in Washington. But she also criticized the group. When Louisa Butler and other black women stayed away from meetings where speakers insulted blacks from the dais, Julia wrote, "I cannot blame them. . . . They can hardly think that Mrs. Stanton & Miss Anthony are their friends from the way they speak of the Negro." She confronted Anthony about the situation: "Had good talk with her [Anthony] about suffrage matters &c., and about the reasons colored people not attending convention."[31]

By 1890 Julia admitted she was "getting tired," in contrast to Anthony, just five years younger, who "seems as enthusiastic as ever." The problem, Julia concluded, was that "women are so indifferent about suffrage."[32] But true to form, she looked ahead to brighter prospects. She copied into her diary a song her four-year-old grand-niece Inez, granddaughter of her sister Mary, belted out in church in 1891, on Christmas Eve no less:

> I'm but a little midget
> To talk to men like you;
> But listen for a minute
> And I'll tell you what is true.
> I'm going to be a woman
> And vote as well as you.
> And I'll learn while I am growing
> What *voters* ought to do.[33]

Many parishioners must have been appalled, but Julia thought it grand.

The last years of Julia Wilbur's life were hard. She and Frances continued to bicker, and they both suffered from health maladies. Julia persevered, trudging off to work. An 1891 article about the "ladies of the Patent Office" described a line of "delicate porcelains" that included "Miss Julia Wilbur, who harbors the soul of a giant and the spirit of a Savonarola in her tiny frame, the friend and teacher of the Freedman, the lover and abettor of every movement that advances women."[34] Although she often contemplated quitting, she held out for the salary, which decreased to $720 in 1894—just $20 more than she had earned twenty-five years earlier. But she accepted the demotion—"Laborers' pay—better than a *dismissal.*" When she asked about the reason for the decrease, she was told it was to free up money to pay go-getting young men.[35]

Despite the setbacks, hope for a better time marked the life of Julia Wilbur. A few years before she died, she sent a package of old illustrations to the two-year-old daughter of a cousin. She enclosed a note: "As you have seen but just *two* summers & just *two* winters, I suppose you can hardly tell how many more you would like. I have seen threesome & ten summers & winters and have liked them so well that I want a few more of them." To the young girl's mother she added, "I sometimes wonder how things will be a century hence & wish that I had been born a half century later, at least, *that I might be there to see.*"[36]

If she had had her wish and lived beyond her death in 1895, Julia would have seen racism institutionalized in the Supreme Court decision *Plessy v. Ferguson* the following year. She would have voted after ratification of the Nineteenth Amendment in 1920 and lived through two world wars. For every disappointment she would have seen progress. But if she had been born fifty years later, as she wrote her cousin, she would have entered the world in 1865, not 1815. She would have missed the struggle against slavery and the Civil War.

Epilogue

"The Burial Was at Avon"

Julia Wilbur died on June 6, 1895. In jagged handwriting, she wrote her last diary entry on April 5: "Hazy. Fine. Cold. Slept till 12, I guess & then till 2 a.m. Milk & crackers did well. Long night, miserable morning. Could hardly dress myself. No life in me till a.m. to do anything."[1]

This devoted diary keeper must have been gravely ill not to jot at least a few words after that. Her body was sent by train to New York, probably arranged by her sister Frances, and buried in the family plot in Avon that she had often visited and tended. An obituary read as follows:

PASSED TO HER REWARD

Miss Julia A. Wilbur, formerly of Avon, NY, a clerk for many years in the Patent Office, died at her home in Washington, June 6th of influenza and results, aged 80 years. Sprung from sturdy Quaker stock, she early in life took up arms against slavery. For many years she engaged in active partisan labor for the cause of freedom, and was intimately associated with all the great anti-slavery leaders and workers of the time. The breaking out of the war brought her to Washington where she labored long for the amelioration of the negroes and the relief of the sick and wounded soldiers. After the war she was appointed a clerk in the patent office, which position she held until her death. The burial was at Avon.[2]

Despite her continual worries about money, Julia left an estate worth $12,000 (about $350,000 today), all willed to Frances.

In the tradition of families sometimes not getting all the details just so, Inez Monroe Steere passed on the following about her great-aunt's life: "During the war, Miss Wilbur gave up her prosperous select school in New York and went to Washington DC to engage in voluntary service for the freedmen who thronged the city in those dark days. She had charge of the dispensing of Red Cross supplies and often went right into the battlefield to help nurse the wounded."[3] Julia's real story was extraordinary enough without the embellishment of battlefield nursing and supply deliveries.

The fate of some of the other people in these pages is noted below.

Family

Frances Hartwell and Family

After Julia's death Frances moved from Washington to the home of their sister-in-law Charlotte Wilbur Griffin in Rochester and died there on March 19, 1902. The 1880 census lists her as "divorced," but she identified herself as "widowed" in 1900. Abner Hartwell, her former husband, remarried a war widow with two small sons in 1866. They moved to Michigan to farm.

Charlotte Wilbur Griffin and Family

Julia's energetic sister-in-law Charlotte maintained her wig and ornamental hair business until her death in 1907, outliving her first husband Theodore (who died in 1858) and second husband Lewis (who died in 1884). As Julia had long ago feared, beautiful Mary Julia (the daughter of Charlotte and Theodore) had a rocky life, marrying three times, finally seemingly stable with her third husband, William Norman. Mary Julia bore a son with her first husband; the child was mostly raised by grandmother Charlotte in Rochester.

Mary Van Buskirk and Family

After leaving military service, Joseph Van Buskirk became a successful lumberman in Harrisville, Michigan. The grand home the family built on the shore of Lake Huron in the 1870s is now an inn. Joseph died in 1905 of heart failure; Mary, in 1928. Their great-grandson Douglas Steere took possession of Julia Wilbur's diaries and donated them to Haverford College, where he was a longtime philosophy professor and author. Julia would have been proud: among his many accomplishments he helped organize Quaker relief efforts in Europe after World War II.

Freda Bigelow and Family

Freda taught at the New York Juvenile Asylum at least until 1900. In 1910, age fifty-four, she lived with her two younger half-sisters, a teacher and a stenographer, on Manhattan's Upper West Side. By 1930 she was a resident at the Miriam Osborn Memorial Home, then a home for elderly indigent women, in Westchester County, from where she died in 1933.

For all Julia complained about the harshness of Freda's father and stepmother, Revilo and Nancy Bigelow, their obituaries treat them as quite mild-mannered. Revilo died in 1896 from surgery complications. After farming in Groveland (where Julia had vainly tried to visit Freda), this "kindly, unpretentious man" was a justice of the peace and a janitor in a village school. Likewise, when Nancy died in 1902, the *Livingston Republican* described her as a "kind, motherly woman and a generally esteemed citizen."[4]

Henry and Ann Wilbur

Julia's brother and sister-in-law moved around after they left the family farm in Rush. The 1870 census lists them at the Burdick Hotel in Kalamazoo, Michigan, he as a hardware clerk and she as a milliner. They returned to New York at some point before Henry's death in 1877. The *Tonawanda Evening News* reported the following on August 19, 1914: "Mrs. Henry Wilbur died in Avon last week. She owned a parrot for the past 25 years. It was her desire that the bird be killed and buried with her. It was done."

Stephen Wilbur

Julia's father died in 1872. Despite his long-standing eye issues and frail constitution, he outlived three wives. In his will he distributed two-twelfths of his assets to each of his children, except that he gave Julia and Frances other property and bequeathed nothing to Henry, who had received support from him earlier.[5] He also gave one-twelfth to his daughter-in-law Charlotte and one-twelfth to his granddaughter Freda, the next of kin of his two children, son Theodore and daughter Sarah, who preceded him in death.

Abolitionist Friends and Colleagues

Harriet Jacobs and Family

Harriet moved from Cambridge, Massachusetts, to Washington in 1877, where she lived until her death in 1897. In Cambridge she operated a boarding house that attracted Harvard students and faculty. To her delight her brother John S. Jacobs, who lived in Australia and England for decades, returned to the United States in 1873. He, his British wife, and their family moved to Cambridge, where he died suddenly in 1877, possibly leading Harriet to move.

In Washington Harriet operated two boarding houses and ran a small catering business (among other jobs) to survive over the years. Daughter Louisa cared for her mother until her death (including surgery in 1894 for breast cancer) and became matron of the National Home for the Relief of Destitute Colored Women and Children and of a residence hall at Howard University. At age seventy-five, Louisa moved north to become a companion to the daughter of Cornelia Willis, the woman who had helped Harriet gain legal freed status in the 1850s. Harriet, John S., and Louisa Jacobs are buried together at Mount Auburn Cemetery in Cambridge. A fourth plot, for Harriet's son Joseph, who disappeared from their lives after moving to Australia, remains empty.

Anna Barnes

The former secretary of the Rochester Ladies' Anti-Slavery Society was a niece of Lucretia Mott, the famed Philadelphia Quaker. Her father Silas was a mapmaker nationally known for designing a "terrestrial globe" and was also active in Rochester abolition circles. Widowed after a brief marriage in the 1840s, Anna described herself in an 1888 passport application, at age sixty-four, as five feet, four inches, with a full face, small nose, and gray hair. She stated she needed the document to travel in Europe and parts of Asia and Africa. By then she lived with family members in Toledo, Ohio.

Maria Porter

The former treasurer of the Rochester Ladies' Anti-Slavery Society remained in Rochester, never marrying, a pillar of the community when she died in 1896. Her obituary in the *Rochester Union and*

Advertiser included the following: "Only a few weeks ago an aged colored woman named Harriet Tubman, who used to be a professional smuggler of slaves from the south, called upon Miss Porter and a pleasant time was spent recalling the time when she used to stop at her house with fugitives in charge."[6]

Lucy Colman

Colman, twice widowed and left financially unstable, taught in Rochester in the 1850s, then lectured against slavery and for women's rights. When her daughter died in 1862 while attending the New England Medical College, Frederick Douglass officiated at a memorial ceremony. Colman accompanied Sojourner Truth to meet Abraham Lincoln in 1864 and later recounted that he had treated the African American woman disrespectfully (something Truth did not state herself). Colman lived in Syracuse with a sister after the war, involved in anti-religion, freethinking circles. She published her autobiography in 1891 and died in 1906.

Amy Post

A creator of the Western New York Anti-Slavery Society, pioneer at Seneca Falls in 1848, and early advocate for Harriet Jacobs to write her autobiography, Post received accolades from Rochester in the later years of her life. In 1882 the city publicly celebrated her eightieth birthday, seven years before she died. A historical marker notes the homesite on Rochester's Plymouth Avenue (then 36 Sophia Street) where she and her husband Isaac welcomed so many people.

Susan B. Anthony

Temperance-turned-abolition-and-women's-rights leader Anthony had faith that women's suffrage would come, famously proclaiming, "Failure is impossible" on her eighty-sixth birthday in 1906.[7] She died shortly afterward, fourteen years before passage of the Nineteenth Amendment, which became known as the Susan B. Anthony Amendment. Her home in Rochester, New York, is open to the public.

Frederick Douglass

Douglass remained a leading civil rights leader and public figure until his death in February 1895. In 1872 a suspicious fire that destroyed his

Rochester home led him to move his family permanently to Washington. His first wife, Anna, died in 1882; his second marriage, to Helen Pitts in 1884, was controversial because of her age (she was about twenty years younger than he) but mostly because of her race (white). In his later years Douglass served as U.S. marshal and recorder of deeds for the District of Columbia and as minister-general to Haiti, among other positions. On the day he collapsed and died, he had attended the convention of the National American Woman Suffrage Association. His two homes in Washington are open to the public.

Julia Griffiths Crofts

The British woman who took Rochester by storm returned to England in 1855. She married Rev. Henry O. Crofts in 1859 and remained an active abolitionist. After her husband died, she ran a girls' boarding school, then served as a governess, where her independent views caused her to lose her job. Financial hardship resulted. In 1886 Frederick and Helen Douglass visited Crofts in England, something she had long hoped for. She died in 1895, the same year as Julia Wilbur and Frederick Douglass.

Alexandria Military and Civilians

John Slough

The military governor of Alexandria was appointed chief justice of New Mexico territory after the war. In 1868 an argument with a member of the Territorial Senate escalated, and the other man shot Slough. According to one Ohio news report, harkening back to his days as a combative state legislator, "He was of a quarrelsome disposition, had been in 'hot water' at Santa Fe for some weeks, quarreled with the Court, with the Legislature, and has met the fate of his perverseness."[8] Two years later Slough's widow successfully received $5,000 from an accident insurance policy.

John C. Wyman

The first provost marshal whom Julia Wilbur encountered in Alexandria remained in the military through May 1865. He later recounted that he accompanied Lincoln's casket on its train journey to Illinois, describing it as "attending a funeral all the time for three weeks."[9]

He remained active in the Republican Party and was elected to the Rhode Island General Assembly in the 1880s from the aptly named town of Lincoln. He married social activist and author Lillie Buffum Chace, who grew up in a family that harbored escaping slaves before the war and who helped preserve records of the abolitionist movement.

H. H. Wells

The provost marshal who replaced Wyman in February 1863 became provost marshal of general defenses south of the Potomac in 1865. He was involved in the hunt for John Wilkes Booth and the interrogation of his co-conspirators. He served for two years as military reconstruction governor of Virginia in Richmond, then U.S. attorney for eastern Virginia, with his son Henry Jr. as assistant. In 1878 father and son formed their own law firm in Washington. An indication of their success is that noted architect Adolf Cluss designed the son's home at 428–430 M St. NW.

Albert Gladwin

After the war the former superintendent of contrabands was serving in Manchester, across the river from Richmond, when Julia and Harriet saw him. At some point afterward the American Baptist Publication Association sent him to Laramie, Wyoming Territory, possibly as a missionary to Indians. He died there in 1869 at age fifty-four, and his body was returned to his home state of Connecticut for burial. The November 16, 1871, *Alexandria Gazette* published a long list of unclaimed letters in the post office, including one addressed to him.

George Seaton

Seaton, Julia's first landlord in Alexandria, illustrates the path some free black men took after the Civil War until Jim Crow reigned in Virginia and elsewhere. A builder and entrepreneur, he was one of the first African American members of the Virginia General Assembly and served on the grand jury that indicted Jefferson Davis for treason. In 1866 he moved from the house on St. Asaph Street (where Julia stayed) to a larger one nearby on South Royal Street. By the mid-1870s he had suffered serious health and financial losses, and he died, with his family surrounding him, in 1881.

Chauncey Leonard

The L'Ouverture Hospital chaplain, who possibly organized the effort to gain proper burials for U.S. Colored Troops, contracted dysentery in 1865 in Alexandria. He fought for a pension for many years, although his ability to work as a minister in Pennsylvania, Massachusetts, and Rhode Island may have hampered his success. In 1889 at a national encampment of the Grand Army of the Republic, the large group of Union veterans, the Rhode Island delegation nominated Leonard to serve as chaplain-in-chief. He died in 1892 in Providence.

Edwin Bentley

Bentley, the L'Ouverture Hospital's surgeon in charge, remained in the army, concurrently serving as physician and professor, until the 1880s. He served in Washington, where he became Howard University's first professor of anatomy, and northern California. After being assigned to Little Rock in 1878, he helped found the University of Arkansas's School of Medicine. In 1869 body parts were found in his former residence in Connecticut that were traced to the fact that during the war, Bentley had sent home "numerous amputated limbs where the operation possessed a scientific interest."[10]

John Bigelow

The surgeon and a partner purchased Clermont, the very property that had housed the smallpox hospital where Bigelow had attempted to move healthy orphans, for a bargain-basement price. When they tried to take possession of it in 1865, they found the main house had burned to the ground. The original owner's son successfully sought legal redress to return Clermont to his family. Bigelow noted all he received from his venture was "a costly and unsuccessful litigation."[11]

Places

More than 150 years after the Civil War, *Alexandria, Virginia*, and *Rochester, New York*, take pride in their places in U.S. history. They feature many historic sites, historical markers, and other connections to the past. Both have dealt with economic and social change over the years, including problems exacerbated by inequality and injustice. Yet through the streets of Old Town Alexandria or across Rochester's Genesee River bridges, the spirit and bravery of nineteenth-century reformers like Julia Wilbur live on.

ACKNOWLEDGMENTS

To help me make sense of things and keep me on track, I have many people to thank, beginning with colleagues at Alexandria Archaeology. Former city archaeologists Pamela Cressey and Francine Bromberg provided initial guidance, background information, and excitement about my discoveries. Current staff and volunteers have been equally enthusiastic.

The Quaker & Special Collections staff at Haverford welcomed me when I visited and quickly responded when I emailed questions. Current curators Sarah Horowitz and Mary Crauderueff and former curators Diana Franzuhoff Peterson and Ann Upton tend a well-organized space for research.

After reading about Rochester from afar, I gained so much more from walking around and researching at close range. Through a fortuitous set of circumstances (*bshert* in Yiddish), the family of the Livingston County deputy historian owns the property that includes the Wilburs' farmhouse, still standing. Great thanks to Holly Watson and Clara Mulligan, who had documented the history of their farm for placement on the National Register, for letting me visit and sharing many useful nuggets of information. Livingston County historian Amie Alden, Rush Town historian Susan Mee, Avon historian Maureen Kingston, Avon Historical Society secretary Joan Reid, Rochester historian Christine Ridarsky, and the helpful staff in the Rochester Public Library also pointed me to useful information about the area's rich past. Lori Birrell and Melinda Wallington guided me through the collections at the University of Rochester. Ed Daniels, an attorney at McConville Considine Cooman and Morin PC, saw me loitering outside the Talman Building in downtown Rochester on a Friday evening at dusk. He connected me to his colleague Kevin Cooman, who shared information about the place where Frederick Douglass published the *North Star* and where their law firm is headquartered. Thanks also to Ruth Thaler-Carter for inviting me to speak at a conference that brought me to upstate New York in fall of 2015.

Monroe and Livingston Counties are justifiably proud of their history, as these people exemplify.

Research staff at the Library of Congress, National Archives in Washington and College Park, Local History/Washingtonia Room in the District of Columbia Public Library, Virginia Historical Society, and Library of Virginia were also generous with their time and expertise, especially as I ventured into new areas of inquiry for me, such as Richmond right after the Civil War. Staff in the Office of Historic Alexandria and the Local History and Special Collections at the Alexandria Public Library, especially Julia Downie, also provided ideas and support. Behind the scenes, staff members in the Alexandria, Arlington, and Fairfax library systems transferred many books from one branch to another for my convenience.

The William Clements Library at the University of Michigan holds the files of the Rochester Ladies' Anti-Slavery Society, including annual reports and letters that Julia Wilbur wrote. My thanks to the staff, including curator Cheney Schopieray and reference specialist Janet Bloom, for tending and sharing these valuable papers with me and many other researchers.

When I ventured to the Friends Historical Library at Swarthmore College, Chris Densmore helped me make best use of limited time. Via phone and email, John McClure from the Virginia Historical Society, Janet Winfield from the American Baptist Historical Society, Dawn Srock from the Office of the Niagara County Clerk, Nancy Horan from the New York State Library, Nancy Pope from the National Postal Museum, and Heather Oswald from Emory University (and others I may have inadvertently omitted) provided just-in-time information on many topics.

I particularly value meeting two descendants of the Wilbur family, both proud of their ancestor and generous in sharing what they have gathered. From Charles Lenhart, a descendant of Julia's uncle, I learned so much—from the genealogy of the family to background about social and religious movements in nineteenth-century upstate New York. His map took me right to the Wilbur family graves in the sprawling Avon Cemetery. He also connected me with historians Nancy Hewitt and Judith Wellman, whose breadth of knowledge was matched by their encouragement of my project. Kevin West, a descendant of Julia's sister Elizabeth, told me (among other tidbits) about the death wish of Julia's sister-in-law Ann, who requested the murder of, and co-burial with, her pet parrot. Later in my project, Josh Anderson, descendant of Mary, generously shared family lore, too.

Many people reviewed all or parts of my manuscript and pointed out errors of fact, interpretation, or plain old confusion. My gratitude to Mary Lynn Bayliss, Gordon Berg, Mary Collins, Cathy Curtis, Audrey Davis, Carol Faulkner, Sharon Hannon, Nancy Hewitt, Scott Korb, Charles Lenhart, Kate Masur, Wally Owen, Ted Pulliam, and Jean Fagan Yellin. Some I knew, but others I contacted out of the blue, and I appreciate their taking time from their own work to look at mine. Any remaining errors or obfuscations are my fault, not theirs. Others who provided valuable background include Char McCargo Bah, Tim Dennee, Peggy Harlow, Anita Henderson, Charles Joyce, Molly Kerr, Michelle Krowl, Chandra Manning, Lillian Patterson, Peggy Wagner, and Paul Watson.

Appreciation goes to Sharon Hannon, with whom I set writing goals and reported progress each month, a favor I expect to repay soon. My friend Diane Kehlenbrink linked me with her sister Leslie Higgins, who hosted me at her family's home when I researched at Haverford. Ron and Wesley Ann Godard hosted me in Richmond, and MacClurg Vivian did so in Rochester, providing hospitality and the lay of the land.

While I researched, I found giving presentations great opportunities because people's interest confirmed Julia Wilbur "deserved" a book and because their questions guided me in what to include or not. Thanks go to the Alexandria Black History Museum, Alexandria Historical Society, Alexandria Library, Society for Women and the Civil War, Surratt House, and Patrick Henry Library in Fairfax County, Virginia, among others.

Ruth Reeder, Jen Barker, and Rebecca Siegal at Alexandria Archaeology helped get the word out and organize what became known as the "Julia Wilbur Volunteers," who transcribed and proofread the second set of diaries. They included Lori Arbuckle, Gale Carter (and her students at East Chicago High School), Melissa Carter,

Laci Chelette, Tom D'Amore, Christopher Goodwin, Jill Grinsted, Tom Gross, Janet Hughes, Maureen Lauran, Donna Martin, Wendy Miervaldis, Patty Morison, Mary Jane Nugent, Kim Ormiston, Trudy Pearson, Janet Penn, Mary Ray, Diane Riker, Kelly Rooney, Elizabeth Schneider, Cindy Slaton, Rachel Smith, Jeanne Springman, Karen White, and Christina Wingate.

A special note of thanks to Donna Martin, who became almost as, or even as, obsessed with Julia as I have been and took on much additional transcribing and proofreading. Anna Lynch proofread the pocket diary transcriptions, shared information (such as on early African American schools), and let me join her on several research trips to the city clerk's office.

Fellow writers Joanne Lozar Glenn, Kaaren Christopherson, Beth Kalikoff, the Monday-by-Midnight group, and many members of the Freelance Brunch Bunch empathized with my bouts of writing angst. Thanks to Martha McGloin, who came from Toronto to Rochester, fitting her schedule to accommodate mine, and to Rayna Aylward, Linda Cahn, Joan Ehrlich, Nancy Light, Merianne Liteman, Chira Rosen, Susan Ruberry, and the Havurah, Mahj, and Ramparts groups, among many friends who cheered me on. I make my living as a freelance writer and editor, and several long-standing clients accommodated their schedules to meet mine. I appreciate their flexibility, knowing they have their own deadlines to meet.

My shift to biographer was helped by a 2014 workshop at the Writer's Center in Bethesda, Maryland, taught by Ken Ackerman (although he would hate this passive-voice sentence). Ken pushed our small group to refine our ideas to tell a compelling story, an aim that I hope I have achieved. He also encouraged us to attend an annual conference sponsored by the Washington Independent Review of Books, where I met agent Roger Williams. After I made my pitch, I peeked across the table to his notebook, where he checked "agent-ready" next to my name. Even if we hadn't worked together, his little checkmark validated me tremendously. Since then Roger has helped me navigate the proposal and publication process, while continuing to ask what I plan to write next.

When I joined the Washington Biographers Group and the Biographers International Organization (BIO), I learned from the tops in the field, through formal presentations and informal conversations. Also through BIO I met fellow researcher and writer Christina Karas. Luckily for me, Christina moved from Massachusetts to Michigan and helped me access the Rochester Ladies' Anti-Slavery Society materials at the Clements Library in Ann Arbor.

I have greatly enjoyed working with the editors and other staff at Potomac Books/University of Nebraska Press, from their initial enthusiasm for my proposal to this final product. Bojana Ristich carefully edited my manuscript, delving into the details while keeping the big picture in mind.

Thanks go to my cousin Jerome Fisher, an ophthalmologist who offered a retrospective diagnosis of Stephen Wilbur's eye problems. My sister and brother-in-law Debra and Robert Ballen and my sons, Zack and Jacob, patiently heard about "my person" (i.e., Julia) whenever any remotely relevant topic came up. As proof that the best way to figure out how to explain something is to tell it to your mother, Joyce Tarnapol, my mother, adeptly listened and asked questions. Finally, my husband, Bill, offered the time, space, and never-ending enthusiasm and support to turn my vaguely formed intention into action.

APPENDIX

Abbreviated Wilbur Family History

Julia Wilbur's parents: Mary Lapham (1790–1834) and Stephen Wilbur (1787–1872), married in 1810; Stephen married Sally Rundell Tanner (1788–1857) in 1836 and Laura Winegar (1799–1870) in 1859[1]

Angeline Wilbur (1812–91); married Alfred Van Wagoner (~1815–81) in 1833

    Three sons died in early childhood, all in 1842

    Surviving son Theodore (1842–1927); married with six children

Elizabeth Wilbur (1812–79); married Morgan Van Wagoner (1809–90) in 1833

    Ten children (one died in infancy)

Julia Wilbur (1815–95)

Theodore Wilbur (1817–58); married Charlotte Sears (1829–1907) in 1846; Charlotte married Lewis Griffin (~1825–84) in 1860

    Theodore (1850–1913); unmarried

    Mary Julia (1848–1923); married William Milstead (1840–1930) in 1864, John Hawley (1848–73) in 1869, and William Norman (?–1910) in 1883; one son with first husband

Frances (1819–1902); married Abner Hartwell (1819–1905) in 1839; separated and/or divorced ~1864

    No children; Abner remarried in 1866 and raised two stepsons

Henry (1821–77); married Ann Austin (1827–1914) in 1846

    No known children

Sarah (1824–58); married Revilo Bigelow (1820–98) in 1855

    Revilo married Nancy Sinclair Haynes (1824–1902) in 1859 and had two daughters

Alfreda (Freda) (1856–1933); unmarried

Sarah (1858)

William Penn (1826–1907); married Henrietta Fletcher (1838–80) in 1858

Four children

Flora Elma, known as Ella (1828–1913); married Joseph Albertson (1826–99) in 1856

No known children

Mary (1834–1926); married Joseph Van Buskirk (1837–1905) in 1857

Minnie (1858–1930); four children; grandmother of Douglas Steere

Stewart (1861–1913)

NOTES

Prologue

1. *Alexandria Gazette* (hereafter *Gazette*), April 15, 1865.

2. Julia Wilbur Large Diary (hereafter JWLD), April 15, 1865, MC.1158, Quaker & Special Collections, Haverford College (hereafter Haverford).

3. *Gazette*, April 17, 1865.

4. JWLD, April 16, 1865.

5. JWLD, April 15, 1865.

6. JWLD, April 16, 1865.

7. *Gazette*, April 17, 1865.

8. JWLD, April 18, 1865.

9. Procession described in Hodes, *Mourning Lincoln*, 146; JWLD, April 19 and 20, 1865.

10. JWLD, April 21, 1865.

11. In her *Reminiscences*, Colman does not mention the hair. She does recount she received a piece of the coffin and its inside lining, which she gave away, as well as one of Lincoln's nightshirts, given to her by Mrs. Lincoln—in Colman's opinion, "a rather strange article to give one as a keepsake, but Mrs. Lincoln was a very strange woman" (77).

12. Julia Wilbur to Mary Van Buskirk, April 26, 1865, MC.1158, Haverford.

13. JWLD, June 4, 1851.

14. Thirteenth Annual Report of the Rochester Ladies' Anti-Slavery Society, 24, RLASS papers, University of Michigan, William L. Clements Library (hereafter UM).

1. "A Peculiar Period"

1. Quoted in May, "A University Dream That Failed," 160.

2. Quoted in Biddle, *Captain Hall in America*, 97.

3. Offices of the Board of Education, "A History of the Public Schools of Rochester, New York," 8–9.

4. P. Smith, *General History of Duchess County*, 300.

5. Handwritten notes by Julia Wilbur, dated 1883, in Series I, Box 2, Douglas V. and Dorothy M. Steere papers, HC.Coll.1174, Haverford.

6. JWLD, July 12, 1851.

7. JWLD, March 31, 1848.

8. JWLD, August 15, 1845.

9. JWLD, May 18, 1850. In 1851 abolitionist and women's rights leader Abby Kelley Foster stated, "Women revolt at the idea of marrying for the sake of a home, for the sake of a support—of marrying the purse instead of the man." Reality often allowed no option (http://www.wwhp.org/Resources/WomansRights/akfoster_1851.html).

10. JWLD, March 31, 1848.

11. Advertised in Rochester Business Directory, 1857, 71; available online through the Central Library of Rochester and Monroe County, http://www3.libraryweb .org/lh.aspx?id=1095.

12. JWLD, October 25, 1845.

13. Quoted in McElroy, "Social Control and Romantic Reform," 24. While evangelism caught hold, it should be noted that Quakers, Unitarians, and Catholics also flourished without conversion or spiritual rebirth.

14. According to Wellman ("Crossing over Cross"), Finney used the term "burned district" in his 1876 memoir—that is, after his preaching there was no "fuel" left in the form of unconverted individuals. Wellman explains that historian Whitney Cross adapted the term "burned-over district" to describe the area in this time period, and it has become widespread.

15. JWLD, November 1, 1844. The aftermath became known as "the Great Disappointment."

16. JWLD, September 26, 1847.

17. Pegram, *Battling Demon Rum*, 10, citing historian W. J. Rorabaugh.

18. JWLD, July 21, 1844.

19. Quoted in Barry, *Susan B. Anthony*, 51.

20. Quoted in Barry, *Susan B. Anthony*, 68. The convention language went too far for many of the women attendees, who were more interested in temperance than women's rights.

21. See Hewitt, *Women's Activism and Social Change*, 130–35, for background on these events.

22. *New York Daily Tribune*, August 10, 1857. A history of the New York State Teachers Association, published in 1883, attributes introduction of the two resolutions to Anthony.

23. Julia Wilbur Journal Briefs (hereafter JWJB), 24. In the 1880s Julia went through her old diaries to excerpt noteworthy entries that she called "Journal Briefs." They are on legal-sized sheets of paper and span 1844 to 1862. Julia numbered the top of each page, cited here for easier retrieval.

2. "Slavery Is an Evil"

1. Lampe, *Frederick Douglass*, 276.

2. Mary Fitzhugh Talman and two sisters were involved in abolitionism themselves and through marriage to prominent abolitionists. Her sister Ann married Gerrit Smith; sister Elizabeth married James Birney. The Talman Building stands in downtown Rochester.

3. JWLD, July 23, 1845.

4. *Rochester Daily Advertiser*, July 25, 1845.

5. Hewitt, *Women's Activism and Social Change*, 22

6. Fish Family Papers, 1770–1915, A.F53, Department of Rare Books, Special Collections, and Preservation, University of Rochester, River Campus Libraries (hereafter UR).

7. Patenaude, "Bound by Pride and Prejudice," table 1.

8. Slavery was legal in New York State until 1827. Most notably, Sojourner Truth was born into slavery in Ulster County circa 1797.

9. Cohen, "Clip Not Her Wings," 11.

10. *Rochester Daily Democrat*, September 24, 1835.

11. For the text of Walker's *Appeal*, see http://www.pbs.org/wgbh/aia/part4/4h2931t .html. For Garrison, see Mayer, *All on Fire*, xv.

12. JWLD, May 11, 1852.

13. U.S. Census Bureau, Statistics of Slaves, http://www2.census.gov/prod2/decennial /documents/00165897ch14.pdf.

14. Second Annual Meeting of the Western New York Anti-Slavery Society, February 5–6, 1845; reported in *National Anti-Slavery Standard*, March 6, 1845.

15. Parker, *Rochester*, 258.

16. F. Douglass to Amy Post, April 28, 1846, Post Family Papers Project, UR.

17. Quoted in Parker, *Rochester*, 257.

18. *North Star*, April 20, 1849.

19. JWLD, February 18, 1848; *North Star*, March 9, 1849, 2. The article, "a brief account of the events, labors, and impressions connected with the lecturing tour of the last two weeks," does not include a description of East Avon. Douglass does describe an unfriendly reception in Avon on February 5.

20. Fifth Annual Meeting of the Western New York Anti-Slavery Society; reported in *North Star*, December 29, 1848.

21. JWLD, May 19, 1849.

22. JWLD, June 17, 1849.

23. JWLD, June 25, 1849.

24. JWLD, July 20, 1849.

25. "Colored School Meeting," *North Star*, December 21, 1849.

26. *North Star*, May 15, 1851.

27. Quoted in Cohen, "Clip Not Her Wings," 61.

28. In *Women's Activism and Social Change*, historian Nancy Hewitt distinguishes between the "ultrist" or more radical orientation of the WNYASS versus the "perfectionist" or more moderate leanings of the RLASS.

29. J. Griffiths to Gerrit Smith, quoted in Hewitt, *Women's Activism and Social Change*, 150.

30. Frederick Douglass to Mrs. S. D. Porter, March 27, 1852; reprinted in the First Report of the Rochester Ladies' Anti-Slavery Society, RLASS papers, UM.

31. JWLD, June 4, 1852.

32. Constitution of the Rochester Ladies' Anti-Slavery Society.

33. Second Report of the Rochester Ladies' Anti-Slavery Society, 1.

34. Fourth Annual Report of the Rochester Ladies' Anti-Slavery Society, 2.

35. Letter from J. Griffiths to William Lloyd Garrison, August 5, 1852. Available through Internet Archive, http://archive.org/details/lettertomydearsioogrif.

36. J. Griffiths to W. L. Garrison, August 5, 1852. Available through Internet Archive, http://archive.org/details/lettertomydearsioogrif.

37. Treasurer's Report, Eighth Annual Report of the Rochester Ladies' Anti-Slavery Society, 3.

38. Julia Griffiths to Amy Post, October 16, 1852, Post Family Papers Project, UR.

39. JWLD, September 30, 1853.

40. JWLD, June 30, 1855.

41. JWLD, February 8, 1856.

42. Two years later Julia Griffiths was not listed as an RLASS officer. Wilbur was corresponding secretary, and Anna Cornell Barnes was recording secretary. Later Barnes was Wilbur's main point of contact when she worked in Alexandria.

43. JWLD, June 4, 1852.

44. Cohen, "Clip Not Her Wings," 81.

45. JWLD, March 1, 1856.

46. W. Nell to Amy Post, April 12, 1856, Post Family Papers Project, UR.

47. JWLD, November 21, 1857.

48. JWLD, May 9, 1858.

3. "My Plans Overthrown"

1. JWLD, June 30, 1855.

2. JWLD, May 9, 1858.

3. Julia Wilbur Pocket Diary (hereafter JWPD), May 3, 1858.

4. JWLD, July 2, 1859.

5. Quoted in "Third Presbyterian Active in Abolition," *Rochester Democrat and Chronicle*, June 7, 2010.

6. JWJB, 29.

7. JWLD, September 11, 1858.

8. The overall mortality rate in Rochester in 1850 was 145 infant deaths per 1,000 live births, compared to 7 per 1,000 today. Figure for 1850 cited in Higgins et al., "The Poor in the Mid-Nineteenth-Century Northeastern United States," 167; current figure (higher than the national average) from "Gone Too Soon," *Rochester Democrat and Chronicle*, September 23, 2012.

9. JWLD, May 9, 1858.

10. JWPD, July 18, 1859.

11. JWPD, August 26, 1859.

12. JWLD, September 11, 1859.

13. JWJB, 34.

14. JWJB, 35.

15. JWLD, December 31, 1859.

16. JWLD, January 10, 1860.

17. JWLD, March 7, 1860.

18. JWLD, March 8, 1860.

19. JWLD, March 15, 1860.

20. JWLD, July 18, 1860.

21. JWLD, April 1, 1860.

22. JWLD, June 21, 1858, and May 9, 1859.

23. As sociologist Claude Fischer notes, "Typically, an elite of merchants, lawyers, doctors, manufacturers, financiers, and, in the countryside, farmers with large holdings formed the leading circles in American communities. . . . But those images hide our view of most rural and small-town Americans, who were transient" (*Made in America*, 123).

24. JWLD, October 1, 1860.

25. JWLD, July 25, 1860. See also http://www.syracuseuniversitypress.syr.edu /spring-2009/irish-bridget.html.

26. JWLD, April 17, 1860.

27. U.S. Federal Census, 1860, on Ancestry.com.

4. "At Alexandria"

1. *Gazette*, October 20, 1859.

2. Figures from the 1860 census; reprinted in Provine, *Alexandria County, Free Negro Register*. Statewide, slaves outnumbered free blacks almost ten to one—five hundred thousand slaves and fifty-eight thousand free blacks out of a total of about 1.6 million in the most populous state in what became the Confederacy the following year.

3. "Letter to the Wife of John Brown," November 23, 1859, *Weekly Anglo-African*, December 17, 1859; in Quarles, *Blacks on John Brown*, 16–19.

4. *Gazette*, April 3, 1852.

5. *Gazette*, November 7, 1859.

6. Washington's comments reprinted in W. F. Smith and Miller, *A Seaport Saga*, 15–17.

7. A replica of the torn-down house at 508 Cameron Street was built in the 1960s. Mick Fleetwood of the band Fleetwood Mac rented it in the 1990s. It remains a private residence.

8. Marquis de Chastellux, *Travels in North America*, vol. 3, *1780–1782*; in *Travelers' Accounts of the Historic Alexandria Waterfront (1624–1900)*, 20.

9. Brissot de Warville, *Nouveau voyage dans les États-Unis*; in *Travelers' Accounts of the Historic Alexandria Waterfront (1624–1900)*, 35.

10. Quoted in *Virginia Gazette and Alexandria Advertiser*, April 21, 1791; in T. M. Miller, *Pen Portraits*, 38.

11. Observer's account from 1827 in Artemel, Crowell, and Parker, *The Alexandria Slave Pen*, 26–27.

12. Observer's account from 1835 in Artemel, Crowell, and Parker, *The Alexandria Slave Pen*, 32–33.

13. This agent, George Kephart, partnered with James Birch and also sold part of the property to Charles Price. These transactions explain the sign "Price, Birch and Co., Dealers in Slaves," which remained painted on the brick front in the 1860s. It shows up in several iconic pictures taken during the Civil War. A portion of the

Franklin and Armfield establishment stands at 1315 Duke Street, where it houses the Northern Virginia Urban League and Freedom House Museum. Bruin's building, 1707 Duke Street, houses a real estate agency and has a historical marker and a statue of Mary and Emily Edmonson.

14. Deyle, *Carry Me Back*, 4.

15. Quoted in Bedell, "Archaeology of the Bruin Slave Jail," 47.

16. Quoted in Pulliam, "The Civil War Comes to Duke Street," 31.

17. Manumission is the formal emancipation of an enslaved person by the slave owner.

18. Quoted in Carothers, *Quakers Living in the Lion's Mouth*, 134.

19. *Alexandria Gazette*, September 28, 1860.

5. "Civil War Is Upon Us"

1. Lincoln received 975 votes more than his opponents out of a total of 7,893 in Rochester; most Republicans had earlier supported William Seward, New York's governor, as their candidate for the nomination. Also a state amendment that would have granted state suffrage to all African American men, removing a property requirement set only for blacks, lost in the city by 1,629 votes (McKelvey, "Rochester's Part in the Civil War," 1961).

2. JWLD, November 6, 1860.

3. Douglass's reaction reported by David Blight, *New York Times Opinionator*, December 28, 2010; *Gazette*, December 21, 1860.

4. JWLD, December 22, 1860.

5. JWLD, December 30, 1860.

6. Harper, *The Life and Work of Susan B. Anthony*, 1:210–11.

7. *Rochester Union and Advertiser*, January 12, 1861.

8. JWLD, March 8, 1861.

9. JWLD, March 11, 1861.

10. JWLD, March 12, 1861.

11. JWLD, March 13, 1861.

12. *Gazette*, November 15, 1860. Bell received 911 votes in the city of Alexandria. Countywide (to include current-day Arlington) Lincoln received 16 votes and Bell 1,012. Across the state Bell and pro-slavery John Breckinridge were neck and neck, with about 44 percent each; Lincoln received about 1 percent of the total votes cast in Virginia.

13. Described in the memoirs of Edgar Warfield, one of the two organizers (*Manassas to Appomattox*).

14. Robertson, *Civil War Virginia*, 15.

15. New Orleans was by far the largest Southern city, with a population of about 168,000. Within the top ten, with far smaller populations, were Richmond, Petersburg, Norfolk, and Wheeling (which was in Virginia before the formation of West Virginia the following year).

16. Quoted in Robertson, *Civil War Virginia*, 13.

17. Warfield, *Manassas to Appomattox*, 23.

18. For a fuller description, see McPherson, *Battle Cry of Freedom*, and Goodheart, *1861*.

19. *Gazette*, April 18, 1861.

20. *Washington Herald*, as reported in *Gazette*, May 16, 1861.

21. "The Town Is Took," John Ogden to Mary P. Ogden, in *Alexandria History*, 10, Alexandria Historical Society, http://www.alexandriahistorical.org/Resources /Documents/1981_AlexHistory.pdf.

22. Diary of Judith Brockenbrough McGuire; in Davis and Robertson, *Virginia at War 1861*, 163.

23. *Life of James W. Jackson*, 13.

24. "Marshall House Flag," New York State Military Museum and Veterans' Research Center, http://dmna.ny.gov/historic/btlflags/other/CSA_MHF1995.3033 .htm.

25. JWLD, April 19, 1861.

26. McKelvey, "Rochester's Part in the Civil War"; *Rochester Union and Advertiser*, April 19, 1861; *Democrat and American*, April 19, 1861.

27. JWLD, April 20, 1861.

28. JWLD, May 3, 1861.

29. JWLD, April 7, 1861.

30. JWLD, May 2, 1861.

31. "The Town Is Took," John Ogden to Mary P. Ogden, in *Alexandria History*, 10.

32. *Harper's Weekly*, June 8, 1861.

33. JWPD, May 29, 1861; Judith McGuire diary, May 25, 1861, in Davis and Robertson, *Virginia at War 1861*, 169; Henry Whittington diary, May 24, 1861, original at Alexandria Public Library, Local History/Special Collections.

34. "Church Records Speak," Lancaster at War, November 20, 2014, http://www .lancasteratwar.com/2014/11/church-records-speak-lancasters.html.

35. R. Wilson, *Mathew Brady*, 87.

36. As reported in Poland, *The Glories of War*, 23.

37. The cemetery still exists, but Jackson's body was disinterred and reburied with his wife's elsewhere in Fairfax County.

38. Quoted in U.S. War Department, *The War of the Rebellion*, series 1, vol. 2, ch. 9, 41. The news about Ellsworth was already known.

39. Henry Whittington diary, May 25, 1861, Alexandria Public Library, Local History/Special Collections.

40. Special dispatch to the *New York Tribune*; reprinted in *Rochester Union and Advertiser*, May 25, 1861.

6. "My Way Seems Clear to Go"

1. JWLD, May 9, 1861.

2. JWLD, July 23, 1861.

3. Quoted in Barnes, "Rochester's Congressmen Part I," 19.

4. JWLD, July 30, 1861.

5. JWLD, June 3, 1861.

6. Barham, *Descriptions of Niagara*, 20.

7. JWLD, August 26, 1861.

8. JWLD, September 20, 1861; History of Old Fort Niagara, http://www.oldfort niagara.org/history.

9. JWLD, September 1, 1861.

10. By the end of the Civil War Lincoln had proclaimed two other fast days, while Jefferson Davis called for a total of ten, according to Frank, *The World of the Civil War*, 570.

11. JWLD, September 26 and October 1, 1861.

12. JWLD, August 1, 1861. Henry Wise was the governor of Virginia at the time of the John Brown raid in Harpers Ferry. In part because of Wise's feuding with another Southern general, western Virginia fell into Union hands. Florence was one of Julia's nieces, the daughter of her brother William Penn.

13. Quoted in "The Duties of Women in the Present Crisis."

14. JWLD, November 28, 1861.

15. JWLD, November 28, 1861.

16. JWLD, January 1, 1862.

17. Estimates from Lehrman Institute, http://www.mrlincolnandfreedom.org /inside.asp?ID=30&subjectID=3.

18. Historian Thavolia Glymph, "'This Species of Property,'" refers to contraband-*ists* in recognition of their taking action; Glymph's is one example of many in which more recent historians have reconsidered the movement from slavery to freedom.

19. From a January 14, 1862, speech; full text in University of Rochester Frederick Douglass Project, http://rbscp.lib.rochester.edu/4381.

20. Wagner, Gallagher, and Finkelman, *Library of Congress Civil War Desk Reference*, 11. In 1831 Virginia prohibited the teaching of "slaves, free negroes, or mulattoes to read or write." As a free black, Mary Chase may have been educated in a hidden school in Alexandria or Washington.

21. "Mission to the Freed 'Contrabands' at Fortress Monroe, VA."

22. JWLD, January 1 and 12, 1862.

23. JWLD, February 27, 1862.

24. JWLD, February 11, 1862.

25. For context about a "good death," see Faust, *This Republic of Suffering*, 6–31.

26. JWLD, March 12, 1862.

27. JWLD, May 28, 1861.

28. JWLD, August 27, 1862.

29. Quoted in Scott, *Forgotten Valor*, 349.

30. JWLD, June 16, 20, and 22, 1862.

31. JWLD, July 9, 1862.

32. JWLD, August 2, 1862.

33. JWLD, August 12, 1862. The report of the McClellan requisitioning was widespread. See, for example, *Daily Evansville Journal*, August 11, 1862, 2, in a short article that begins "McClellan's officers do not suffer for something to drink."

34. JWLD, August 16, 1862.

35. The 1861–62 RLASS annual report itemized expenses of $488, most of which went to fugitive slaves, and a surplus in the treasury of $671.31.

36. Jacobs, "Life among the Contrabands."

37. Secretary's Report, Twelfth Annual Report, Rochester Ladies' Anti-Slavery Society, 1863, RLASS papers, UM.

38. JWLD, September 27 and October 8, 1862.

39. JWLD, October 17, 1862.

40. JWLD, October 22, 1862.

7. "What a Place I Have Found"

1. *Gazette*, October 23, 1862.

2. "Miniature mountains . . ." is from *Philadelphia Inquirer*, reprinted in *Gazette*, August 10, 1863. "I expected to find . . ." is from Manley Stacey Civil War Letters, December 15, 1862, Historical Society of Oak Park and River Forest, Illinois.

3. JWLD, October 22, 1862.

4. Quoted in Brownstein, "The Willard Hotel."

5. Julia Wilbur to Anna Barnes, October 24, 1862, UM.

6. JWPD, October 24, 1862.

7. Flyer, National Freedman's Relief Association of the District of Columbia, April 1862; available online at http://www.nytimes.com/1862/05/03/news/national -freedman-s-relief-association-of-the-district-of-columbia.html.

8. JWJB, October 25, 1862; Julia Wilbur to Amy Post, November 5, 1862, UR.

9. Julia Wilbur to Amy Post, November 5, 1862, UR.

10. JWLD, October 24, 1862.

11. *Evening Star*, October 26, 1862.

12. JWLD, October 25, 1862.

13. JWLD, October 25, 1862.

14. JWLD, October 28, 1862.

15. In the late 1700s the academy had a section set aside for indigent students that Washington helped support during his lifetime; he also left twenty shares of Bank of Alexandria stock (then worth about $4,000) to the school in his will. Robert E. Lee attended as a paying student from 1820 to 1823 (Serverian, "Alexandria Academy").

16. For descriptions, see Department of Education, *Special Report*, 283–93.

17. JWLD, October 28, 1862.

18. JWLD, October 30, 1862.

19. JWLD, October 25, 1862.

20. JWLD, November 19, 1862.

21. Letter from William Henry Channing to "Miss Chase," November 4, 1862, in Swint, *Dear Ones at Home*, 19.

22. *Gazette*, April 3, 1852. The street number was 69 when Julia lived there; it is now 323 South Asaph and is a private residence.

23. JWJB, 84.

24. American Baptist Publication Society, *Thirty-Ninth Annual Report*, 44. A colporter (sometimes spelled colporteur from the French) was someone who distributed books and pamphlets, often religious in nature.

25. JWLD, November 6, 1862.

26. Julia Wilbur to Anna Barnes, November 25, 1862, UM; JWLD, November 19, 1862.

27. Here and in the following paragraph, Julia Wilbur to Abraham Lincoln, November 7, 1862, and Wyman to Slough, November 24, 1862, filed with W-1263 1862, Letters Received, ser. 12, RG 94 [K-55], National Archives (hereafter NARA); Mary Todd Lincoln to Abraham Lincoln, November 3, 1862, Abraham Lincoln Papers, Series 2, General Correspondence, 1858–1864, Library of Congress.

28. Frobel, *The Civil War Diary of Anne S. Frobel*, 136.

29. Heintzelman, quoted in Freedom: A Documentary History of Emancipation, Freedmen and Southern Society Project, University of Maryland, series 1, vol. 2, *Wartime Genesis of Free Labor*, 277; quartermaster reports, Entry 225, Box 22, letters of December 8 and 11, 1862, RG 92, NARA.

30. After the war William McVeigh brought suit against the government to reclaim his property; the suit eventually made it way to the U.S. Supreme Court (*U.S. v. McVeigh*, 1871).

31. Quoted in Marks, *The Peninsula Campaign in Virginia*, 21.

32. Quoted in Harrison, "Atop an Anvil," 143–44.

33. Lowry in Davis and Robertson, *Virginia at War 1861*, 63.

34. Stanton to Saxton, May 28, 1862, in U.S. War Department, *The War of the Rebellion*, series 1, vol. 51, ch. 63, 641.

35. "Alexandria: Inquiry into the Military Administration of," Reports of Committees of the Senate of the United States for the First Session of the Thirty-Eighth Congress, 54.

36. *Gazette*, August 26, 1862.

37. Lt. Charles E. Grisson, June 2, 1863, in T. M. Miller, *Murder and Mayhem*, 123.

38. JWLD, November 24, 1862.

39. Department of Education, *Special Report*, 287.

40. Julia Wilbur to Anna Barnes, November 12, 1862, UM.

41. *Gazette*, December 12, 1839; Wise, *The Life of Henry A. Wise*, 214.

42. Henry Whittington diary, November 27, 1862, Alexandria Public Library, Local History/Special Collections. Jefferson Davis had declared a day of Thanksgiving, though marked by fasting rather than feasting, in September 1862. In 1863 Lincoln issued a proclamation uniformly marking Thanksgiving as the last Thursday in November.

43. Quoted in *Gazette*, November 28, 1862.

44. McPherson, *Battle Cry of Freedom*, 791–93, describes the parole system and why it broke down in 1863.

45. Comments about Thanksgiving here and below in JWLD, November 27, 1862. Background about De Korponay in Orr, *Last to Leave the Field*, 66.

46. JWLD, December 19, 1862.

47. Quoted in Munroe, *Adventures of an Army Nurse in Two Wars*, 56; Alcott, "Hospital Sketches," 42.

48. *Gazette*, December 22, 1862; JWLD, December 21, 1862. The database compiled by Alexandria Library Special Collections of people taking the oath lists 1,200 individuals, but Deborah Stabler is not among them (see Oath of Allegiance in Virginia, 1862–1865, under Genealogy Online Indexes).

49. JWLD, December 21, 1862.

50. JWLD, December 31, 1862.

8. "Mrs. J and I"

1. Julia's quotes in this paragraph and the following from JWLD, January 1 and 2, 1863.

2. JWLD, January 7, 1863.

3. John C. Babcock to Mrs. Horace Clark, December 26, 1861, Civil War Manuscripts 33, Library of Congress.

4. JWLD, January 9, 1863.

5. JWLD, January 14, 1863.

6. Julia Wilbur to Anna Barnes, January 15, 1863, UM.

7. Background information about Jacobs's early life comes principally from Jacobs, *Incidents in the Life of a Slave Girl*, and Yellin, *Harriet Jacobs*. Multiple editions of *Incidents* are now in print; page citations here are from a book published in 1969 by the Negro History Press.

8. Jacobs, *Incidents in the Life of a Slave Girl*, 44.

9. Jacobs, *Incidents in the Life of a Slave Girl*, 85.

10. Jacobs, *Incidents in the Life of a Slave Girl*, 149.

11. *American Beacon*, July 4, 1835; reprinted in Yellin, *Harriet Jacobs*; photo insert after p. 265. Harriet's parents, grandmother, and other family members were fathered by white men, hence "mulatto" in the ad.

12. Child held the copyright, and authorship became muddled over the years, but Child praised the manuscript and told Jacobs, "I have very little occasion to alter the language." Yet from shortly after Jacobs's death in 1897 through the 1980s, prevailing opinion was that the book was a novel written by Child. Through a multi-year effort, Jean Fagan Yellin established Jacobs as the author of *Incidents* and connected the book's contents with fact.

13. JWLD, May 19, 1861.

14. Jacobs, "Life among the Contrabands."

15. Jacobs, "Life among the Contrabands."

16. JWLD, November 26, 1862.

17. Second Report of a Committee of the Representatives of New York Yearly

Meeting of Friends upon the Conditions and Wants of the Colored Refugees, 4, https://archive.org/details/secondreportofcooosoci.

18. H. Jacobs to Amy Post, December 8, 1862, UR.

19. Julia Wilbur to Anna Barnes, January 15, 1863, UM.

20. As Julia wrote to Barnes, "There is a great deal of sickness among Northerners, I am told. The water here is bad" (November 25, 1862, UM). Julia was often ill too.

21. JWLD, January 27, 1863; Julia Wilbur to Amy Post, January 23, 1863, UR.

22. Julia Wilbur to Anna Barnes, December 22, 1862, UM.

23. *Gazette*, February 2, 1863.

24. A court of inquiry formed to consider the charges and went on for several days and almost eighty pages of charges and countercharges. *Proceedings of a Court of Inquiry Which Convened at Alexandria Virginia by Virtue of the Following Special Order* (Special Order No. 30, February 7, 1863); available online through Fold3.

25. Julia Wilbur to Emily Howland, February 5, 1863; reprinted in Yellin, *Harriet Jacobs Family Papers*, 439–40. Testimony of Lewis McKenzie, *Proceedings of a Court of Inquiry Which Convened at Alexandria Virginia by Virtue of the Following Special Order* (Special Order No. 30, February 7, 1863); available online through Fold3.

26. H. H. Wells to J. Slough, February 10, 1863, Pt. 4, E.1526, Lts. Sent 1862–64 (Alex.), RG 393, NARA.

27. *Gazette*, March 10, 1863. (Like most official notices, this one appeared over multiple days, including the date cited here.)

28. JWPD, February 18, 1863.

29. For an account of this meeting, discussed here and in the following paragraph, see Julia Wilbur to Anna Barnes, February 27, 1863, UM.

30. Report of Julia Wilbur, Twelfth Annual Report of the Rochester Ladies' Anti-Slavery Society, 12, RLASS papers, UM.

31. *Gazette*, March 6, 1863.

32. JWPD, January 21, 1863: "Dr. Bigelow of N.Y. has come, but I presume he will not stay. I hope he will not, I don't like him. Too important entirely. Oh! Such people! Such people!"

33. H. H. Wells, February 12, 1863, Pt. 4, E.1526, Lts. Sent 1862–64 (Alex.), RG 393, NARA.

34. Julia Wilbur to Anna Barnes, February 27, 1863, UM.

35. See Goldman and Schmalstieg, "Abraham Lincoln's Gettysburg Address."

36. Report of Julia Wilbur, Twelfth Annual Report of the Rochester Ladies' Anti-Slavery Society, 14.

37. J. Dennis Jr. to Julia Wilbur, January 21, 1863, UM.

38. Report of Julia Wilbur, Twelfth Annual Report of the Rochester Ladies' Anti-Slavery Society, 14.

39. Julia Wilbur to Anna Barnes, February 27, 1863, UM.

40. For measurements: Norcom's runaway notice for Jacobs described her as five feet, four inches and "corpulent." On January 24, 1863, Julia measured herself at the

Smithsonian—five feet, 107 pounds. Julia Wilbur to Anna Barnes, March 10, 1863, UM; JWPD, March 7, 1863.

41. Julia Wilbur to Anna Barnes, March 10, 1863, UM.

42. Julia Wilbur to Anna Barnes, March 10, 1863, UM.

43. Harriet Jacobs to Lydia Child, March 18, 1863, in Yellin, *Harriet Jacobs Family Papers*, 470.

44. Julia Wilbur to Amy Post, February 20, 1863, UR.

45. Julia Wilbur to Sarah Wistar Cope, February 7, 1863, in Yellin, *Harriet Jacobs Family Papers*, 444.

46. Yellin, *Harriet Jacobs Family Papers*, 486.

47. Julia Wilbur to Anna Barnes, March 10, 1863, UM.

48. See, for example, Faulkner, *Women's Radical Reconstruction*.

49. Julia Wilbur to Anna Barnes, March 10, 1863, UM.

50. Julia Wilbur to Anna Barnes, December 22, 1862, UM.

51. Julia Griffiths Crofts to Anna Barnes, February 20, 1863, in Yellin, *Harriet Jacobs Family Papers*, 447.

52. Julia Wilbur to Anna Barnes, March 10, 1863, UM.

9. "An Interfering . . . Person"

1. Julia Wilbur to Amy Post, November 5, 1862, UR.

2. Julia Wilbur to Anna Barnes, February 27, 1863, UM.

3. "Early Baptists in Connecticut," by Rev. Henry Jones, 1861, http://baptist historyhomepage.com/connect.early.baptists.html.

4. Livermore, *A History of Block Island*, 257.

5. Recounted in Albert Gladwin, "Brief Biographies," in Yellin, *Harriet Jacobs Family Papers*, lxvii–lxviii.

6. Julia Wilbur to Anna Barnes, February 27, 1863, UM.

7. Department of Education, *Special Report*, 287.

8. "Relief of the Freed People: From A. Gladwin," *Friends Review*, December 27, 1862.

9. JWLD, March 12, 1863.

10. JWLD, April 5, 1863.

11. Julia Wilbur to Emily Howland, February 5, 1863; reprinted in Yellin, *Harriet Jacobs Family Papers*, 439–40.

12. JWLD, November 22, 1863.

13. Quoted in Swint, *Dear Ones at Home*, 24–25.

14. *Gazette*, March 11, 1863.

15. Records of the U.S. Continental Commands, Part 1, Entry 5451, Papers Relating to Refugees and Prisoners, 1861–1865, RG 393, NARA.

16. Noted in *Evening Star*, April 11, 1863, 3.

17. JWLD, April 28, 1863.

18. JWPD, March 17, 1863.

19. JWLD, May 16, 1863.

20. Roswell Farnham to Laura (his sister), Special Collections, University of Vermont, http://cdi.uvm.edu/collections/item/cwuvmfarnham134; Julia Wilbur to Anna Barnes, February 27, 1863, UM.

21. JWLD, April 4, 1863.

22. JWLD, April 12, 1863.

23. Civil Defenses of Washington, https://www.nps.gov/cwdw/learn/history culture/index.htm.

24. *Gazette*, April 4, 1863.

25. *Gazette*, March 16 and 28, 1863.

26. *Gazette*, March 9, 10, 11, 14, and 30, 1863; "because he talks so much" is from JWLD, March 8, 1863.

27. Julia Wilbur to Esther Titus, February 20, 1863, in Post Family Papers Project, UR; estimates about population from Artemel, Crowell, and Parker, *The Alexandria Slave Pen*.

28. Julia Wilbur to Amy Post, November 5, 1862, UR.

29. JWLD, March 26, 1863.

30. *Harper's Weekly*, December 18, 1858.

31. JWLD, March 26, 1863.

32. JWLD, March 30, 1863.

33. Anna M. C. Barnes to Abraham Lincoln, March 31, 1863, B0427 1863, Records of the Office of the Secretary of War, Letters Received, RG 107 [L-23], NARA.

34. Julia Wilbur to P. H. Watson, April 1, 1863, W-394 1863, Records of the Office of the Secretary of War, Letters Received, RG 107 [L-23], NARA.

35. H. H. Wells to J. Slough, April 11, 1863, W-394, 1863, Records of the Office of the Secretary of War, Letters Received, RG 107 [L-23], NARA.

36. H. H. Wells to J. Slough, April 12, 1863, W-394, 1863, Records of the Office of the Secretary of War, Letters Received, RG 107 [L-23], NARA.

37. JWLD, April 14, 1863.

38. Julia Wilbur to Hon. E. Stanton, March 24, 1863, W-477, 1863, Records of the Office of the Secretary of War, Letters Received, RG 107 [L-23], NARA.

39. Julia did not hear about the response Barnes received until May 20, when she wrote, "Sorry I have not known this before, I might have counteracted some of the bad effects of his [Wells's] mis-statements and misapprehensions" (JWLD, May 20, 1863).

40. Albert Gladwin to Lt. Col. H. H. Wells, April 11, 1863; Wells to Slough, April 8, 1863, W-394, 1863, Records of the Office of the Secretary of War, Letters Received, RG 107 [L-23], NARA.

41. JWLD, May 6, 1863.

10. "I Wish to . . . Fight It Through"

1. JWLD, July 9, 1863.

2. JWLD, June 14, 1863; *Home Evangelist*, March 1863, 10; Gladwin in Twentieth Annual Report, American Baptist Free Mission Society, 9.

3. "The Freedmen at Alexandria. Their Improved Condition and Character," *New York Evening Post*, May 2, 1863.

4. *Anglo-African*, November 14, 1863; in Yellin, *Harriet Jacobs*, 169.

5. JWLD, May 16, 1863; *Rochester Democrat*, May 22, 1863.

6. Wheelock, *Boys in White*, 96.

7. JWLD, May 21, 1863.

8. *Liberator*, June 5, 1863.

9. Julia Wilbur to "My Dear Secretary," May 12, 1863, UR.

10. JWLD, May 26, 1863.

11. JWLD, May 26, 1863. The establishment on South Fairfax Street may have been trying to expand its business. On April 14, 1863, the Leslie House placed an ad in the *Gazette*: "Wanted at the Leslie House two good WHITE GIRLS for dining room and chamber work. Apply at the Leslie House, No. 14 South Fairfax Street."

12. JWLD, May 25, 1863.

13. JWLD, June 11, 1863.

14. JWLD, June 22, 1863.

15. JWLD, July 4 and July 5, 1863.

16. For quotes in this and the following paragraph, JWLD, July 7, 1863.

17. Spann, *Gotham at War*, 93

18. JWLD, June 1, 1863.

19. Frobel, *The Civil War Diary of Anne S. Frobel*, May 25, 1863.

20. All quotes in this paragraph are from Riker, "This Long Agony," 2–3.

21. Henry Whittington diary, July 6, 1863, Alexandria Public Library, Local History/Special Collections; *Gazette*, July 6, 1863.

22. *Gazette*, July 10, 1863; Slough quoted in Riker, "This Long Agony," 8.

23. JWLD, July 20, 1863.

24. JWLD, July 15 and 16, 1863.

25. JWLD, July 23, 1863; JWPD, August 4, 1863.

26. JWPD, July 27, 1863.

27. "List of Exemptions," *Lockport Daily Journal*, August 18, 1863.

28. Julia Wilbur to Anna Barnes, August 8, 1863, UM.

29. JWLD, August 16, 1863.

30. Excerpt of letter from Harriet Jacobs to Julia in letter from Julia Wilbur to Anna Barnes, August 8, 1863, UM. This is the only known surviving correspondence between Jacobs and Wilbur.

31. Julia Wilbur to Anna Barnes, October 2, 1863, UM. Milly and Julia Wilbur Washington are recorded in Pippinger, *Alexandria, Virginia Death Records*, as dying in the summer of 1863, no specific date given.

32. JWPD, August 27, 1863.

33. Quotes in this paragraph are from Report of Julia Wilbur, Twelfth Annual Report of the Rochester Ladies' Anti-Slavery Society, 6–20, RLASS papers, UM.

34. JWPD, September 21, 1863.

35. JWLD, September 26, 1863.

11. "Will It Pay?"

1. Amy Post to Isaac Post, n.d., Post Family Papers Project, UR.

2. JWLD, November 1, 1863. According to Randolph, *The Virginia Housewife*, a well-known nineteenth-century housekeeping book, a shote is a "fat young hog, which, when the head and feet are taken off, and it is cut into four quarters, will weigh six pounds per quarter"—quite a delicacy indeed.

3. JWLD, October 30, 1863.

4. Samuel May Jr. to the editor of the *National Anti-Slavery Standard*, October 24, 1863. May referred to Jacobs as "Linda," her pseudonym as author of *Incidents in the Life of a Slave Girl*.

5. JWLD, October 22 and 31 and November 3, 1863; Jacobs and Jacobs, "Letter from Teachers of the Freedmen."

6. Samuel Shaw to Dr. J. R. Bigelow, June 1, 14, 1863, filed with G-42 1863, Letters Received, ser. 360, Colored Troops Division, RG 94 [B-29], NARA; reprinted in Freedom: A Documentary History of Emancipation, Freedmen and Southern Society Project, University of Maryland, series 1, vol. 2, *Wartime Genesis of Free Labor*, 299.

7. A. A. Graves to National Freedman's Relief Association, September 12, 1863; reprinted in Freedom: A Documentary History of Emancipation, Freedmen and Southern Society Project, University of Maryland, series 1, vol. 2, *Wartime Genesis of Free Labor*, 302.

8. G. Buckingham and George E. H. Day, Freedman's Association, to Secretary of War, October 1, 1863, in Letters Received by the Office of the Adjutant General, Main Series 1861–1863, M669, Roll 225, RG 94, NARA.

9. W. Gwynne to J. Slough, October 1, 1863; reprinted in Freedom: A Documentary History of Emancipation, Freedmen and Southern Society Project, University of Maryland, series 1, vol. 2, *Wartime Genesis of Free Labor*, 299.

10. J. Slough to Asst. Adjt. General, October 1, 1863; reprinted in Freedom: A Documentary History of Emancipation, Freedmen and Southern Society Project, University of Maryland, series 1, vol. 2, *Wartime Genesis of Free Labor*, 299.

11. Julia Wilbur to Anna Barnes, October 2, 1863, UM.

12. JWLD, October 22, 1863.

13. JWLD, March 17, 1864; Thirteenth Annual Report of the Rochester Ladies' Anti-Slavery Society, 17, RLASS papers, UM.

14. JWLD, March 15 and May 21, 1864; Sixteenth Annual Report of the Rochester Ladies' Anti-Slavery Society, 27.

15. JWLD, November 3 and 4, 1863.

16. Julia Wilbur to Anna Barnes, November 20, 1863, UM.

17. Harriet Jacobs to Hannah Stevenson, March 10, 1864; in Yellin, *Harriet Jacobs*, 172.

18. JWLD, November 21, 1863.

19. Julia Wilbur to Anna Barnes, November 20, 1863, UM.

20. *American Baptist*, February 9, 1864; reprinted in Yellin, *Harriet Jacobs Family Papers*, 540.

21. JWLD, March 27, 1864.

22. JWLD, January 3, 1864.

23. *Gazette*, November 28, 1863; JWLD, November 28, 1863.

24. Winkle, *Lincoln's Citadel*, 342.

25. This area was considered Alexandria County until 1920, when the jurisdiction took on the name "Arlington" in recognition of Arlington House, the Lee-Custis home, within its borders.

26. JWLD, June 26, 1863.

27. See Reidy, "Coming from the Shadow of the Past," for a description of Freedman's Village.

28. JWLD, December 3, 1863.

29. JWLD, December 8, 1863.

30. JWLD, December 10, 1863; Amy Post to Isaac Post, n.d., Post Family Papers, UR.

31. Third Report of a Committee of the Representatives of New York Yearly Meeting of Friends upon the Condition and Wants of the Colored Refugees, 7–8, https://archive.org/details/ASPC0001938700.

32. Julia Wilbur to Anna Barnes, November 20, 1863, UM; JWLD, December 23, 1863.

33. JWLD, December 12 and 19, 1863.

34. JWLD, January 1 and 2, 1864.

35. JWLD, January 2, 1864.

36. JWLD, January 30, 1864.

37. Letter reprinted in *National Anti-Slavery Society Standard*, April 16, 1864. For an account of the establishment and control of the school, see Yellin, *Harriet Jacobs*, 176–79.

38. JWLD, January 9, 1864; Jacobs and Jacobs, "Letter from Teachers of the Freedmen."

39. Yellin, *Harriet Jacobs*, 176–79; *Christian Recorder*, March 21, 1863. In November 1864 twelve named Quartermaster laborers "and many others" officially complained their wages were being garnished to pay for freedmen's relief while the wages of whites were not. No change, or even response, was reported. Reprinted in Freedom: A Documentary History of Emancipation, Freedmen and Southern Society Project, University of Maryland, series 1, vol. 2, *Wartime Genesis of Free Labor*, 353–54.

40. *Anti-Slavery Society Standard*, April 16, 1864.

41. *New York Times*, February 3, 1864; final report included in The Reports of Committees of the Senate of the United States for the First Session of the Thirty-Eighth Congress, "Alexandria. Inquiry into the Military Administration of the City of," 54.

42. Reports of Committees of the Senate of the United States for the First Session of the Thirty-Eighth Congress, "Alexandria. Inquiry into the Military Administration of the City of," 54.

43. JWLD, February 13, 1864.

44. *Gazette*, February 18 and 23, 1864; no date given for original *Times* article.

45. JWLD, February 13, 1864.

46. JWLD, March 17, 1864. Mahala Grady's trail disappears, although the 1880 census lists a married black woman of the right age, with a teenage son, named Mahala Murphy in Alexandria. It would be nice to think she married and had a child.

47. JWLD, April 19, 1864.

48. JWLD, April 19, 1864.

49. Thirteenth Annual Report of the Rochester Ladies' Anti-Slavery Society, 8.

50. Julia Wilbur to Anna Barnes, March 5, 1864; Thirteenth Annual Report of the Rochester Ladies' Anti-Slavery Society, 4.

51. JWLD, February 28 and 29, 1864.

52. Julia Wilbur to Anna Barnes, March 5, 1864.

53. JWLD, April 27, 1864.

54. JWLD, May 1, 1864.

55. JWLD, May 27–June 5, 1864.

12. "As Good a Spot"

1. For a description of hospitals, see Alexandria Archaeology, http://www.alexandriava.gov/historic/civilwar/UnionHospitals.aspx?id=70778.

2. Dorwart, *Death Is in the Breeze*, 20, 28.

3. Estimate based on Albert Gladwin's record of deaths, begun in March 1863. The full name of his document, known informally as the "Gladwin Record," is "Book of Records, Containing the Marriages and Deaths That Have Occurred, within the Official Jurisdiction of Rev. A. Gladwin: Together with any Biographical or Other Reminisces That May Be Collected, Alexandria, Va." Some 1,200 people are estimated to have died before the record began. See Pippinger, *Alexandria, Virginia Death Records, 1863–1868 (the Gladwin Record) and 1869–1896.*

4. JWLD, October 25, 1862.

5. JWLD, October 28, 1862.

6. JWLD, February 3, 1863.

7. JWLD, May 1, 1863.

8. Woolsey, *Hospital Days*, 20–27; Wheelock, *Boys in White*, 47; Civil War Diary of Isaac Tucker, available online through the Wisconsin Veterans Museum, http://www.wisvetsmuseum.com/exhibitions/online/Isaac_Tucker/.

9. Brockett and Vaughan, *Women's Work in the Civil War*, 220; Wheelock, *Boys in White*, 39–40.

10. William Taylor, September 28, 1862, transcribed in the William and Mary Digital Archive, https://digitalarchive.wm.edu/bitstream/handle/10288/1499/Taylor 18620928.pdf?sequence=5; Anne Reading, November 26, 1862, in Irwin, "Bandages and Broken Bones," 13; JWLD, December 2, 1862.

11. JWLD, April 19, 1863.

12. Julia Wilbur to Anna Barnes, November 20, 1863, UM.

13. JWLD, February 13, 1864.

14. JWLD, February 16, 1864.

15. JWLD, February 15, 1864.

16. JWLD, March 17 and May 31, 1864.

17. JWLD, April 13, 1864.

18. JWLD, June 16, 1864.

19. JWLD, November 16, 1862.

20. JWLD, December 17, 1862; *Gazette*, September 12, 1863, and June 27, 1864; E. Miller, "Volunteers for Freedom," part I, 1. For background on notification (or lack thereof) to family members of their loved ones' casualties, see Faust, *This Republic of Suffering*, ch. 4.

21. JWLD, February 5, 1864.

22. *Gazette*, March 4, 1864; Gladwin to Slough, December 16, 1864, Letters Received, 1862–1865, Records of the Military Governor of Alexandria, Entry 2053, RG 393, NARA.

23. JWLD, April 10, 1864.

24. For an account of the rediscovery of the Gladwin Record, rededication of the cemetery site, and genealogical research conducted by Char McCargo Bah, who has identified more than one thousand descendants to date, see https://www.alex andriava.gov/FreedmenMemorial.

25. JWLD, May 5, 1864.

13. "Things as Usual, Quite Unsettled"

1. JWLD, July 28–30, 1864; JWPD, September 23, 1864.

2. According to research conducted by the current property owner, Stephen Wilbur bought 124 acres of land for $2,000 on July 1, 1828. Between 1813 and 1828 the land went through five different transactions. Before 1813 James Wadsworth owned the land—it was one of his descendants, James G. Wadsworth, who was military governor when Julia first came to Washington in 1862. Wilbur sold 94.1 acres on March 31, 1864, for $6,116 to Aaron Barber.

3. JWLD, March 24 and April 6, 1864.

4. JWPD, September 1, 1864. Map, Livingston County, 1872, Caledonia 001, Canawaugus, East Avon, Littleville; originally published by F. W. Beers, available in Historic Map Works, Rare Historic Maps Collection.

5. JWLD, September 11, 1864.

6. JWLD, September 2, 1849, March 22, 1851, and October 25, 1856.

7. JWLD, September 21, 1864.

8. JWLD, December 22, 1860, November 14, 1863, and February 22, 1864.

9. JWLD, October 14, 1864.

10. Fite, *Social and Industrial Conditions*, 263; *Soldier's Aid* 2, no. 4 (September 7, 1864): 28; "Civil War Medicine and the Rochester General Hospital," online exhibit, http://www.rochestergeneral.org/about-us/rochester-general-hospital/about -us/rochester-medical-museum-and-archives/online-exhibits/civil-war-medicine -and-the-rochester-city-hospital/.

11. The New York State Constitution at the time (article II, section 1) required a voter (male, twenty-one years of age and older) to have lived in the state for one year and, if he had within New York, in a new county at least four months. The sec-

tion also imposed a property requirement on blacks, no matter how long they had lived in the state or a particular county. Voters defeated a change to this requirement in 1860. By moving to Avon from Rush, the Wilburs moved from Monroe County to Livingston County.

12. JWLD, October 26, 1864. Tubman's request for a pension took years and was resolved in 1899 but on the grounds that she was a war widow rather than for her own accomplishments.

13. JWLD, November 3, 1864.

14. JWLD, November 8, 1864.

14. "Flung My Flag to the Breeze"

1. Diary of Francis H. Snow, August–September 1864, Records of the Office of the Chancellor, Kenneth Spencer Research Library, University of Kansas. The Union losses were 3,800 wounded, lost, or captured; the Confederate losses, 1,500. Several hundred USCT were captured, then killed (Wolfe, "Battle of the Crater").

2. Quoted in *Anglo-African*, September 3, 1864, reprinted in Yellin, *Harriet Jacobs Family Papers*, 578–81; Yellin, *Harriett Jacobs*, 183–84

3. JWPD, August 24, 1864.

4. A. Gladwin to J. Slough, August 5, 1864, and September 2, 1864; certificates by "Edgar, Surgeon" and "Dr. Brown, 37 Park Row, NY, room 24," September 2 and 30, 1864. In Union Provost Marshal's File of One-Name Papers re: Citizens, Gim-Gn, Roll #105, RG 109, NARA.

5. JWLD, November 9 and 12, 1864.

6. JWLD, November 17, 1864.

7. JWLD, December 5, 1864.

8. JWLD, December 1, 1864.

9. Quoted in *Liberator*, January 13, 1865; reprinted in Yellin, *Harriet Jacobs Family Papers*, 609–11.

10. JWLD, December 15, 1864.

11. "The Government Attempts at Negro Colonization," *New York Times*, April 5, 1864.

12. Chauncey Leonard to Adjutant General Lorenzo Thomas, January 31–May 31, 1865, L-287 1865, Letters Received, ser. 12, RG 94 [K-524], NARA.

13. JWLD, December 26 and 27, 1864.

14. A copy of the petition, rolled up, is in the file General Correspondence and Reports Relating to National and Post Cemeteries, RG 576, Records of the Office of the Quartermaster General, NARA.

15. J. G. C. Lee to Montgomery Meigs, Depot Quartermaster's Office, Alexandria, VA, December 28, 1864, Entry 576, RG 92, NARA.

16. JWLD, December 27, 1864.

17. JWLD, December 28, 1864.

18. Barber, *Alexandria in the Civil War*, 98.

19. Quoted in U.S. War Department, *The War of the Rebellion*, series 1, vol. 43, part 2, Correspondence, etc., October 16, 1864, 388–89.

20. *Gazette*, January 3, 1865.

21. JWLD, January 1, 1865.

22. JWLD, January 9, 1865.

23. JWLD, January 13, 1865.

24. Winkle, *Lincoln's Citadel*, 342. Letter to James Ferree from C. A. Dana, Adjutant Secretary of War, January 1865, in Letters Received by the Office of the Adjutant General, Main Series, 1861–1870, M619, 1865, Roll 334, 53-W (1865), RG 94, NARA.

25. JWLD, January 16, 1865.

26. JWLD, January 29, 1865.

27. JWLD, January 28, 1865.

28. Fourteenth Annual Report of the Rochester Ladies' Anti-Slavery Society, 9, RLASS papers, UM.

29. Julia Wilbur to Maria Porter, February 8, 1865, UM; JWLD, February 2, 1865.

30. JWLD, February 3, 1865.

31. Julia Wilbur to Maria Porter, February 8, 1865, UM.

32. JWLD, February 17, 1865.

33. JWLD, March 4, 1865.

34. "Miss Wilbur's Report," March 31, 1865, in *Pennsylvania Freedmen's Bulletin* 1, no. 2 (April 1865).

35. JWLD, March 23, 1865.

36. Thirteenth Annual Report of the Rochester Ladies' Anti-Slavery Society, 23–24.

37. JWLD, April 3, 1865.

38. JWLD, April 4, 1865.

39. JWLD, April 4, 1865. For more information on Lewis, see Henderson, "Maria Lewis."

40. JWLD, April 9, 10, and 14, 1865.

15. "The Paraphernalia of War"

1. JWLD, May 17, 1865.

2. Julia Wilbur to Maria Porter, April 27, 1865, UM.

3. Lankford, *Richmond Burning*, 22.

4. Quoted in Lankford, *Richmond Burning*, 71.

5. McGuire, reprinted in Davis and Robertson, *Virginia at War 1865*, 192–93.

6. JWLD, May 18, 1865.

7. JWLD, May 18, 1865.

8. Wilbur, "Richmond."

9. JWLD, May 18, 1865. See also http://www.encyclopediavirginia.org/Lumpkin _s_Jail.

10. Wilbur, "Richmond."

11. Report of Julia Wilbur, Fourteenth Annual Report of the Rochester Ladies' Anti-Slavery Society, 19–21, RLASS papers, UM.

12. JWLD, June 14, 1865.

13. JWLD, May 19 and 22, 1865. Gladwin at some point after this went west as a missionary under Baptist auspices.

14. JWLD, June 19, 1865; *Evening Star,* June 28, 1865, 2. The trial began on May 9 and concluded on June 28, followed by sentencing on June 29–30 and execution on July 7.

15. According to historian Jim Downs, "The distress and medical crises that freed slaves experienced were a hidden cost of war and an unintended consequence of emancipation" (*Sick from Freedom,* 7). Downs estimates these deaths in the tens of thousands.

16. For a summary of how historians have interpreted Reconstruction, see Foner, *Reconstruction.*

17. Quoted in Downs, *Sick from Freedom,* 73.

18. See, for example, Faulkner, *Women's Radical Reconstruction,* 83–99.

19. "Miscellaneous Reports and Lists," Records of the Assistant Commissioner for the District of Columbia, Bureau of Refugees, Freedmen and Abandoned Lands, M1055, Roll 21, RG 105, NARA.

20. According to Harrison, "The African American population of the District increased from 14,316 in 1860 to 28,663 in 1867. At least two-thirds were recent migrants unfamiliar with urban life and the working of an urban economy" (*Washington during Civil War and Reconstruction,* 61).

21. Bvt. Brig. Gen. C. H. Howard to Pastors of Black Churches, October 15, 1866; reprinted in Freedom: A Documentary History of Emancipation, Freedmen and Southern Society Project, University of Maryland, series 3, vol. 2, *Land and Labor, 1866–1867,* 830–32.

22. JWLD, March 16 and April 2, 1866.

23. Report of Julia Wilbur, Sixteenth Annual Report of the Rochester Ladies' Anti-Slavery Society, 8–9. Examples of letters to the Freedmen's Bureau are in Freedom: A Documentary History of Emancipation, Freedmen and Southern Society Project, University of Maryland, series 3, vol. 2, *Land and Labor, 1866–1867*—related to the South, for example, on p. 426 and related to the North on pp. 871–73.

24. Julia Wilbur to James McKim, January 10, 1866, Samuel J. May Anti-Slavery Collection, Division of Rare and Manuscript Collections, Cornell University.

25. JWLD, January 12, 1866.

26. John V. Vandenburgh, quoted in Harrison, *Washington during Civil War and Reconstruction,* 84.

27. JWLD, February 5, 1866; Julia Wilbur Report, 2nd District, January 19, 1866, M1055, Reel 19, RG 105, NARA; JWLD, December 30, 1866, and January 4, 1867.

28. JWLD, January 26, 1866.

29. Sixteenth Annual Report of the Rochester Ladies' Anti-Slavery Society, 11; for example, according to Harrison, the Pennsylvania Association of Freedmen supported seventeen teachers, the New England Friends distributed clothing, and the Philadelphia Friends ran a soup kitchen (*Washington during Civil War and Reconstruction,* 53).

30. Painter, *Sojourner Truth*, 219; M. Washington, *Sojourner Truth's America*, 330–31; Sojourner Truth to Josephine Griffing, March 30, 1867, Post Family Papers Project, UR.

31. On June 30, 1866, for example, Frances reported to Robert Corson, corresponding secretary of the association, that the three schools she oversaw enrolled 178 children between the ages of six and fifteen ("Report of Mrs. Hartwell, Teacher of Industrial Schools," *Pennsylvania Freedmen's Bulletin*, October 1866, 11).

32. JWLD, December 4 and 25, 1866.

33. JWLD, January 21 and 22, 1869.

34. JWLD, June 26, 1867.

35. JWLD, December 6, 1865.

36. Julia Wilbur to James McKim, January 10 and 29, 1866, Cornell University; JWLD, May 4, 1867.

37. JWLD, May 31, 1866. The book was *The Public Life of John Brown*, published in 1860 by James Redpath.

38. One of Brown's group, John Cook, moved to Harpers Ferry in 1858 to scout out the area. He boarded with a pro-slavery woman named Mrs. Kennedy and in the process married her daughter Virginia. Neither woman was involved in the plot, but according to historian Tony Horwitz (*Midnight Rising*, 266–67), Virginia knew about it. Virginia moved to Boston after her husband's execution.

39. JWLD, June 1 and 15, 1866.

40. In Fourth Report of a Committee of the Representative of New York Yearly Meeting of Friends upon the Condition and Wants of the Colored Refugees; reprinted in Yellin, *Harriet Jacobs Family Papers*, 828–30.

41. JWLD, October 11, 1867. For details on Jacobs's experiences in Savannah and Edenton, see Yellin, *Harriett Jacobs*.

42. One of the most notable cases of public-transport segregation at the time occurred in Alexandria. A black U.S. Capitol employee named Catherine Brown was injured when forcibly removed from the ladies' car in Alexandria in February 1868. She sued the Baltimore and Ohio Railroad in a case that went to the Supreme Court (Masur, "Patronage and Protest in Kate Brown's Washington," 1061–66). JWLD, October 12, 1867.

43. JWLD, October 10, 1865.

44. For a description of the trial, see D. O. Stewart, *Impeached*. JWLD, March 22 and May 7 and May 16, 1868.

45. Graf, *The Papers of Andrew Johnson*, 7:656–58; *Gazette*, May 4, 1865.

46. Quoted in *Gazette*, July 7, 1865.

47. JWLD, October 11, 1865.

48. JWLD, June 21, 1866.

49. JWLD, August 23, 1866.

50. JWLD, September 18, 1865, and August 23, 1866; Seventeenth Annual Report of the Rochester Ladies' Anti-Slavery Society, 27.

16. "That I Might Be There to See"

1. JWLD, July 1, 1869.

2. U.S. Commissioner of Patents, *Annual Report of the Commissioner of Patents for the Year 1869*, 1:16. On July 1, 1869, the Patent Office went from hiring women to work as copyists in their own homes to having them come to the office, in six rooms set aside for them in the basement. Julia became part of this group of office workers.

3. Aron, *Ladies and Gentlemen of the Civil Service*, 40–61.

4. JWLD, May 4, 1869. The patronage system apportioned most federal jobs by congressional district. Although Julia did not write about enlisting a congressman on her behalf, she was identified as "Julia A. Wilbur, New York" throughout her career at the agency.

5. JWLD, April 26, 1869.

6. See Masur, *An Example for All the Land*, for background on the brief period until the District of Columbia became a territory with a government appointed by Congress.

7. JWLD, June 3, 1867; Sixteenth Annual Report of the Rochester Ladies' Anti-Slavery Society, 22, RLASS papers, UM.

8. Noted in JWLD, April 22, 1869.

9. *National Republican*, April 26, 1869; *New York Herald*, April 23, 1869.

10. JWPD, August 17, 1876; Records of the Office of the Secretary of the Interior, Records of the Appointments Division, Register of Reports Concerning Employees, 1875–1877, Department of the Interior (Patent Office), RG 48, NARA. Unfortunately only the register survives and not the reports themselves.

11. JWLD, March 6, 1872.

12. JWLD, June 2 and September 7, 1872.

13. JWPD, January 21, 1874.

14. JWPD, December 7, 1876.

15. JWPD, December 31, 1876.

16. JWPD, March 22, 1881. For a description of some of the treatments, see the New York Historical Society *From the Stacks* blog, http://blog.nyhistory.org/electric-medicine/.

17. JWPD, April 17, 1883.

18. JWPD, November 1, 1877.

19. In 1967 a mayor and city council system was instituted, appointed by the president. Direct elections for local officials in the District of Columbia only began again in 1974.

20. "The New Washington," 643.

21. JWPD, July 6, 1874.

22. For example, see JWPD, July 27, 1881, and March 7, 1883. For background on these money-lending practices, see Aron, *Ladies and Gentlemen of the Civil Service*, 178–81.

23. JWLD, September 6, 1872.

24. JWPD, September 16, 1885.

25. *Evening Star,* January 28, 1886. The *Official Register of the United States Containing a List of the Officers and Employees in the Civil, Military, and Naval Service on the First of July, 1887* lists Julia as earning $1,000 per year.

26. Article in *Women's Tribune* reprinted in the *Lima (OH) News,* July 15, 1895, and other newspapers.

27. JWPD, July 27, 1886.

28. Wheelock, *Boys in White;* JWPD, November 7, 1886.

29. Mary Van Buskirk, September 18, 1881, Box 4, Julia Wilbur papers, MC.1158, Haverford.

30. As a few examples of many, Julia was part of a group (though not a speaker) that met with the Senate Judiciary Committee about suffrage in 1871, member of a Decoration Day Committee in 1880, and auditor of the National Woman Suffrage Association in 1888. At the 1888 NWSA convention, she was one of at least fifteen women given a special seat on stage as a "pioneer" of the movement.

31. JWPD, January 17 and 18, 1874.

32. JWPD, February 21, 1890, and January 16, 1892.

33. Memoranda page, back of 1891 JWPD.

34. "In the Patent Office," *Chatauquan;* reprinted in *Inter Ocean* (Chicago), June 6, 1891. Girolamo Savonarola was a fifteenth-century Italian cleric who fought for reforms within the Catholic Church until he was executed.

35. JWPD, July 26 and 30, 1894.

36. Copy of letter written January 21, 1890, back of JWPD. This is one of Julia's very few personal letter excerpts that survives. She would have been older than "threesome & ten" when she wrote it in 1890, at age seventy-five.

Epilogue

1. JWPD, April 5, 1895.

2. *Avon Herald,* June 19, 1895.

3. Note written by Inez Monroe Steere, Box 6, Julia Wilbur papers, MC.1158, Haverford.

4. *Livingston Republican,* August 6, 1896, and September 11, 1902.

5. JWLD, March 4, 1872.

6. *Rochester Union and Advertiser,* December 14, 1896.

7. Quoted in Harper, *The Life and Work of Susan B. Anthony,* 3:1408–9.

8. *Highland Weekly News* (Hillsborough OH), January 16, 1868.

9. Quoted in Ellis, "John Crawford Wyman, 1822–1900."

10. *Sacramento Daily Union,* April 15, 1869.

11. Quoted in Kaye, "Property of Citizens of Alexandria City and Fairfax County," 47.

Appendix

1. The information in the appendix is from Wilbur descendants Charles Lenhart and Kevin West, based on their genealogical research.

BIBLIOGRAPHY

Archival Sources

ORIGINAL WRITING BY JULIA WILBUR

Haverford College, Quaker & Special Collections
  HC.Coll.1174: Douglas V. and Dorothy M. Steere papers, Series I, Box 2
  MC.1158: Julia Wilbur papers
    Journal Briefs, 1844–1862
    Large Diaries, 1844–1873
    Pocket Diaries, 1856–1895
University of Michigan, William L. Clements Library
  Rochester Ladies' Anti-Slavery Society (RLASS) papers, 1851–1868

OTHER SOURCES

Alexandria Public Library, Local History/Special Collections
  Green Family Collection photographs
  Henry Whittington diary
  Isabel (Emerson) Otis Price personal memoirs
American Baptist History Association
  American Baptist Free Mission Society annual reports
  Home Evangelist
Black Abolitionist Archive, University of Detroit Mercy, http://research.udmercy
  .edu/find/special_collections/digital/baa/.
Central Library of Rochester and Monroe County, Local History Division
  Maps, photographs, city newspapers, city directories
Civil War Washington, Center for Digital Research in the Humanities, University
  of Nebraska–Lincoln, http://civilwardc.org/.
Cornell University, Division of Rare and Manuscript Collections
  Samuel J. May Anti-Slavery Collection
District of Columbia Public Library, Special Collections
  Maps, photographs, vertical files
Documenting the American South, University of North Carolina, http://docsouth
  .unc.edu/.
Emory University, Stuart A. Rose Manuscript, Archives, and Rare Book Library
  Robert Langmuir African American photograph collection, circa 1840–2000
Freedom: A Documentary History of Emancipation, Freedmen and Southern Soci-
  ety Project, University of Maryland.
  Series 1, volume 2: *Wartime Genesis of Free Labor: The Upper South*. Edited by Ira
    Berlin, Steven Miller, Joseph Reidy, and Leslie Rowland. Cambridge: Cam-
    bridge University Press, 1993.

Series 2: *The Black Military Experience*. Edited by Ira Berlin, Joseph Reidy, and Leslie Rowland. Cambridge: Cambridge University Press, 1982.

Series 3, volume 1: *Land and Labor, 1865*. Edited by Steven Hahn, Steven Miller, Susan O'Donovan, et al. Durham: University of North Carolina Press, 2008.

Series 3, volume 2: *Land and Labor, 1866–1867*. Edited by Rene Hayden, Anthony Kaye, Kate Masur, et al. Durham: University of North Carolina Press, 2013.

Historical Society of Oak Park and River Forest, Illinois

Manley Stacey Civil War Letters, 1862–1863

Library of Congress—Geography and Map Division, Newspapers and Periodicals, Prints and Photographs Division, Manuscript Division

Abraham Lincoln Papers

Civil War Manuscripts 33, John C. Babcock, 1855–1913

Civil War Manuscripts 582, James Morrison MacKaye, 1805–1888

Civil War Manuscripts 781, Roberts Family, 1734–1944

Civil War Manuscripts 989, James Thomas Ward, 1820–1897

Library of Virginia

51450: Letters of Frederick C. Hale, 1862–1865

Livingston County Historian's Office

Property deeds and will for S. Wilbur, county newspapers

Monroe County, Surrogate's Court

Wills of C. Griffin, L. Griffin, F. Hartwell, J. Wilbur

National Archives, I and II (NARA)

RG 48: Department of the Interior (Patent Office)

RG 92: Records of the Office of the Quartermaster General

RG 94: Records of the Office of the Adjutant General, 1780s–1917

RG 103: Records of the Field Offices for the State of Virginia, Bureau of Refugees, Freedmen, and Abandoned Lands, 1865–1872

RG 105: Records of the Bureau of Refugees, Freedmen, and Abandoned Lands, 1861–1879

RG 107: Records of the Office of the Secretary of War

RG 393: Records of the U.S. Continental Commands, 1821–1920

Swarthmore College, Friends Historical Library

RG 5/066: Emily Howland Family papers, 1827–1929

University of Kansas, Kenneth Spencer Research Library

Diary of Francis H. Snow, Records of the Office of the Chancellor

University of Rochester, River Campus Libraries, Department of Rare Books, Special Collections, and Preservation

Benjamin Fish letters, Fish Family Papers, 1770–1915

Frederick Douglass Project, Frederick Douglass Papers

Porter Family Papers

Post Family Papers Project, Isaac and Amy Post Family Papers

Virginia Historical Society

Bibliography

Mss 1 H6795, Section 34: Hoge Family papers, 1804–1938

Mss 5: 1 C2467: Sarah S. Carter diary

Published Sources

Abbott, Karen. *Liar, Temptress, Soldier, Spy: Four Women Undercover in the Civil War.* New York: HarperCollins, 2014.

Adams, Michael C. C. *Living Hell: The Dark Side of the Civil War.* Baltimore: Johns Hopkins University Press, 2014.

Alcott, Louisa May. "Hospital Sketches." In *The Sketches of Louisa May Alcott.* Forest Hill NY: Ironweed Press, 2001.

American Baptist Publication Society. *Thirty-Ninth Annual Report.* Philadelphia, 1863.

Ammons, Elizabeth, ed. *Harriet Beecher Stowe's Uncle Tom's Cabin.* New York: Oxford University Press, 2007.

Applegate, Debby. *The Most Famous Man in America: The Biography of Henry Ward Beecher.* New York: Three Leaves Press, 2006.

Aptheker, Herbert. "Negro Casualties in the Civil War." *Journal of Negro History* 32, no. 1 (January 1947): 10–80.

Aron, Cindy Sondik. *Ladies and Gentlemen of the Civil Service: Middle-Class Workers in Victorian America.* New York: Oxford University Press, 1987.

Artemel, Janice, Elizabeth Crowell, and Jeff Parker. *The Alexandria Slave Pen: The Archaeology of Urban Captivity.* Washington DC: Engineering-Science, 1987.

Ash, Martha Montague. "The Social and Domestic Scene in Rochester, 1840–1860." *Rochester History* 18, no. 2 (1956): 1–20.

Atwater, Edward, and Lawrence A. Kohn. "Rochester and the Water Cure: 1844–1854." *Rochester History* 32, no. 4 (1970): 1–27.

Bacon, Margaret Hope. *Valiant Friend: The Life of Lucretia Mott.* New York: Walker Publishing, 1980.

Baker, James W. *Thanksgiving: The Biography of an American Holiday.* Durham: University of New Hampshire Press, 2009.

Barber, James G. *Alexandria in the Civil War.* Lynchburg VA: H. E. Howard, 1988.

Barbour, Hugh, ed. *Quaker Crosscurrents: Three Hundred Years of Friends in the New York Yearly Meetings.* Syracuse NY: Syracuse University Press, 1995.

Bardaglio, Peter. "The Children of Jubilee: African American Childhood in Wartime." In *Divided Houses: Gender and the Civil War,* edited by Catherine Clinton and Nina Silber. Oxford: Oxford University Press, 1992.

Barham, William. *Descriptions of Niagara.* Gravesend, England: Compiler, 1847.

Barnes, Joseph. "Rochester's Congressmen Part I, 1789–1869." *Rochester History* 61, no. 3 (1979): 1–24.

Barnett, Teresa. *Sacred Relics: Pieces of the Past in Nineteenth-Century America.* Chicago: University of Chicago Press, 2013.

Baron, Erika Lea. "Building Separate Spheres: The Life of Julia Wilbur." Senior dissertation, Haverford College, 1989.

Barry, Kathleen. *Susan B. Anthony: A Biography*. New York: New York University Press, 1988.

Bedell, John. "Archaeology of the Bruin Slave Jail (Site 44ax0172)." Prepared by the Louis Berger Group for Columbia Equity Trust, 2010.

Berkin, Carol. *Civil War Wives*. New York: Alfred A. Knopf, 2009.

Bernstein, Peter. *The Life and Times of George Seaton*. Publication Number 121. Alexandria VA: Alexandria Archaeology, 2001.

Biddle, Richard. *Captain Hall in America*. Philadelphia: Carey and Lea, 1830.

Blight, David. *Frederick Douglass' Civil War: Keeping Faith in Jubilee*. Baton Rouge: Louisiana State University Press, 1989.

———. *Race and Reunion: The Civil War in American Memory*. Cambridge MA: Belknap Press of Harvard University Press, 2001.

Bollet, Alfred. *Civil War Hospitals: Challenges and Triumphs*. Tucson AZ: Galen Press, 2002.

Breault, Judith Colucci. *The World of Emily Howland: Odyssey of a Humanitarian*. Millbrae CA: Les Femmes, 1976.

Brockett, Linus Pierpoint, and Mary Vaughan. *Women's Work in the Civil War: A Record of Heroism, Patriotism, and Patience*. Philadelphia: Zeigler, McCurdy, 1867. https://archive.org/details/womansworkincivi5900broc.

Brownstein, Elizabeth Smith. "The Willard Hotel." *White House History* 31 (n.d.).

Bryant, Tammy. "Documentary Study of the 1300 Block of Duke Street, Alexandria, Virginia." Prepared by Thunderbird Archeology for Van Metre Companies, 2007.

Calvit, Elizabeth. "USDI/NPS NRHP Multiple Property Documentation Form: African American Historic Resources of Alexandria, Virginia." Washington DC, 1994; updated 2001.

Carbado, Devon, and Donald Weise, eds. *The Long Walk to Freedom: Runaway Slave Narratives*. Boston: Beacon Press, 2012.

Carothers, A. Glenn. *Quakers Living in the Lion's Mouth: The Society of Friends in Northern Virginia, 1730–1864*. Gainesville: University Press of Florida, 2012.

Carpenter, Daniel, and C. Moore. "When Canvassers Became Activists: Antislavery Petitioning and the Political Mobilization of American Women." *American Political Science Review* 108, no. 3 (2014): 479–498.

Cheever, Susan. *Louisa May Alcott: A Personal Biography*. New York: Simon and Schuster, 2010.

Chen, Xi. "The Making of John B. Gough (1817–1886): Temperance, Evangelical Pageantry, and the Conservatism of Popular Reform in Victorian Society." PhD dissertation, University of Washington, 2013.

Cimbala, Paul, and Randall Miller, eds. *The Great Task Remaining before Us: Reconstruction as America's Continuing Civil War*. New York: Fordham University Press, 2010.

Claxton, Melvin, and Mark Puls. *Uncommon Valor: A Story of Race, Patriotism and Glory in the Final Battles of the Civil War*. Hoboken NJ: John Wiley and Sons, 2006.

Clinton, Catherine. *Harriet Tubman: The Road to Freedom*. New York: Little, Brown, 2004.

———. *Mrs. Lincoln: A Life*. New York: HarperCollins, 2009.

Cohen, Gretchen W. "Clip Not Her Wings: Female Abolitionists in Rochester, New York, 1835–1868." Master's thesis, City College of New York, 1994.

Collins, Gail. *America's Women: 400 Years of Dolls, Drudges, Helpmates, and Heroines*. New York: William Morrow, 2003.

Colman, Lucy. *Reminiscences*. Buffalo NY: H. L. Green, 1891.

Connery, William S. *Northern Virginia 1861*. Civil War Sesquicentennial Series. Charleston SC: History Press, 2011.

Conway, Moncure D. *Testimonies Concerning Slavery*. London: Chapman and Hall, 1864.

Coon, Anne. "The Magnetic Circle; the Bloomer Costume." *Rochester History* 57, no. 3 (1995): 1–28.

Coster, Sarah. "Nurses, Spies and Soldiers: The Civil War at Carlyle House." *Carlyle House Docent Dispatch*, March 2011.

Cressey, Pamela, Francine Bromberg, and Laura Triesch. "Contraband and Freedmen's Cemetery, Alexandria, Virginia." Site #44AX0179NDHR #1 00-01 21-1085. National Register of Historic Places, Places/Registration Form, 2012. https://www.nps.gov/nr/faq.htm#citation.

Cromwell, T. Ted, and Timothy Hills. "Phase III Mitigation of the Bontz Site (44AX103) and the United States Military Railroad Station (44AX105)." Submitted to the Virginia Department of Transportation, 1989.

Dammann, G., and A. Bollet. *Images of Civil War Medicine*. New York: Demos, 2008.

Davis, William C., and James I. Robertson Jr., eds. *Virginia at War 1861*. Lexington: University Press of Kentucky, 2005.

———. *Virginia at War 1862*. Lexington: University Press of Kentucky, 2007.

———. *Virginia at War 1863*. Lexington: University Press of Kentucky, 2008.

———. *Virginia at War 1864*. Lexington: University Press of Kentucky, 2009.

———. *Virginia at War 1865*. Lexington: University Press of Kentucky, 2011.

DeBats, Donald, et al. "Voting Viva Voce: Unlocking the Social Logic of Past Politics." http://sociallogic.iath.virginia.edu/project_intro.

Deck, Alice. "Whose Book Is This? Authorial versus Editorial Control of Harriet Brent Jacobs' *Incidents in the Life of a Slave Girl*." *Women's Studies International Forum* 10, no. 1 (1987): 33–40.

Dennee, Timothy. "African-American Civilians and Soldiers Treated at Claremont Smallpox Hospital, Fairfax County, Virginia, 1862–1865." Alexandria: Friends of Freedmen's Cemetery, 2008. http://www.freedmenscemetery.org/resources/documents/claremont.pdf.

———. *Convalescent Soldiers in L'Ouverture Hospital "Express Our Views" on Burial Location*. Freedmen's Series, no. 1. Alexandria VA: Office of Historic Alexandria, 1997. http://www.freedmenscemetery.org/resources/documents/contrabandhospital.pdf.

———. "A House Divided Still Stands: The Contraband Hospital and Alexandria Freedmen's Aid Workers." Friends of Freedmen's Cemetery, 2011. http://www.freedmenscemetery.org/resources/documents/contrabandhospital.pdf.

Department of Education. *Special Report of the Commission of Education on the Condition and Improvement of the Public Schools in the District of Columbia.* Washington DC: Government Printing Office, 1871.

Deyle, Steven. *Carry Me Back: The Domestic Slave Trade in American Life.* New York: Oxford University Press, 2005.

Dickey, J. D. *Empire of Mud: The Secret History of Washington, DC.* Guilford CT: Lyons Press, 2014.

Dols, Jonathan R. "Military Occupation and Cultural Perceptions: Union Soldiers in Alexandria, Virginia, 1861–1865." Dissertation, U.S. Military Academy, 1990.

Dorwart, Bonnie Brice. *Death Is in the Breeze: Disease during the American Civil War.* Frederick MD: NMCWM Press, 2009.

Downs, Jim. "The Other Side of Freedom: Destitution, Disease, and Dependency among Freedwomen and Their Children during and after the Civil War." In *Battle Scars: Gender and Sexuality in the American Civil War,* edited by Catherine Clinton and Nina Silber. New York: Oxford University Press, 2006.

———. *Sick from Freedom: African-American Illness and Suffering during the Civil War and Reconstruction.* New York: Oxford University Press, 2012.

Dudden, Faye. *Fighting Chance: The Struggle over Woman Suffrage and Black Suffrage in Reconstruction America.* New York: Oxford University Press, 2011.

"The Duties of Women in the Present Crisis." *Soldier's Aid* 1, no. 1 (June 19, 1863).

Eggener, Keith. *Cemeteries.* New York and Washington: W. W. Norton and Library of Congress, 2010.

Ellis, Robert. "John Crawford Wyman, 1822–1900." Northborough Historical Society. http://northboroughhistoricalsociety.org/Historian/Historian_articles/John_Wyman.html.

Fahs, Alice. "The Feminized Civil War: Gender, Northern Popular Literature, and the Memory of the War, 1861–1900." *Journal of American History* 85, no. 4 (March 1999): 1461–94.

Farmer-Kaiser, Mary. "'With a Weight of Circumstances like Millstones about Their Necks': Freedwomen, Federal Relief, and the Benevolent Guardianship of the Freedmen's Bureau." *Virginia Magazine of History and Biography* 115, no. 3 (2007): 412–42.

Faulkner, Carol. *Lucretia Mott's Heresy: Abolition and Women's Rights in Nineteenth-Century America.* Philadelphia: University of Pennsylvania Press, 2011.

———. *Women's Radical Reconstruction: The Freedmen's Aid Movement.* Philadelphia: University of Pennsylvania Press, 2004.

Faust, Drew Gilpin. *This Republic of Suffering.* New York: Alfred A. Knopf, 2008.

Fee, Frank E., Jr. "To No One More Indebted: Frederick Douglass and Julia Griffiths, 1849–63." *Journalism History* 37, no. 1 (2011): 12–26.

Fischer, Claude. *Made in America: A Social History of American Culture and Character*. Chicago: University of Chicago Press, 2010.

Fisher, Donald. "The Civil War Draft in Rochester: Part One." *Rochester History* 53, no. 1 (1991): 1–24.

———. "The Civil War Draft in Rochester: Part Two." *Rochester History* 53, no. 2 (1991): 1–32.

Fite, Emerson Davis. *Social and Industrial Conditions in the North during the Civil War*. New York: MacMillan, 1910.

Foner, Eric. *Gateway to Freedom: The Hidden History of the Underground Railroad*. New York: W. W. Norton, 2015.

———. *Reconstruction: America's Unfinished Revolution 1963–1877*. New York: HarperCollins, 1988.

———. *A Short History of Reconstruction, 1863–1877: Updated Edition*. New York: Harper Perennial, 2015.

Frank, Lisa Tendrich, ed. *The World of the Civil War: A Daily Life Encyclopedia*. Santa Barbara CA: Greenwood, 2015.

Fraser, Nancy, and Linda Gordon. "A Genealogy of Dependency: Tracing a Keyword of the U.S. Welfare State." *Signs: Journal of Women in Culture and Society* 19, no. 2 (1994): 309–36.

Frobel, Anne. *The Civil War Diary of Anne S. Frobel: Of Wilton Hill in Virginia*. With introduction and appendixes by Mary H. and Dallas M. Lancaster. McLean VA: EPM Publications, 1992.

Frothingham, Octavius Brooks. *Memoir of William Henry Channing*. Cambridge MA: Riverside Press, 1886.

Furguson, Ernest. *Freedom Rising: Washington in the Civil War*. New York: Vintage Books, 2004.

Geisberg, Judith. *Civil War Sisterhood: The U.S. Sanitary Commission and Women's Politics in Transition*. Boston: Northeastern University Press, 2000.

———, ed. *Emilie Davis's Civil War: The Diaries of a Free Black Woman in Philadelphia, 1863–1865*. University Park: Pennsylvania State University, 2014.

Glymph, Thavolia. "'This Species of Property': Female Slave Contrabands in the Civil War." In *A Woman's War: Southern Women, Civil War, and the Confederate Legacy*, edited by Edward D. C. Campbell Jr. and Kim Rice. Richmond: Museum of the Confederacy and University Press of Virginia, 1997.

Goldman, Armond S., and Frank C. Schmalstieg. "Abraham Lincoln's Gettysburg Address." *Journal of Medical Biography* 15 (2007): 104–10.

Goodheart, Adam. *1861: The Civil War Awakening*. New York: Alfred A. Knopf, 2011.

———. "How Col. Ellsworth's Death Shocked the Union." Smithsonian.com, March 30, 2011. http://www.smithsonianmag.com/history/how-col-ellsworths-death-shocked-the-union-1277063/.

Goodwin, Doris Kearns. *Team of Rivals*. New York: Simon and Schuster, 2005.

Gordon, Ann D., ed. *The Selected Papers of Elizabeth Cady Stanton and Susan B. Anthony.* Vol. 6, *1895 to 1906.* New Brunswick NJ: Rutgers University Press, 2013.

Graf, Leroy, ed. *The Papers of Andrew Johnson.* Vol. 7, *1864–1865.* Knoxville: University of Tennessee Press, 1986.

Greenly, Mark. *Those upon Whom the Curtain Has Fallen: Past and Present Cemeteries of Alexandria, Virginia.* Publication 88. Alexandria VA: Alexandria Archaeology, 1996.

Grier, Katherine C. *Pets in America: A History.* Chapel Hill: University of North Carolina Press, 2006.

Groth, Michael. "Slaveholders and Manumission in Dutchess County, New York." *New York History* 78, no. 1 (1997): 33–50.

Hamm, Thomas D. *The Quakers in America.* New York: Columbia University Press, 2003.

Harper, Ida Husted. *The Life and Work of Susan B. Anthony.* Indianapolis: Bowen-Merrill, 1899.

Harrison, Noel. "Atop an Anvil: The Civilians' War in Fairfax and Alexandria Counties, April 1861–April 1862." *Virginia Magazine of History and Biography* 106, no. 2 (1998): 133–64.

Harrison, Robert. *Washington during Civil War and Reconstruction.* New York: Cambridge University Press, 2011.

———. "Welfare and Employment Policies of the Freedmen's Bureau in the District of Columbia." *Journal of Southern History* 72, no. 1 (2006): 75–110.

Harrold, Stanley. *Subversives: Antislavery Community in Washington, D.C., 1828–1865.* Baton Rouge: Louisiana State University Press, 2003.

Haviland, Laura. *A Woman's Life Work.* Cincinnati: Walden and Stowe, 1882.

Henderson, Anita. "Maria Lewis." In *Battle of Waynesboro*, edited by Richard G. Williams Jr. Charleston SC: History Press, 2014.

Hewitt, Nancy. "Amy Kirby Post: Of Whom It Was Said, 'Being Dead, yet Speaketh.'" *University of Rochester Library Bulletin* 37 (1984). http://rbscp.lib.rochester.edu/4018.

———. "Seeking a Larger Liberty: Remapping First Wave Feminism." In *Women's Rights and Transatlantic Slavery in the Era of Emancipation*, edited by James Brewer and Kathryn Kish Stewart. New Haven CT: Yale University Press, 2007.

———. "The Spiritual Journeys of an Abolitionist: Amy Kirby Post, 1802–1889." In *Quakers and Abolition*, edited by Brycchan Carey and Geoffrey Plank. Champaign-Urbana: University of Illinois Press, 2014.

———. *Women's Activism and Social Change: Rochester, New York, 1822–1872.* Lanham MD: Lexington Books, 2001.

Higgins, Rosanne, Michael Haines, Lorena Walsh, and Joyce Sirianni. "The Poor in the Mid-Nineteenth-Century Northeastern United States." In *The Backbone of History: Health and Nutrition in the Western Hemisphere*, edited by Richard Steckel and Jerome Rose. Cambridge: Cambridge University Press, 2002.

Hine, Darlene Clark, and Kathleen Thompson. *A Shining Thread of Hope*. New York: Broadway Books, 1998.

History of Oneida County, New York. Philadelphia: Everts and Fariss, 1878.

Hodes, Martha. *Mourning Lincoln*. New Haven CT: Yale University Press, 2015.

Horwitz, Tony. *Midnight Rising: John Brown and the Raid That Sparked the Civil War*. New York: Henry Holt, 2011.

Hunt, Sanford B. "The Negro as Soldier." *Anthropological Review* 7, no. 24 (1869): 40–54.

Hurst, Harold. "The Merchants of Pre-Civil War Alexandria: A Dynamic Elite in a Progressive City." *Records of the Columbia Historical Society* 52 (1989): 327–43.

Irwin, Margaret Garrett, ed. "Bandages and Broken Bones: The Civil War Diary of Anne Reading." *Alexandria Chronicle* 3, no. 2 (1995): 1–21.

Jackson, Debra. "A Cultural Stronghold: The 'Anglo-African' Newspaper and the Black Community of New York." *New York History* 85, no. 4 (2004): 331–57.

Jacobs, Harriet. *Incidents in the Life of a Slave Girl*. Detroit: Negro History Press, reprinted 1969.

———. "Life among the Contrabands." *Liberator*, September 5, 1862.

Jacobs, Harriet, and Louisa Jacobs. "Letter from Teachers of Freedmen." *National Anti-Slavery Standard*, April 16, 1864.

Jaquette, Henrietta Stratton, ed. *Letters of a Civil War Nurse: Cornelia Hancock, 1863–1865*. Lincoln: University of Nebraska Press, 1998.

Johnston, Allan John. "Surviving Freedom: The Black Community of Washington DC, 1860–1880." PhD dissertation, Duke University, 1980.

Jones, Jacqueline. *Saving Savannah: The City and the Civil War*. New York: Alfred A. Knopf, 2008.

Jordan, Ervin L., Jr. *Black Confederates and Afro-Yankees in Civil War Virginia*. Charlottesville: University Press of Virginia, 1995.

Joyce, Charles. "Freedmen Warriors, Civil Rights Fighters." *Military Images* (Autumn 2016): 42–48.

Kaye, Ruth Lincoln. "Property of Citizens of Alexandria City and Fairfax County Confiscated by the Federal Government during the Civil War." *Yearbook of the Historical Society of Fairfax County, Virginia* 30 (2006): 7–64.

Kirk, Highland Clare. *A History of the New York State Teachers' Association*. New York: E. L. Kellogg, 1883.

Klingaman, William. *Abraham Lincoln and the Road to Emancipation: 1861–1865*. New York: Viking, 2001.

Kundahl, George C. *Alexandria Goes to War*. Knoxville: University of Tennessee Press, 2004.

Lampe, Gregory. *Frederick Douglass: Freedom's Voice, 1818–1845*. Lansing: Michigan State University Press, 1998.

Lankford, Nelson. *Richmond Burning: The Last Days of the Confederate Capital*. New York: Viking Penguin, 2002.

Larson, Kate Clifford. *Bound for Freedom: Harriet Tubman, Portrait of an American Hero*. New York: Ballentine, 2004.

Lee, J. G. C. "The Alexandria Quartermaster's Depot during the Civil War." *Journal of the Military Service Institution of the United States* 39 (1906): 13–21.

Leech, Margaret. *Reveille in Washington: 1860–1865*. New York: New York Review of Books, 1941.

Leepson, Marc. "The First Union Civil War Martyr." *Alexandria Chronicle* (Fall 2011): 1–4.

Leonard, Elizabeth. *Yankee Women: Gender Battles in the Civil War*. New York: W. W. Norton, 1994.

Levy, George, and Paul Tynan. "Campgrounds of the Civil War." *Rochester History* 66, no. 3 (2004): 1–24.

Life of James W. Jackson: The Alexandria Hero, the Slayer of Ellsworth, the First Martyr in the Cause of Southern Independence. Richmond: West and Johnston, 1862.

Livermore, Samuel Truesdal. *A History of Block Island*. Hartford CT: Case, Lockwood and Brainard, 1877.

Long, Di. "Divorce in New York from 1850s to 1920s." Master's thesis, University of Georgia, 2013.

Lowe, Richard. "Another Look at Reconstruction in Virginia." *Civil War History* 32, no. 1 (1986): 56–76.

Lynch-Brennan, Margaret. *The Irish Bridget: Irish Immigrant Women in Domestic Service in America, 1840–1930*. Syracuse NY: Syracuse University Press, 2009.

Mahood, Wayne. *General Wadsworth: The Life and Wars of Brevet General James S. Wadsworth*. Boston: Da Capo Press, 2003.

Manning, Chandra. *Troubled Refuge: Struggling for Freedom in the Civil War*. New York: Alfred A. Knopf, 2016.

———. "Working for Citizenship in Civil War Contraband Camps." *Journal of the Civil War Era* 4, no. 2 (2014): 172–204.

Mansfield, Betty. "That Fateful Class: Black Teachers of Virginia's Freedmen, 1861–1882." PhD dissertation, Catholic University, 1980.

Marcotte, Bob. "The University of Rochester and the Civil War: Three Heroes at Gettysburg." Based on a talk delivered at the University of Rochester, December 17, 2002.

Marks, James Junius. *The Peninsula Campaign in Virginia, or Incidents and Scenes on the Battlefield and in Richmond*. Philadelphia: J. B. Lippincott, 1864.

Masur, Kate. *An Example for All the Land: Emancipation and the Struggle for Equality in Washington, D.C.* Chapel Hill: University of North Carolina Press, 2010.

———. "Patronage and Protest in Kate Brown's Washington." *Journal of American History* 99, no. 4 (2013): 1047–71.

———. "'A Rare Phenomenon of Philological Vegetation': The Word 'Contraband' and the Meanings of Emancipation in the United States." *Journal of American History* 93, no. 4 (2007): 1050–84.

Mauro, Charles V. *The Civil War in Fairfax County.* Charleston SC: History Press, 2006.

May, Arthur. "A University Dream That Failed." *New York History* 48, no. 2 (1967): 160–81.

Mayer, Henry. *All on Fire: William Lloyd Garrison and the Abolition of Slavery.* New York: St. Martin's Press, 1998.

McCord, T. B., Jr. *Across the Fence, but a World Apart: The Coleman Site, 1796–1907.* Alexandria VA: Alexandria Archaeology, 1985; reprinted 2006.

McElroy, James. "Social Control and Romantic Reform in Antebellum America: The Case of Rochester, New York." *New York History* 58, no. 1 (1977): 16–46.

McIntosh, Linda. "Virginia's Reactions to John Brown's Raid on Harper's Ferry, October 16–18, 1859." Honors thesis, University of Richmond, 1972.

McIntosh, W. H. *History of Monroe County, New York.* Philadelphia: Everts, Ensign, and Everts, 1877.

McKelvey, Blake. "Lights and Shadows in Local Negro History." *Rochester History* 21, no. 4 (1959): 1–27.

———. "Rochester's Mid Years: Center of Genesee County Life: 1854–1884." *Rochester History* 2, no. 3 (1940): 1–24.

———. "Rochester's Part in the Civil War." *Rochester History* 23, no. 1 (1961): 1–24.

———. "Rochester's Public Schools: A Testing Ground for Community Policies." *Rochester History* 31, no. 2 (1969): 1–28.

———. "A Sesquicentennial Review of Rochester's History." *Rochester History* 24, no. 3 (1962): 1–40.

McKivigan, John, and Heather Kaufman, eds. *In the Words of Frederick Douglass.* Ithaca NY: Cornell University Press, 2012.

McMillan, Sally G. *Seneca Falls and the Origins of the Women's Rights Movement.* New York: Oxford University Press, 2008.

McPherson, James. *Battle Cry of Freedom.* New York: Oxford University Press, 1988.

———. *Ordeal by Fire: The Civil War and Reconstruction.* New York: Alfred A. Knopf, 1982.

———. *The Struggle for Equality: Abolitionists in the Civil War and Reconstruction.* Princeton NJ: Princeton University Press, 1964.

Melder, Keith. "Angel of Mercy in Washington: Josephine Griffing and the Freedmen, 1864–1872." *Records of the Columbia Historical Society* 63/65: 242–72.

Miller, Edward, Jr. "Volunteers for Freedom: Black Civil War Soldiers in Alexandria National Cemetery, Parts I and II." *Historic Alexandria Quarterly* (Fall/Winter 1998).

Miller, T. Michael, ed. *Murder and Mayhem: Criminal Conduct in Old Alexandria, Virginia, 1749–1900.* Bowie MD: Heritage Books, 1988.

———. *Pen Portraits of Alexandria, Virginia, 1739–1900.* Bowie MD: Heritage Books, 1987.

———. "Trial of Gladwin." Alexandria VA: Office of Historic Alexandria, n.d.

"Mission to the Freed 'Contrabands' at Fortress Monroe, VA." *American Missionary*, October 1, 1861.

Mitchell, Reid. *Civil War Soldiers: Their Expectations and Experiences*. New York: Viking Penguin, 1988.

Munroe, James Phinney, ed. *Adventures of an Army Nurse in Two Wars: Edited from Diary and Correspondence of Mary Phinney Baroness Von Olnhausen*. Boston: Little, Brown, 1903.

Murphy, Deidre, and Sarah Sidman. "From Slavery to War: The History of 1315 Duke Street." 1988.

Nathans, Sydney. *To Free a Family: The Journey of Mary Walker*. Cambridge MA: Harvard University Press, 2012.

Nelson, Scott, and Carol Sheriff. *A People at War: Civilians and Soldiers in America's Civil War*. Oxford: Oxford University Press, 2007.

Nevins, Allan, ed. *George Templeton Strong, Diary of the Civil War 1860–1865*. New York: MacMillan, 1962.

"The New Washington." *Century Magazine* 27, no. 5 (March 1884).

Nudelman, Franny. "Harriet Jacobs and the Sentimental Politics of Female Suffering." *ELH* 59, no. 4 (Winter 1992): 939–64.

O'Brien, John. "Reconstruction in Richmond: White Restoration and Black Protest, April–June 1865." *Virginia Magazine of History and Biography* 89, no. 3 (1981): 259–81.

Office of Historic Alexandria. African American Historic Resources of Alexandria, Virginia. New submission: National Register of Historic Places: National Park Service, U.S. Department of the Interior, 2001–2004.

Offices of the Board of Education. "A History of the Public Schools of Rochester, New York, 1813–1935." http://www.libraryweb.org/~digitized/books/History_of_the_Public_Schools_of_Rochester_NY.pdf.

Official Register of the United States Containing a List of the Officers and Employees in the Civil, Military, and Naval Service on the First of July, 1887. Vol. 1. Washington DC: Government Printing Office, 1887.

Oller, John. *American Queen: The Rise and Fall of Kate Chase Sprague*. Boston: Da Capo Press, 2014.

Orr, Timothy, ed. *Last to Leave the Field: The Life and Letters of First Sergeant Henry Hayward*. Knoxville: University of Tennessee Press, 2011.

Painter, Nell Irvin. *Sojourner Truth: A Life, a Symbol*. New York: W. W. Norton, 1996.

Palmer, Erwin. "A Partnership in the Abolition Movement." *University of Rochester Library Bulletin* 26, nos. 1 and 2 (1970–71). http://rbscp.lib.rochester.edu/3476.

Parker, Jenny Marsh. *Rochester: A Story Historical*. Rochester: Scranton, Wetmore, 1884.

Patenaude, Monique. "Bound by Pride and Prejudice: Black Life in Frederick Douglass's New York." PhD dissertation, University of Rochester, 2012.

Paullin, Charles. "Alexandria County in 1861." *Records of the Columbia Historical Society, Washington, D.C.* 28 (1924): 107–31.

Peck, Garrett. *Walt Whitman in Washington, D.C.* Charleston SC: History Press, 2015.

Peck, William Farley. *History of Rochester and Monroe County, New York, from the Earliest Historic Times to the Beginning of 1907.* New York: Pioneer Publishing, 1908.

Pegram, Thomas R. *Battling Demon Rum: The Struggle for a Dry America, 1800–1933.* Chicago: Ivan R. Dee, 1998.

Pippinger, Wesley. *Alexandria, Virginia Death Records, 1863–1868 (the Gladwin Record) and 1869–1896.* Westminster MD: Family Line Publications, 1995.

Poland, Charles, Jr. *The Glories of War: Small Battles and Early Heroes of 1861.* Bloomington IN: AuthorHouse, 2006.

Poole, Robert M. *On Hallowed Ground: The Story of Arlington National Cemetery.* New York: Walker Publishing, 2009.

"Progress of the Electric Telegraph." *Atlantic Monthly* 5 (March 1860): 290–98.

Provine, Dorothy S., ed. *Alexandria County, Free Negro Register, 1779–1861.* Bowie MD: Heritage Books, 1990.

Pryor, Elizabeth Brown. *Clara Barton: Professional Angel.* Philadelphia: University of Pennsylvania Press, 1987.

Pulliam, Ted. "The Civil War Comes to Duke Street." *Alexandria Chronicle* (2011): 5–14.

———. *Historic Alexandria: An Illustrated History.* Alexandria VA: Office of Historic Alexandria, 2011.

Quarles, Benjamin, ed. *Blacks on John Brown.* Urbana: University of Illinois Press, 1972.

Randolph, Mary. *The Virginia Housewife.* Baltimore: Plaskitt, Fite, 1838. http://digital.lib.msu.edu/projects/cookbooks/html/books/book_10.cfm.

Redkey, Edwin. "Black Chaplains in the Union Army." *Civil War History* 33, no. 4 (1987): 331–50.

Reidy, Joseph. "Coming from the Shadow of the Past: The Transition from Slavery to Freedom at Freedmen's Village, 1863–1900." *Virginia Magazine of History and Biography* 95, no. 4 (1987): 403–28.

Reisen, Harriet. *Louisa May Alcott: The Woman behind Little Women.* New York: Henry Holt, 2009.

Reynolds, David S. *Mightier Than the Sword: Uncle Tom's Cabin and the Battle for America.* New York: W. W. Norton, 2011.

Ricks, Mary Kay. *Escape on the Pearl.* New York: HarperCollins, 2007.

Riker, Diane. "Fitzgerald's Warehouse: King and Union Streets." In *Studies of the Old Waterfront.* Alexandria VA: Office of Historic Alexandria, 2008.

———. "'This Long Agony': A Test of Civilian Loyalties in an Occupied City." *Alexandria Chronicle* (Spring 2011): 1–12.

Roberts, Cokie. *Capital Dames: The Civil War and the Women of Washington, 1848–1868.* New York: HarperCollins, 2015.

Robertson, James I., Jr. *Civil War Virginia: Battleground for a Nation.* Charlottesville: University of Virginia Press, 1991.

Rodriguez, Junius, ed. *Encyclopedia of Emancipation and Abolition in the Transatlantic World*. Vols. 1–3. New York: Routledge, 2007.

Rosenberg-Naparsteck, Ruth. "A Growing Agitation: Rochester before, during, and after the Civil War." *Rochester History* 46, nos. 1 and 2 (1984): 140.

Russell, William Howard. *My Diary North and South*. Boston: T. O. H. P. Burnham, 1863.

Sauffer, John. *The Black Hearts of Men: Radical Abolitionists and the Transformation of Race*. Cambridge MA: Harvard University Press, 2001.

Schermerhorn, Calvin. "Capitalism's Captives: The Maritime United States Slave Trade, 1807–1850." *Journal of Social History* 47, no. 4 (2014): 897–921.

Schmitt, Victoria Sandwick. "Rochester's Frederick Douglass: Part One." *Rochester History* 67, no. 3 (2005): 1–28.

———. "Rochester's Frederick Douglass: Part Two." *Rochester History* 67, no. 4 (2005): 1–32.

Schweninger, Loren. "The Roots of Enterprise: Black-Owned Businesses in Virginia, 1830–1880." *Virginia Magazine of History and Biography* 100, no. 4 (1992): 515–42.

Scott, Robert Garth, ed. *Forgotten Valor: Memoirs, Journals and Civil War Letters of Orlando B. Willcox*. Kent OH: Kent University Press, 1999.

Scully, Pamela, and Diana Paton, eds. *A Nation's Sin: White Women and U.S. Policy toward Freedpeople*. Durham NC: Duke University Press, 2005.

Serverian, W. "Alexandria Academy." In George Washington Digital Encyclopedia, edited by Joseph Stoltz III. Mount Vernon Estate.

Silber, Nina. *Daughters of the Union: Northern Women Fight the Civil War*. Cambridge MA: Harvard University Press, 2005.

Smith, Bruce. "Benjamin Hallowell of Alexandria: Scientist, Educator, Quaker Idealist." *Virginia Magazine of History and Biography* 85, no. 3 (1977): 337–61.

Smith, Philip. *General History of Duchess County, 1609 to 1876*. Pawling NY: self-published, 1877.

Smith, William Francis, and T. Michael Miller. *A Seaport Saga: A Portrait of Old Alexandria, Virginia*. Virginia Beach: Donning, 1989.

Spann, Edward. *Gotham at War: New York City, 1860–1865*. Wilmington DE: Scholarly Resources, 2002.

Spring, Joel. *The American School, 1642–2000*, 5th ed. Boston: McGraw-Hill Higher Education, 1997.

Stalcup, Brenda, ed. *Women's Suffrage, Turning Points in World History*. San Diego CA: Greenhaven Press, 2000.

Steckel, Richard. "The Health and Mortality of Women and Children, 1850–1860." *Journal of Economic History* 48, no. 2 (1988): 333–45.

Stewart, David O. *Impeached: The Trial of President Andrew Johnson and the Fight for Lincoln's Legacy*. New York: Simon and Schuster, 2009.

Stewart, James Brewer, and Kathryn Kish, eds. *Women's Rights and Transatlantic Slavery in the Era of Emancipation*. New Haven CT: Yale University Press, 2007.

Stowe, Harriet Beecher. *A Key to Uncle Tom's Cabin*. Boston: John P. Jewett, 1858.

Struble, Joseph P. "Captured Images: The Daguerreian Years in Rochester, 1840 to 1860." *Rochester History* 62, no. 1 (2000): 1–24.

Swanson, James. *Bloody Times: The Funeral of Abraham Lincoln and the Manhunt for Jefferson Davis*. New York: HarperCollins, 2010.

Sweig, Donald. "Alexandria to New Orleans: The Human Tragedy of the Interstate Slave Trade, Parts 1 to 4." *Alexandria Gazette Packet*, 2014.

Swint, Henry, ed. *Dear Ones at Home: Letters from Contraband Camps*. Nashville TN: Vanderbilt University Press, 1966.

Symonds, Henry Clay. *Report of a Commissary of Subsistence, 1861–1865*. Self-published, 1888.

Taylor, Bayard. *Hannah Thurston: A Story of American Life*. New York: G. P. Putnam, 1864.

Taylor, Kay Ann. "Mary S. Peake and Charlotte L. Forten: Black Teachers during the Civil War and Reconstruction." *Journal of Negro Education* 74, no. 2 (2005): 124–37.

Thomas, Emory M. *Robert E. Lee: A Biography*. New York: W. W. Norton, 1995.

Toler, Pamela. *Heroines of Mercy Street: The Real Nurses of the Civil War*. New York: Little, Brown, 2016.

Townsend, George Albert. *Campaigns of a Non-Combatant and His Romaunt Abroad during the Civil War*. New York: Blelock, 1866.

Traum, Sarah, Joseph Balicki, and Brian Corle. *Documentary Study, Archeological Evaluation and Management Plan for 1323 Duke Street*. Alexandria VA: John Milner Associates, 2007.

Travelers' Accounts of the Historic Alexandria Waterfront (1624–1900). Organized by Kelsey Ryan for the Office of Historic Alexandria, 2009.

Twelve Years a Slave and Other Slave Narratives (N. Turner, F. Douglass, S. Truth, S. Northup, H. Jacobs). Introduction by Rebecka Rutledge Fisher. New York: Fall River Press, 2015.

U.S. Commissioner of Patents. *Annual Report of the Commissioner of Patents for the Year 1869*. Vol. 1, *Report to the 41st Congress, 2d Session*. Washington DC: Government Printing Office, 1871. https://babel.hathitrust.org/cgi/pt?id=njp.32101049919135;view=1up;seq=7.

U.S. National Park Service, National Capital Region and CEHP Incorporated. "A Historic Resources Study: The Civil War Defenses of Washington: Parts I and II." https://www.nps.gov/parkhistory/online_books/civilwar/index.htm.

U.S. Sanitary Commission. *Documents of the U.S. Sanitary Commission*. Vol 1. New York, 1866.

U.S. War Department. *The War of the Rebellion: A Compilation of the Official Records of the Union and Confederate Armies*. Series 1, vol. 2. Washington DC: Government Printing Office, 1880–91. http://ebooks.library.cornell.edu/m/moawar/waro.html.

———. *The War of the Rebellion: A Compilation of the Official Records of the Union and Confederate Armies*. Series 1, vol. 43, part 2. Washington DC: Government Printing Office, 1893. http://ebooks.library.cornell.edu/m/moawar/waro.html.

Van Tuyll, Debra Reddin, Nancy McKenzie Dupont, and Joseph Hayden. *Journalism in the Fallen Confederacy*. New York: Palgrave MacMillan, 2015.

Vorenberg, Michael. "Abraham Lincoln and the Politics of Black Colonization." *Journal of the Abraham Lincoln Association* 14, no. 2 (1993): 22–45.

Wagner, Margaret, Gary Gallagher, and Paul Finkelman, eds. *Library of Congress Civil War Desk Reference*. New York: Simon and Schuster, 2002.

Warfield, Edgar. *Manassas to Appomattox: The Civil War Memoirs of Pvt. Edgar Warfield, 17th Virginia Infantry*. McLean VA: EPM Publications, 1936; reprinted 1996.

Washington, Margaret. *Sojourner Truth's America*. Champaign-Urbana: University of Illinois Press, 2009.

Washington, V. F. *Eagles on Their Buttons: A Black Infantry Regiment in the Civil War*. Columbia: University of Missouri Press, 1999.

Watson, Holly Cameron, Clara Mulligan, Barbara Scott, and Mike Mulligan. "The Perry House." Avon Historic Properties Project. Avon NY, 2009.

Wellman, Judith. "Crossing over Cross: Whitney Cross's Burned-over District." *Reviews in American History* 17, no. 1 (1989): 169–74.

———. "Women's Rights, Republicanism, and Revolutionary Rhetoric." *New York History* 69, no. 3 (1988): 352–84.

Welter, Barbara. "The Cult of True Womanhood: 1820–1860." *American Quarterly* 18, no. 2 (1966): 151–74.

Wheelock, Julia. *Boys in White, the Experience of a Hospital Agent in and around Washington*. New York: Lange and Hillman, 1870.

Wilbur, Julia. "Richmond." *Pennsylvania Freedmen's Bulletin* 1, no. 3 (August 1, 1865).

Wilson, Gregory F. *Jonathan Roberts: The Civil War's Quaker Scout and Sheriff*. North Charleston SC: CreateSpace, 2014.

Wilson, Robert. *Mathew Brady: Portraits of a Nation*. New York: Bloomsbury USA, 2013.

Winch, Julie. *Between Slavery and Freedom: Free People of Color in America from Settlement to the Civil War*. Lanham MD: Rowan and Littlefield, 2014.

Winkle, Kenneth. *Lincoln's Citadel: The Civil War in Washington, DC*. New York: W. W. Norton, 2013.

Wise, Barton Haxall. *The Life of Henry A. Wise of Virginia, 1806–1876*. New York: MacMillan, 1899.

Wolfe, Brendan. "Battle of the Crater." *Encyclopedia of Virginia*. Virginia Foundation for the Humanities in partnership with the Library of Virginia. http://www.encyclopediavirginia.org/Crater_Battle_of_the.

Woolsey, Jane Stuart. *Hospital Days: Reminiscence of a Civil War Nurse*. 1868; Roseville MN: Edinburgh Press, 1996.

Yellin, Jean Fagan. *Harriet Jacobs: A Life*. Cambridge MA: Basic Civitas, 2004.

———, ed. *The Harriet Jacobs Family Papers*. Vols. 1 and 2. Chapel Hill: University of North Carolina Press, 2008.

————. "Written by Herself: Harriet Jacobs' Slave Narrative." *American Literature* 53, no. 3 (November 1981): 479–86.

Zeitz, Joshua. *Lincoln's Boys: John Hay, John Nicolay, and the War for Lincoln's Image.* New York: Viking, 2014.

INDEX

abolition movement, 15, 20–35; attitude of, toward African Americans, 92; Frederick Douglass and, 20–21, 25–33, 57, 58; Julia Wilbur and, 18–21, 23–24, 26, 58; at start of Civil War, 57–58; William Lloyd Garrison and, 23–25, 31–32, 107

Alcott, Louisa May, 99

Alexander, John, 45

Alexandria Academy (Old Schoolhouse), 86, 89–91, 108, 110, 145, 249n15

Alexandria National Cemetery. *See* Soldiers' Cemetery

Alexandria Rifles, 44, 59

Alexandria VA: after Civil War, 207–8, 230–31; concerns for rebel attack on, 134–36; in early 1860s, 59, 86–87, 245n15; guerillas and, 184–85; history of, 44–47; inquiry into military administration in, 156–58; during Reconstruction, 207–8; "secesh" ordered expelled from, 138–39; slave pen in, 49, 87, 108, 126, 128, 132, 148, 150, 154, 157–58, 180, 208; slave trade and, 47–50; smallpox and, 98, 114–15, 121, 162–63, 165–66, 230; at start of Civil War, 59–62; Union military presence in, 2, 64–67, 82–83, 86, 93–95, 98–99, 124–30

American Anti-Slavery Society, 23

American Baptist Free Mission Society, 120

American Colonization Society, 23, 181

American Missionary Society, 74

American Union Commission, 196

American Woman Suffrage Association (AWSA), 220

AME Zion Church, 22, 57

Anderson, Eliza, 203, 212

Anderson, Robert, 60

Anthony, Susan B., 17–19, 21, 57, 68, 149, 203, 220, 227

Arlington House, 46, 82, 141, 152, 257n25

Armfield, John, 47–49, 245n13

Aron, Cindy Sondik, 210, 217

Autographs for Freedom, 31–32

Baker, Charles, 218

Baker, George, 84

Baldwin, Jeremiah, 205

Banks, Nathaniel, 86, 92

Barber, James, 184

Barnes, Anna Cornell: Julia Wilbur's correspondence with, 79, 84, 91, 103, 109, 116, 118, 134, 141, 147, 150, 154, 159–60, 165; Julia Wilbur's visit to, 139–40, 175; later life of, 226; letter of, to Abraham Lincoln, 127–30; RLASS and, 78, 244n42

Barnes, Silas, 226

Barton, Clara, 203, 210, 215

Beecher, Henry Ward, 32

Bell, John, 59, 246n12

Benevolent Society of Alexandria for Ameliorating and Improving the Condition of the People of Color, 50

Bentley, Edwin, 167–68, 178, 181–82, 230

Bethel AME Church, 151

Bigelow, Alfreda (Freda): Julia Wilbur's care for and separation from, 35–43, 56–57, 68, 71, 77, 90, 100, 131, 140, 154, 176, 183, 217; Julia Wilbur's reunion with, 213–15; later life of, 225; Stephen Wilbur's will and, 225

Bigelow, John, 112, 115, 230; Julia Wilbur's work and, 113–14, 144–47; treatment of freedmen by, 128, 141, 165–66, 167

Bigelow, Nancy Sinclair Haynes, 39, 40, 214, 225

Bigelow, Revilo, 35, 38–41, 43, 214, 215, 225

Bigelow, Sarah Alice, 35, 36–37

Bigelow, Sarah Wilbur, 13, 16, 39, 225; birth of, 11; death of, 35, 36, 63, 75, 173; marriage of, 34, 36

Booth, John Wilkes, 2, 190, 229

Bowen, Sayles, 211

Bradley, Amy, 165

Brady, Mathew, 65

Breed, Daniel, 141, 152, 187